MW00559962

The publisher gratefully acknowledges the generous support of the Simpson Humanities Endowment Fund of the University of California Press Foundation.

Waiting for Verdi

Waiting for Verdi

ITALIAN OPERA AND POLITICAL OPINION, 1815–1848

Mary Ann Smart

UNIVERSITY OF CALIFORNIA PRESS

University of California Press, one of the most distinguished university presses in the United States, enriches lives around the world by advancing scholarship in the humanities, social sciences, and natural sciences. Its activities are supported by the UC Press Foundation and by philanthropic contributions from individuals and institutions. For more information, visit www.ucpress.edu.

University of California Press
Oakland, California

Library of Congress Cataloging-in-Publication Data

Names: Smart, Mary Ann, author.
Title: Waiting for Verdi : Italian opera and political opinion, 1815–1848 / Mary Ann Smart.
Description: Oakland, California : University of California Press, [2018] | Includes bibliographical references and index. |
Identifiers: LCCN 2017055321 (print) | LCCN 2017056879 (ebook) | ISBN 9780520966574 () | ISBN 9780520276253 (cloth : alk. paper)
Subjects: LCSH: Opera—Political aspects—Italy—19th century. | Verdi, Giuseppe, 1813–1901—Influence. | Verdi, Giuseppe, 1813–1901—Criticism and interpretation. | Opera—Political aspects—France—Paris—19th century.
Classification: LCC ML3918.O64 (ebook) | LCC ML3918.O64 S63 2018 (print) | DDC 782.10945/09034--dc23
LC record available at https://lccn.loc.gov/2017055321

Manufactured in the United States of America

25 24 23 22 21 20 19 18
10 9 8 7 6 5 4 3 2 1

For Pat and John

CONTENTS

ILLUSTRATIONS

FIGURES

EXAMPLES

TABLES

ACKNOWLEDGMENTS

I began thinking about some of the personalities, issues, and events at the center of *Waiting for Verdi* during a sabbatical year spent in Bologna, the same year my daughter Clara was born in that city's welcoming Villa Erbosa. That has meant that almost every page of this book bears some mark of a memorable experience, and many of its ideas were first sketched during satisfying (and often also challenging) family sojourns, that year in Bologna, and later on summer research trips to Naples and Genoa, on the trail of Rossini and Donizetti, and of Giovanni and Agostino Ruffini. During those times in Italy, I benefited hugely from conversations and meals with friends old and new. Susan Rutherford shared coffee and conversation and her vast knowledge of the nineteenth-century press. Scrolling through microfilms became a pleasure when she was sitting at the next machine. Fabrizio della Seta saw something in this project at an early stage and invited me to teach his wonderful students at the Facoltà di musica in Cremona (University of Pavia), where many of these ideas were tried out for the first time. Anselm Gerhard attended some of those meetings and offered more brilliant ideas than I was able to incorporate in these pages. I am grateful to Carlotta Sorba for her boundless hospitality, and for the intellectual openness that made her eager to spend time talking through our views of opera and politics. I hope these pages show that we agree far more than not. Marco Capra shared his incomparable knowledge of the nineteenth-century press and introduced me to the wonderful collection of the Centro internazionali di ricerca sui periodici musicale (CIRPeM). Always and everywhere, Emanuele Senici has been a dear friend, an encouraging and exigent reader, and an inspiring example. His own publications have been points of reference throughout, reminding me of the pleasures and insights that flow from that magical combination of engagement with historical sources and imaginative, informed speculation.

While those brief and intense periods of living in Italy may have given these pages a special texture, Berkeley is home, and this book would not exist without the precious influence of my brilliant and generous colleagues and students at Berkeley. For several years I had the privilege of occupying the office next door to Katherine Bergeron, whose intense and original engagement with documents and other traces of the past shaped the way I approached this project. The late Wendy Allanbrook sometimes seemed to understand better what I was writing than I did myself. I continue to ponder some of the questions she asked about early drafts of these chapters, and I have not stopped missing her presence among us. Richard Taruskin's indelible injunction to write the history of what works have meant, rather than what they mean, has been energizing, if occasionally paralyzing. At many Friday night dinners and, more recently, on walks at Point Isabel, we have exchanged ideas about articles we've read and talks we've heard. Those energetic conversations about the state of our field have left many traces in these pages.

Berkeley has also been a place for enjoyable and mind-expanding collaborations on writing and teaching. I would not have enjoyed work on the last stages of the book half as much without the friendship of Nicholas Mathew, always ready with a new idea for an event, a considered opinion on something he has read or heard, discerning comments on chapter drafts, and a clear vision of the ethical stakes of writing about music, history, and politics. I learned much from teaching with Hannah Ginsborg, and her kind and persistent interest in the progress of the manuscript is the reason that it was completed when it was. I first encountered many of the texts central to chapters 1 and 2 during a graduate seminar cotaught with Albert Ascoli, and our conversations about writing and about literature have continued to energize and inform my work. The chance to share ideas and exchange work with James Davies has, several times over, changed the way I think and write about music; I would be pleased if even a little of his passion, and his tireless quest for ideas about music that are new and true and not trivial, had rubbed off on me. I am also grateful to Bonnie Wade for her steadfast support, consistently good advice, and for her example as a productive, inventive, and endlessly curious scholar and writer. I have derived a deep pleasure from my work with the editorial board of *Representations* over the past several years; the book would be much less were it not for the valuable comments and ideas of several board members who read an early version of chapter 6. I also gained much in motivation and in substance from the writing group convened by Deirdre Loughridge, and Deirdre's own discerning readings contributed enormously to the clarity of the first few chapters.

I have been fortunate to teach and make friends with many remarkable graduate students at Berkeley, and there is not a page in this book that does not bear the mark of conversations with them. I cannot adequately mark the contributions to my thinking made by former and current students. Melina Esse, Adeline Mueller, Laura Protano-Biggs, Emily Richmond-Pollock, Arman Schwartz, and Benjamin Walton may have begun as Berkeley graduate students, but they quickly became valued colleagues whose own work and reactions to mine have sustained and defined this project in enjoyable and mind-expanding ways. Melanie Gudesblatt, Edward Jacobson, and Alessandra Jones all read parts of the manuscript and offered valuable feedback.

The ideas contained in these pages are the product of innumerable conversations and e-mail exchanges with friends and colleagues, old and new. Roger Parker read every word and prompted me to strengthen arguments and rethink details, all the while proclaiming his utter lack of interest in the subject. This project could not have existed without the example of his work and of his way of working; but his contributions go further that. I could try to enumerate the moments when Roger's curiosity or skepticism or belief in the project made a difference; but what I would be describing is quite simply friendship, of the kind that can make scholarly work so satisfying. Among the many people whose reactions to written or spoken versions of these chapters changed the way they have emerged, I remember especially stimulating questions and ideas from Nicholas Baragwanath, Gregory Bloch, Majel Connery, John Davis, Philip Gossett, Rebecca Harris-Warwick, Sarah Hibberd, Francesco Izzo, Axel Körner, David Levin, Adrian Lyttelton, Roger Moseley, David Rosen, Susan Rutherford, Gary Tomlinson, Francesca Vella, Claudio Vellutini, and Flora Willson; but no doubt I have overlooked some who shared their thoughts and knowledge with me. I owe the book's title to a chance remark made by Alex Rehding over lunch in Harvard Square; he may be appalled that his quick joke became so central to this project.

Research on the book was supported by fellowships from the National Endowment for Humanities, the Townsend Center for the Humanities at Berkeley, and by several other sources at Berkeley. Among the many libraries and archives I consulted during my research, I am especially grateful for the help of librarians and archivists at Bologna's Biblioteca civica del Archiginnasio and Conservatorio di Musica Gioachino Rossini, the library of the Conservatorio San Pietro a Majella in Naples, and of John Roberts, former head music librarian at the Jean Gray Hargrove Library at Berkeley. Chapter 5 first appeared in *19th-Century Music* 34/1 (2010): 39–60, and a portion of chapter 6 was published in the *Journal of Modern Italian Studies* 18/2 (2013): 190–204. I am grateful to the editors and readers of those journals for their comments.

I have thoroughly enjoyed working with Raina Polivka, Mary Francis, and Cindy Fulton at the University of California Press. I'm thankful for their belief in this project and their swift and gracious responses to questions along the way. Copy editor Jeffrey Wyneken improved the manuscript immeasurably with his sharp eye and his great ear for style. Susan Storch prepared the index. David Coll and Scott Rubin engraved the music examples, often working at short notice, and Mark Mueller and Jim Coates cheerfully provided all manner of practical support throughout the research and writing. Thanks also to Edward Jacobson, Peter Mondelli, and Francesca Vella for excellent historical detective work and the choice documentary morsels they threw to me at crucial moments.

My parents, John and Patricia Smart, provided such a loving and intellectually vibrant environment when I was growing up that it has been easy to take their influence for granted at times. But in this project, which draws from both of their fields—literature and history—and which tries to hash out the relations between political change and emotional life, their contributions are very present. As a professor herself and a brilliant reader and writer, my mother modeled commitment to ideas and to finding a strong expressive voice in scholarly writing. Equally embedded in my approach to this material are the bedrock commitments to fairness and to working for social and political change that my parents share. I am also blessed with the best in-laws ever, Rachel and Shale Brownstein, who have over the years joined me at performances and listened to me work through ideas. Rachel, whose own writing has long been an inspiration to me, also commented on drafts of several chapters.

It remains only to thank the two people who have accompanied this project from inception to completion, and without whom the work on it would have been so much less fulfilling. Daniel Brownstein knows far more about Italy than I do, and his curiosity and sense of adventure and hunger for ideas have delighted and emboldened me in travels near and far. Clara Katherine Brownstein long regarded this book—as she did opera—with impatience. But a writer herself now, she has become my favorite companion in marathon writing sessions, a trusted consultant on all manner of questions about style and process, and a model for how to listen to and participate in musical cultures.

ONE

Risorgimento Fantasies

THE SOCIETY OF TRANSCENDENTAL-ROMANTICS

In 1816 and 1817 two competitions were announced in Milan within a little more than a year of each other. One was a serious and official undertaking: the royal theaters of Milan sponsored a contest for a new libretto, promising that the winning entry would be set to music by a composer chosen by theater officials, and given a première at the Teatro alla Scala. No record survives of the winner—it is likely that none was ever declared—but one of the contenders was Giovanni Gherardini's *Avviso ai giudici,* a drama of legal persecution and social injustice set after the French Revolution that eventually became the basis for Rossini's *La gazza ladra.* The competition does not seem to have had the desired rejuvenating effect. On reading the submissions, judge Vincenzo Monti came to the realization that Italian dramatic poetry was in crisis. In a letter to one of his fellow judges, Monti declared that it would take a miracle to overcome the illogical libretti and the musical pretensions that had reduced opera to nothing more than "a monstrous coagulation of words without meaning."[1]

A little over a year later, the Milan-based journal of fashion and culture, the *Corriere delle dame,* announced a competition of its own. Held under the auspices of the impressive-sounding but entirely imaginary "Accademia de' Romantici Transcendentali," this contest advertised that it would identify and reward the best romantic tragedy of the moment.[2] The guidelines for prospective applicants fill more than a page of dense type and amount to a virtual catalogue of romantic affectations. The winning tragedy must denigrate Italy and Italians as much as possible, the list begins, and therefore all the villains of the piece must be Italian. Competing playwrights are advised to have thirty or forty characters die in full view on the stage, to extend the action over "no less than five years, no more than fifty," and to place one scene in Italy and the next in Babylon, or perhaps to divide the action between Mecca and Siberia.

The tongue-in-cheek recommendations go on and on, but all of them engage in this jesting way with the classical unities and with related aesthetic conventions that had long governed the narrative modes of both spoken drama and opera libretti. In a light-hearted vein, the editors of the *Corriere* were fighting back against the encroachment of romantic aesthetics that was beginning to infiltrate Italy from the north, a movement whose new currency was trumpeted most loudly by Madame de Staël's article "On the Manner and the Usefulness of Translations," which had appeared in Italian translation in the first issue of the *Biblioteca italiana* in 1816. In the midst of a generally disparaging evaluation of the current state of Italian literary production, she called for the translation of Shakespeare, Schiller, and other northern authors as the best antidote for Italian backwardness.[3] The sentence about "denigrating Italians" in the *Corriere*'s contest is a clear swipe at Mme. de Staël, and the sarcastic calls for multiple deaths and action that veers wildly across time and space were indirect responses to the dramatic values promoted in her article and represented by the authors she championed.

Mme. de Staël felt no more positive than Monti about the operatic dimension of Italian culture and even went so far as to blame opera for the sad state of the nation's literary tradition. Advocating the translation of a drama by Chateaubriand into Italian, she paused to make a distinction between the sheer quality of Italian music and the frivolity of the social settings in which it is heard:

> I do not doubt that *Athalie* would be appreciated in Milanese theaters, especially if the choruses were accompanied by wonderful Italian music. But they say that in Italy people go to the theater not to listen but to meet and chat with their dearest friends in the boxes. And I will conclude from this that sitting for five hours every evening listening to what passes for words in Italian opera must dull the intellect of the nation, for want of exercise.[4]

With this dismissal of operagoing as both tranquilizing and distracting, Mme. de Staël anticipated—and perhaps also provided the script for—the poet Giacomo Leopardi, who a few years later in 1824 would offer his own scathing evaluation of opera and its effects on Italian society. Leopardi lamented that Italians knew little of the free exchange of opinion or of close interpersonal bonds beyond the family, compared to other European nations:

> Many reasons conspire to deprive Italy of society, not all of which I can enumerate here. The climate, which predisposes Italians to spend most of each day in the open air, and encourages long walks and things like that, the vivacity of the Italian character, which causes citizens to prefer the pleasures of live performance [*spettacoli*] and other delights of the senses to those of the spirit, and that pushes them to pure entertainment divorced from any effort of the soul, as well as to negligence and indolence.... There can be no doubt that the *passeggio* [the public evening walk], the *spettacoli*, and the rituals of the church have nothing at all to do with that type of society that other nations possess. Today the *passeggio*, the theater, and the church are the principal venues for what little society Italy does possess, and indeed they constitute its entirety ... since Italians do not like domestic life, nor do they take pleasure in or excel at conversation. So instead they stroll, they go to the theater and other entertainments, to Mass and to sermons, and to sacred and secular feasts.[5]

Whereas Mme. de Staël imagined Italian audiences lulled into a stupor by five-hour stretches of pretty music, Leopardi characterizes operagoing as a herd activity like promenading through the piazza before dinner or gawking at a religious procession, all activities that militate against independent thought and debate.

Reading Monti, Mme. de Staël, or Leopardi, one might conclude that opera was an entirely negative force in early-nineteenth-century Italy. All agree on the low literary quality of the libretti, and the last two resoundingly blame operatic culture for the deficiencies they observe in civil society and public engagement. Around 1816 this was no trivial matter: the cities and regions of Italy were grappling with the upheavals wrought by the decade-long occupation of much of the peninsula by Napoleonic forces and the political reorganizations imposed by the Congress of Vienna. After 1815 Milan and Venice were subsumed into the Habsburg Kingdom of Lombardy-Veneto, ruled by viceroys appointed by Vienna; Naples and Sicily were returned to the control of the Bourbon king Ferdinand who had governed the city for a turbulent half century before the advent of French rule in 1806; Bologna and its environs became part of the Papal States with Rome; and cities such as Florence reclaimed their status as autonomous duchies. Linguistically, the peninsula remained at least as diverse—a mosaic of regional dialects—so that the language sung on the opera stage would have been one of the few occasions on which audiences scattered across the peninsula enjoyed the same spectacle in the same standard Italian. Enmeshed in such tumultuous change, some among the literati saw an opportunity to reposition Italy in relation to Europe and to restore Italian letters to the widespread renown of the age of Dante or Michelangelo. A scant few among those were also wondering what steps they might take to gain independence from foreign rule or to knit the peninsula's regions into a single entity; but for most the idea of a unified and independent Italy was no more than a shadow, if even that.

From this perspective, the institution of opera would not seem a promising place to begin inquiry into the process of "making Italy" that stretched from 1815 through the unification of the Italian peninsula in 1861. Opera figured in these polemical essays because it was both the central form of entertainment for educated Italians and an important trope in the lively and anxious discourse about the place of Italian culture in a European context. Long before Verdi and the tales of spontaneous patriotic outpouring that rose up around some of his works, opera was heralded as something that Italians did better than anyone else in Europe, and therefore as a medium for projecting Italian character into the world. The primacy of Italian operatic style was rooted in the delivery of cantilena, the smooth, unbroken singing of a melodic line; and such melodies were thought to arise naturally from the inherent musicality of the language: "remarkable for its smoothness and the facility with which it enters into musical composition," as Italian was described in one eighteenth-century geographical compendium.[6] Rossini champion Giuseppe Carpani recast this conviction in more oppositional and more nationalistic terms in the pages of the *Biblioteca italiana* in 1818: "We see two genres of music emerge and contend on the battlefield: the ancient and regular Italian style based on song and melody, and the Romantic German style, poor in cantilena and rich in harmony, full, erudite, capricious."[7] As we shall see in chapter 2, such discourse could be just as debilitating as the conversation about how opera encouraged passivity and dullness of mind. The association between pure, vocally conceived melody and *italianità* could become a prison, with writers on opera circling endlessly around the same narrow lexicon of approved notions, each new work evaluated in relation to a mythical ideal of pure Neapolitan melody.

Yet going to the opera could also feel like the very opposite of imprisonment. In his pseudodiary from 1817, *Rome, Naples, and Florence*, the always effervescent Stendhal tells of being a frequent guest in the box of Ludovico di Breme at La Scala, amid a distinguished company that included Mme. de Staël's Italian translator Pietro Borsieri, philosopher Ermes Visconti, politician and patriot Federico Confalonieri, and revolutionary poet Silvio Pellico. "One never saw women," Stendhal admits; but for female company one could escape to the loge of Nina Viganò, singer and daughter of the choreographer Salvatore. Stendhal's description of the people he met in di Breme's box at La Scala is both energetic and intellectually intense: the fragments of conversation he relays, in fact, mostly concern Mme. de Staël's controversial article on translation, forming a sort of viva voce counterpart to the many weighty responses to that essay that were published in the pages of the *Biblioteca italiana, Il conciliatore,* and in freestanding pamphlets. It is a commonplace that the most important function of opera in the early nineteenth century was as a place of assembly, one of the few venues where large groups could freely gather, mingle, and react to what they saw and heard. But reading Stendhal against Leopardi, one could add that opera houses and the nearby cafés in which performances were dissected the next day were a crucial component of Italy's emerging public sphere, one that was invisible to the reclusive Leopardi.

A striking absence in Stendhal's bright picture of operatic sociability is any mention of music or musicians. He tells us that di Breme was generous enough to welcome Stendhal into his loge as a guest almost every night except Fridays, when the theater was dark; but he never mentions what operas they saw, and they never seem to encounter Rossini or any other musician. When Rossini does make an appearance a few pages earlier in Stendhal's idiosyncratic diary, it is almost in the guise of a jester, or perhaps a caricature of Italian charm and desire: at the Caffè dell'Accademia across from La Scala, the composer is overheard boasting about his conquest of a (married?) countess.[8] The format of *Rome, Naples, and Florence* as combination diary and travelogue makes the juxtaposition seem accidental; but the strict separation of the actual, practical business of making music from matters of the mind is also typical of the book, perhaps even integral to its conception.

IN SEARCH OF POLITICAL MUSIC

Two contests—one genuine, the other satirical, devised entirely to amuse the readership of a fashionable journal. Two manifestos—one penned by a woman of letters of impeccable cosmopolitan credentials, the other by a sheltered Italian from Le Marche. And then the exuberant testimony of Stendhal, an essential voice in operatic history, despite his chronic fallibility. This eclectic sampling puts before us some of the possible contemporary stances about how opera might connect to the public sphere, to political feeling and political thought. At the same time, the project of reading the *Corriere delle dame* in satirical mode alongside the letters of Vincenzo Monti, or juxtaposing the reclusive Leopardi with Stendhal's giddy prose makes clear one of the challenges of narrating the operatic history of early-nineteenth-century Italy, archived as it is in documentary material that is variously indirect, satirical, heavily censored (or self-censored), and oblique.

From our current vantage point it might seem that the historian's task was once much simpler. After the clouds of fascist-era historiography had cleared and before the suspicious mindset and magpie impulses of New Historicism hit musicology, it seemed possible to link specific operas and operatic styles to political events in a relatively straightforward way: one that relied on a distinction—and implicit interdependence—between "text" and "context." The same logic that allowed the linking of Mozart to the Enlightenment, or Beethoven to Napoleon, could authorize the pairing of Verdi "and" the Risorgimento, a dyad based more on contemporaneity and contiguity than on any demonstrable indications that Verdi's operas had affected—or reflected—the thought or action of Italy's period of nation-building.[9] The few instances of more concrete political relevance were worked very hard, none more so than the notorious case of "Va pensiero."

The story went that, inspired by the beauty of the tune and its words voicing the lament of an enslaved people far from their homeland, the audience at the 1842 première of Verdi's *Nabucco* at the Teatro alla Scala spontaneously insisted that the chorus be repeated, defying a police ban on encores. The story of that encore launched a thousand hermeneutic ships before being discredited in 1988 by Roger Parker. When Parker turned to the tome in which the anecdote was first recounted, Franco Abbiati's 1959 Verdi biography, he found that the author had more or less invented the passage, cobbling together bits from two different reviews to attribute to "Va pensiero" an encore that had actually been demanded for another chorus, the Hebrew prayer "Immenso Jeovha."[10] The purported encore was not the only basis for connecting Verdi's early operas to popular patriotic feeling; but it was one of the few instances that pointed toward a concrete audience response rather than the assumed import of words or music. Writing in 1981, David Kimbell took the interpretive leap of faith that is almost inevitable in "Risorgimento" interpretations of the early operas: "*Nabucco* established Verdi in the front rank of Italian composers because in it he showed that his peculiar brand of vehemence and melancholy was ideally matched to expressing the dilemma of contemporary Italy in operatic terms."[11] Philip Gossett, too, seemed to be forcing open a hermeneutic window when he heard what he perceived as a mismatch between words and music in "Immenso Jeovha" as a signal of subversive intent that audiences would have understood.[12] Journalist Alexander Stille exemplified the wide popular uptake of these theories in his 2007 review-essay in the *New Republic,* culminating with those familiar "crowds of patriots" who shouted "Viva Verdi!": "Since political speech was carefully monitored by the powers that controlled most of Italy . . . the cultural expression of italianità became a way of building a political identity while avoiding censorship. The operas of Verdi were commonly regarded as allegories of unification and patriotism."[13]

Probably the most common strategy in connecting Italian opera to politics has been based on morphologies—between the subaltern groups depicted in the early operas of Verdi and the oppression of northern Italians under Austria, but also between musical forms and states of mind. For example, the energy released in the fast concluding section (or "cabaletta") of the standard two-part "double" aria has been heard as a correlate to—and sometimes as a trigger for—the surge of aggression needed to overcome Habsburg domination.[14] Such interpretations falter partly because the similarities of design that seem so obvious to listeners today may not have been perceptible to audiences and writers in the 1830s and 1840s, who were less conditioned to see their own experiences in terms of allegory or abstract structures. To put this another way, the fact that it is *possible* to observe structural similarities between operatic plots or music and contemporary life does nothing to guarantee a relationship of *influence*—or even meaningful connection—between artworks and the offstage world.

This is where *Waiting for Verdi* begins: with the moment when historians acknowledged that listeners from the 1840s did not experience Verdi's operas in terms of analogies between the slaves in *Nabucco*—or the crusaders in *I Lombardi,* or the Aquileians in *Attila*—and northern Italians under Austrian control, nor turn to them at all for messages about politics or everyday life. Keeping these cold, hard facts firmly in view, it is still difficult to dispel completely the sense that Verdi's operas communicated something new and powerful to Italian listeners. The project of this book is to trust that intuition and to pursue it; to add to the documentary record or, more precisely, to access a new archive of historical listening to this music. I approach that challenging task partly by reading a wider range of sources, including texts on aesthetics, literature, and sometimes also science, economics, or anthropology, that were often penned by the same authors who shaped opinion about Verdi and about opera more generally in the journals of the period.

A more fundamental innovation of *Waiting for Verdi* is my decision to push back the start date of the inquiry long before Verdi's *Nabucco.* Not only has much of the reception history of Verdi's early period already been placed under the microscope, but the journalistic and literary discourses of that period are opaque and rigid, chilled by awareness of censorship but also by fatigue or overfamiliarity with assumptions about style and aesthetics that had ossified decades earlier. By beginning from the moment of Rossini's first successes in Naples and Milan around 1815, I aim to explore what opera meant to early-nineteenth-century audiences, what kinds of edification and emotion they believed theatrical experience could and should provide, and how they ranked various forms of mimesis and musical expression. To begin before Verdi also forces a generative reconception of how opera communicates with and about the surrounding world. I want to argue that the social commentary embedded in *La gazza ladra*'s story of a servant unjustly accused of theft, or in the transactions between shipbuilders and Venetian Doge in Donizetti's *Marino Faliero,* opened up new ways for Italians to think about the role of music in shaping their reality, less obvious but perhaps even more powerful than the binaristic struggles that anchored Verdi's early works. These operas and others like them jolted audiences into more active and sympathetic modes of attention in the theater, fostering an engagement that, I argue, was a precondition for a more activist stance outside of the theater. The book ends by returning to Verdi in Milan in the 1840s, to think about how critics and amateurs responded to opera at a time when political discourse was becoming more open and more articulate about unification and about casting off Austrian domination. Just before and during the revolutions of 1848 we begin to see the first instances of operatic music being used in the ways that become common by 1870 or 1880—as part of scripted political demonstrations, as the basis for popular songs and satirical sketches lampooning political leaders.

If differences of opinion about how to hear the evidence of Verdi's early operas and how to read the documentary record have at times divided the community of Verdi scholars, the root of the problem may be a lack of clarity about what makes music "political," or when a musical utterance might be considered to wield political force. This is a question that admits a range of approaches, each with ethical as well as methodological ramifications. Perhaps the lowest threshold, and the easiest to demonstrate, relies on assessing the opinions of composer or librettist about some political situation. By this measure Verdi scores highly, since in his letters of the period he several times expresses support for the 1848 revolutions and for a united, independent Italy. But these scattered statements hardly constitute a coherent political attitude and are in any case irrelevant to any impact the music may or may not have had. More importantly, even music that was commissioned or designed for an explicitly political occasion cannot be assumed to have reliably, completely, or consistently *communicated* whatever its political intentions might have been to its audience.[15] For music to be considered as "political," it should be possible to demonstrate that it has affected some aspect of concrete reality: the experience of hearing the music must have changed events in some fundamental way for listeners. In *Waiting for Verdi* I adopt a reception-based understanding of political music, ultimately referring back to what we can know of the reactions of contemporary listeners and to how those reactions might have been taken up into the collective political imagination.

This may give the impression that the moments that matter most are performances that provoked riots or sparked revolutions—situations that are both extremely rare and often rather random in their choice of musical cue. Famously, a duet from Auber's *La muette de Portici* was used a signal to set off a rebellion in Brussels in 1830.[16] And a chorus from Verdi's *Ernani* was adapted a number of times in 1846–47 to celebrate the new, more progressive pope, and by extension the new freedoms he was expected to introduce. Occasions like these suggest that music had real, sometimes even flamboyant, impact on political life; but the music and the ideas and emotions connected with it tend to be incidental in these situations, usually selected and "weaponized" because of some convenient association between the words and the political cause.

A more commonplace vector of influence between musical experience and the political sphere runs by way of aesthetics and feeling. New representational modes might challenge spectators to react in new ways, or a performance could prompt emotional reactions that changed the way listeners engaged with ideas central to the creation of a nation, ideas such as sympathy, community, progress, tradition, or sacrifice.[17] In these cases, *discourse* is often a crucial term that mediates between inarticulate but intense musical force and political impact: the writings of contemporary listeners (most often journalists but also philosophers and some dilettantes) tend to converge on a few pregnant themes or problems or musical effects, pointing the way toward an understanding of how this music might have acted on groups of listeners and how its power might have been translated into thought and even action.[18]

The allusion to Samuel Beckett's drama of vain anticipation in this book's title is intended both ironically and sincerely. The sensation of "waiting" may capture something of the experience of Italians living in the first half of the nineteenth century, who sought—at first vaguely, then with more purpose— cultural icons and models that would foster a unified national identity and inspire activism. Of course, no one was waiting specifically for Verdi, nor even for the kinds of sounds and situations that his operas pioneered. In that sense my title is more apt as a description of the mindset of the scholars and opera fans who have told this story, over and over, since the 1860s than it is of the pre-1848 historical actors whose voices and actions fill these pages. If Verdi ever did arrive as a symbol of nation, this occurred not so much when his operas began to attract popular and critical acclaim in the 1840s, but fifteen or twenty years later, when the composer and his music were pressed into service as quasi-official signifiers of national pride. In this sense Verdi's arrival was so belated and so gradual as to be almost as anticlimactic as the process dramatized by Beckett. In a more ironic vein, blind anticipation could also be a figure for the efforts of writers on opera since Unification to paste together a coherent narrative of opera's significance—seeking, but never quite seizing, a critical mass of evidence or a truly convincing account of opera's role in the buildup to Unification.

BEFORE "VIVA VERDI"

Long dismissed as a movement of the elites that never succeeded in creating a culture that was both national and truly popular, the Risorgimento has recently been redefined as something more like a mass movement.[19] Its name literally referring to revival, rebirth, resurgence, the term *Risorgimento* gathers together a loose sequence of groups, movements, and social attitudes that worked to foster a shared identity among Italians, nurtured resistance to foreign rule, and eventually made possible the unification of the peninsula into a single state in 1861 (with Rome finally added in 1870). Even if leadership and decision-making were concentrated in the hands of an educated few, the movement was rooted in a set of values shared to some degree by all Italians, regardless of class, social station, or political alignment.[20] Experience of live opera and participation in the conversations that operatic performances stimulated were similarly reserved for an educated elite; but operatic melodies could filter into the piazza, and the aesthetic ideas and social practices promoted by opera were disseminated just as widely, seeping into and gradually reshaping conceptions of what it meant to feel and act, to belong to a group, or to invoke the name of "Italy." In much the same way, the plans of action formulated by a coterie of educated men in northern Italian cities were gradually transformed into widespread, popular, military actions resulting in the unification of the peninsula and the establishment of a constitutional government.

Even leaving aside the challenges of narrating a cultural history that makes room for the political force of musical works, it is difficult to bring the Risorgimento into focus as a single movement or historical progression. Not only did Italy's halting march toward nationhood play out on the split levels of elite and popular action and decision-making, but the movement's cardinal events were different in each of the peninsula's city-states and kingdoms, and its governing ideas changed (at the least) with each decade. One account would involve the uprisings and revolutions that erupted periodically, in 1820, in 1831, more widely and with greater success in 1848, and then decisively in the sustained military engagements between 1859 and 1861. But revolution and eruptions of resistance are not the whole story; at least as significant for a history of cultural forms is the atmosphere of combined secrecy, complacency, and indirect utterance that shaped Italian speech during this period. Planning for revolution was carried out by secret societies such as the Carbonari and by political thinkers operating from safe perches in Switzerland, France, and England. And while resistance activities and speech were suppressed or expressed only in carefully controlled settings, it is also important that between the scattered flares of revolution life was comfortable and even complacent; most Italians lived most of the time in a state of unconflicted acceptance of foreign and absolutist rule, at least until 1848.[21]

Historians Alberto Banti, Paul Ginsborg, and Carlotta Sorba have examined the cultural texts and images that promoted the idea of a unified and autonomous Italy in the popular imagination, which by the late 1850s inspired large numbers of Italians to volunteer for the revolutionary forces and risk their lives for the idea of nation.[22] Banti focuses on a common set of beliefs and rituals around family, gender roles, and religion (many of which play a prominent role in the operas of the time), while Sorba has teased out the multiple levels on which Italian culture and everyday life took on the forms and values of melodrama.[23] In the Risorgimento's final phase, roughly from 1848 until the convening of the first Italian parliament in 1861, this melodramatic populism fused with an increasingly hardy strain of pragmatism, as the deft statesman Camillo Cavour formulated the compromise that would position the Savoy king Vittorio Emanuele II as head of the new constitutional monarchy. What had been a scattered collection of local movements began to converge on a single agenda, led on two planes by charismatic populist hero Giuseppe Garibaldi and by Cavour, whose agenda shared none of the fiery idealism of Giuseppe Mazzini, whose utopian and theocratic vision had been influential before 1848. Once Garibaldi began to amass his army of volunteers and move south in 1859, the quiet laments and elegies of the earlier period were supplanted by more pugnacious songs narrating battles or inciting soldiers to fight, and the slogan "Viva VERDI" began to appear, as an acronym for "Vittorio Emanuele, Re d'Italia."[24]

Cultural messages like the "Viva VERDI" slogan were constructed by individuals or groups who wielded some legislative or communicative power and who had conscious plans to harness artistic works or a composer's image to political (and propagandistic) agendas.[25] Although still active in many cities, censorship was loosened (and during the revolutionary period in 1848 lifted altogether), and the values of what Banti has called the "Risorgimento canon" were broadly disseminated through cheap print products such as dime novels and posters. Before 1848, messages and motivations are more difficult to ascertain; documentation is both sparser and less transparent; and the vectors between music and such concepts as identity, morality, and mimesis were very much up for grabs. Constraints such as censorship and the abstract philosophical and moral tone that prevailed in Italian writing about music collude to render the sources opaque and often contradictory—all of which makes the period before 1848 both difficult to fathom and fascinating as an object of study.

Although the history of Risorgimento is full of nuances and contradictions, musicological approaches to this period in Italian history have largely construed it in baldly heroic terms, figuring the noble, oppressed Italy as bravely casting off Austrian rule, censorship, and oppression. Words like *emancipation* and *oppression* have echoed blithely through the literature, and images of rebels consigned to long terms in the Spielberg prison, plastering the walls of Milan with subversive broadsheets, or facing the firing squad while singing opera—as the Bandiera brothers supposedly did in 1844, with a theme from Mercadante's now-forgotten *Donna Caritea*—have been common coin. Later history shows that nationalism was a no less heady cocktail for Italians than for other European nations. While writing with excitement of opera's role in the crystallization of a national sensibility, I hope also to give suitable weight to the caution and ambivalence with which musicians and intellectuals initially approached the national question, as well as to the spirit of accommodation and even apathy that informed many of their statements.

GUNFIRE IN THE DISTANCE

I'm writing so that you don't worry that I have been killed in the gunfire. I am a man who is worried by few things, in fact, by just one: that is, if an opera of mine goes badly. I don't care about the rest; I live because they let me live, I want to go on living even when I cannot live anymore, etc.[26]

When Gaetano Donizetti wrote home to reassure his family in Bergamo of his safety after the 1831 uprising in Rome, he complained that the government had closed the theaters for a few days. The letter, with its cheerful nod to a "live and let live" philosophy, is stamped with Donizetti's unique combination of whimsical humor and pragmatism. But the proud declaration of indifference to politics, along with a wholehearted commitment to theatrical commerce, could have been uttered by almost any Italian composer of the time. Among scores of letters in which Bellini frets about how each of his new operas will be received, there is just a single one that alludes to the "liberal" politics of the audience for the first performances of *I puritani*, at Paris's Théâtre-Italien.

The overwhelming tone of composers' written statements was resolutely apolitical and somewhat out of step with the mood of the era. Even Verdi, who served as a senator in the first Italian parliament, seems to have noticed and engaged with the Risorgimento selectively, usually keeping practical theatrical and commercial concerns firmly in the foreground. When the 1848 revolutions broke out in Milan and Venice, Verdi was in Paris where he had taken up residence for a combination of professional and personal reasons. He expressed his excitement about the course of events in a letter to librettist Francesco Maria Piave:

You talk to me about music! . . . Do you think that I want to bother myself now with notes, with sounds? There cannot be any music welcome to Italian ears in 1848 except the music of the cannon! I would not write a note for all the money in the world: I would feel immense guilt at using up music paper, which is so good for making shells.[27]

As enthusiastic as Verdi sounds here, his rhetoric coincides with that of Donizetti's letter of 1831 in seeming to treat political action and musical expression as mutually exclusive. Just a few months later, though, Verdi would accept a commission to compose *La battaglia di Legnano,* which would become his most overtly revolutionary opera; in the same year he composed a patriotic hymn to words by Goffredo Mameli (who also wrote the words of the Italian national anthem) at the request of Mazzini.[28] The passionate commitment that led Verdi to devote creative energy to the revolutionary cause in 1848 was sporadic, however, alternating with more sustained moods of pragmatism and disillusionment once the revolutions were suppressed and Austria and the papal government returned to power.[29]

The tendency for composers to keep politics at a safe distance may be rooted in the institutional nature of opera, in which composers had to function partly as self-promoting businessmen, but might equally originate in the structures of musical education. It is not difficult to imagine the ways it would smooth the path of a composer doing business with theaters in multiple cities, under constantly shifting patronage and jurisdiction, to advertise that his primary loyalty was to compositional craft and theatrical impact. And the church- and conservatory-based training most composers received focused on skills and technique, distinct from the breadth of literary and historical knowledge covered at university or *liceo.* This indifference may also be partly a trick of perception: the virtuosic and highly conventional style of bel canto opera may have encouraged some interpreters to highlight composers' apolitical statements as a reflection of the music's style.[30]

Of course, what composers thought and felt is just one angle on the question, and a relatively minor one, as the case of Verdi clearly shows. No matter how explicitly or passionately Verdi supported Mazzini and the revolution in 1848 (or, indeed, before and after), there is scant evidence that audiences at the early performances of his operas perceived the same patriotic or emancipatory tones that many listeners find in them so easily now.[31] As I have already hinted, my focus in these pages will fall not on intention but on the social and intellectual circles in which opera was conceived, discussed, evaluated, and staged; on patterns of circulation; and on reception. The cast of characters in *Waiting for Verdi* is large and varied, and many of its leading figures were polymaths and eccentrics, who were perhaps highly influential for a handful of years but almost completely forgotten since. Because opera was an important economic engine in Italy and across Europe, poets, journalists, and educators could count on work for an opera house to fill in the gaps between more permanent jobs. The margins of operatic history are crowded with stories of librettists and critics who turned to these pursuits after they had been dismissed from another position for their liberal or revolutionary views, or had fled or been exiled for political reasons. The chapters that follow trace the pathways of conversation, collaboration, and economic dependence among these various figures and the textual traces they have left—which include reviews, pamphlets on aesthetics, and private correspondence but also musical works, techniques, and events. The richness and multiplicity of the connections and of the cultural products generated reveals the opera house as an anchor and animating force for the period in a far more active way than has traditionally been described.

Are these connections, then, "networks" and their participants "historical actors"? In a literal sense, definitely not, since much of this book was drafted before I encountered the writings of Bruno Latour or his injunctions to "follow your actors." In another sense, however, musicological writing has for almost twenty years been working with presentiments of and variations on Latour's theory—his ways of tracking the flow and formation of ideas among social actors, his firm resistance to the idea that "society" could be a stable or preexisting concept to which we can relate events and texts, and his conviction that texts (and objects, and events) are not fixed things to be critiqued or deconstructed, but "gatherings" of human thought, effort, and action.[32] The Latourian element in this book has most to do with a notion of historical processes and political imagination as flowing from a tangle of messy, opaque, and often conflicting evidence, rather than from any fixed notion of "society" or "context."[33] Within that fluid and constantly reforming complex of ideas and feelings, musical works and performances serve as sites around which social meaning can converge and crystallize, rather than as screens for interpretation or auratic objects that transport listeners to transcendent states of receptivity to community or patriotic commitment. (To understand "society" in this way perhaps comes especially easily to historians of nineteenth-century Italy, where every time a coherent social unit seems to come into view it is immediately destabilized by some uncooperative or dissenting voice.)

At a few points in each chapter, I venture suggestions that specific operatic scenes or musical passages can be heard as possessing social force, and propose that they were experienced that way by contemporary audiences. Musicologists these days generally trust verbal evidence far more than musical evidence, wary that transfixed by some structural detail or ravishing vocal moment, we might lose touch with the historical listener. Yet written accounts of the musical cultures of the past may not be much more legible than musical works and can be equally prone to misreading. Anyone writing or composing in Italy during the first half of the nineteenth century knew that their words would be scrutinized by censors, but which words, ideas, and images would be forbidden and which permitted was always a bit of a mystery, depending on the mores of the specific city and regime in power, the whims of the censors, and the prestige of the authors.[34] Because of this, writers often stopped before even beginning to write anything that might take a clear position. Such sources need not be distrusted completely, but they certainly need to be *read through*—scanned for subtexts, placed in dialogue with other writings, and creatively interpreted. As I show in some detail in chapter 6, this often entails reading for loose or implicit associations between musical effects and topical issues, or for vignettes and imagery that seem out of place in the discussion of an opera but that point toward some veiled context or concern.

Still, even censored newspaper articles are made of words, whereas musical communication lacks even the imperfect referential stability of a language. In feeling my way toward modes of listening that seem historically responsible, I've been helped by work on a closely related set of issues in literary studies that includes the "distant reading" pioneered by Franco Moretti, Heather Love's advocacy of "thin description," and the "surface reading" theorized by Stephen Best and Sharon Marcus.[35] Moretti's "distant reading" was an early digital humanities project using computer analysis to reveal patterns of diction, syntax, and subject matter in literary texts across styles, periods, and regions. The variant of distant reading that comes into play in *Waiting for Verdi,* without computers and with much smaller amounts of data, resembles a manic collecting spree or hoarding disorder. It involves gathering together as many instances of a single *type* of thing as possible and then reading that assemblage of musical works, or moments from works, as a kind of super- or macro-text. The dispersal into and across multiple examples thwarts any temptation to read operas as coherent, stylistically or structurally unified, generic, or convention breaking. Considering a body of music that features similar gestures or effects unseats the individual composerly voice and allows us to locate a social voice speaking through recurrence, pattern, and convention.

The critical paradigms of "thin description" and "surface reading" have in common an impatience with long-dominant styles of reading that would seize on a few telling moments from a text—inconsistencies, formal tics, or moments of exceptional force—only to treat those moments as "symptoms" of some underlying ideological framework. Although musicology was never quite as ruled by the hegemony of suspicious or symptomatic reading, the hermeneutic turn of the mid-1990s shared some of the same aims and strategies. As in literary studies, the substitution of simple, detailed *description* of events and techniques for more selective, goal-oriented interpretations might have a cleansing or renewing effect. Of course, musicologists have listened to musical surfaces before. More than a decade ago, Wye J. Allanbrook urged scholars of the eighteenth century to "theorize" the "comic surface," by which she meant listening for the kaleidoscopic play of musical topoi that can function as characters or voices in eighteenth-century music, and thinking about the syntactical functions and sequencing of those topoi.[36] The "topoi" of nineteenth-century Italian opera are different—fewer dances, more sighs, swaggers, and storytelling in song—but on some level opera scholars have always known that the surface mattered.[37] Best and Marcus's injunction to read from the surface can also be understood as an invitation to take seriously the messages sent by "surface" elements in music such as instrumentation and timbre, and especially to listen closely to musical moments that depend crucially on evoking a specific timbral world, such as tolling bells and fanfares, but also (for example) the adulterated, hollowed out, or nostalgic effects created when the characteristic contours of a fanfare are rendered in the more intimate timbres of woodwind instruments. Granting weight to such local effects shifts the scale on which we listen, directing attention to moment-to-moment events and away from larger-scale patterns. The vocabulary of musical description lacks terms for that intermediate space of the phrase or the paragraph, which is arguably where some of the most immediate and forceful musical communication occurs. With such a shift of scale, we might begin to probe elements like Donizetti's use of small-scale repetition, or the dramatic pacing of Rossini's operas, a topic that fascinated Stendhal but that is mostly lost to us now.[38]

. . .

Waiting for Verdi begins with a pair of chapters that engage with Rossini, examining how this music signified differently in the classicizing, imperial atmosphere of Naples around 1815 and in the much more progressive climate of Milan, where the first literary debates about romanticism were launched just a few years later. Chapter 2 tackles the knotty problem of whether Italy experienced a "romantic era," and specifically whether Italian opera could ever be said to have dabbled in romanticism.

Until the 1840s Italians writing about music continued to draw heavily on aesthetic assumptions and rhetorical conventions formulated by the Encyclopédistes a half century earlier. The shifting borders and shifting models of subjectivity that arrived with the Napoleonic period and the Congress of Vienna meant that these old assumptions were positioned against a new background and rapidly destabilized, so that for a time there seemed to be no clear consensus on questions such as what kinds of subject matter were suitable for dramatic representation on the stage, how music and words should be combined, or how music acted (or should act) on the listener. Into that mix entered the potent force of romantic thought, which was arguably disseminated most successfully in Italy not by literature or by the heated theoretical debates about literary style that recurred cyclically across the period, but by operas that showcased discrete elements of romantic influence.[39] The impact of romanticism on the Italian nineteenth century has until recently been underestimated, both because romantic thought never fully held sway or unseated classical values in Italy and because of long-standing doubt (extending back to Carl Schmitt in the 1920s) about the potential of romanticism to wield political force. Both Paul Ginsborg and Adrian Lyttelton have countered Schmitt's cynicism, arguing that romanticism, through the very investment in fantasy that Schmitt demeaned, was a crucial force in rewriting the horizon of expectations for Italians, making the impossible seem possible, and ultimately mobilizing popular support for the abstract idea of a unified and autonomous Italy.[40]

My point of entry into the tangled, self-referential, and past-obsessed debates around Italian romanticism comes not via opera, but ballet: the "pantomimic ballets" choreographed by Salvatore Viganò, staged to great acclaim in Milan between about 1815 and 1823. Viganò was the darling of the artistic revolutionaries: while opera is barely mentioned in those early romantic debates, Viganò's ballets are repeatedly praised as ideal examples of a hybrid genre (combining music and dance) and of powerful emotion expressed through the body, without words. Zeroing in on simultaneous performances in 1817 at La Scala of Rossini's *La gazza ladra* and a ballet version of *Otello*, I discuss Viganò's choreography and his use of music by Rossini and others to show why ballet occupied such a central place in these formative debates about innovation and tradition in Italian art. It is tempting to imagine that Viganò stands in for the absent Beethoven: where pure instrumental music had not captured much public interest in Italy, the language of the mute body became another way to circumvent language and to silence the socially contaminated voice. By examining, in parallel, the language used to laud Viganò and the terms that governed the reception of Rossini during this period, this chapter speculates about why music was not yet admitted to romantic discourse.

Chapter 3 takes a new approach to an old question: the relationship between opera and history. It is a commonplace that opera and the novel in Italy became relevant to the national struggle only in the 1840s, as both genres began to represent formative events of the nation's deep history. But opera had already been "historical"—and, I argue, potentially topical—for three decades, staging power relationships between courtiers and monarchs, and the performance of absolute power through plots set at the Tudor court and the Spanish courts of the sixteenth century. Rossini's *Elisabetta, regina d'Inghilterra* (1815) launched a fad for operas about Tudor queens, which eventually produced four separate "Tudor" operas by Donizetti and operas about Mary, Queen of Scots by Mercadante, Carlo Coccia, and many others. The chapter alternates between looking synoptically at the Tudor operas and their reception as a group, construing them as a sort of collective, half-articulate statement about power and statecraft in Restoration Italy, and closer examinations of scenes from a few representative works, especially Rossini's *Elisabetta* and Donizetti's *Maria Stuarda*. What emerges is a clear progression—perhaps not surprisingly—away from allegory and glorification of the monarch toward a darker and more conflicted view of governance.

The book's second main section moves to Paris to consider operas and salon music produced by the sizeable community of Italian political exiles who landed in the French capital after the failed revolutions of 1831. The group encompassed many exiles and expatriates who had fled Italy after the failed uprisings of 1830–31, including librettists Carlo Pepoli (*I puritani*), Agostino Ruffini (*Marino Faliero*), and Giovanni Ruffini (*Don Pasquale*). Singers Giulia Grisi and Luigi Lablache were also important presences, as were Rossini, Bellini, and Donizetti. Chapter 4 addresses the exceptional case of Donizetti's *Marino Faliero*, which provoked an ecstatic response from

Mazzini who greeted it in his "Filosofia della musica" (1836) as the harbinger of a new, "progressive" operatic style. The central section of the chapter asks: Why *Marino Faliero?* What was it about this opera that inspired Mazzini to single it out as an exemplar of the "music of the future"? One answer involves personal and intellectual connections between Mazzini's circle and Donizetti's that have not been much discussed before; but I also show that certain aspects of Donizetti's approach to forms and pacing worked especially well to accommodate Mazzini's expectations for a "progressive" musical style. Perhaps most importantly, the spin on a famous episode of Venetian history offered in Donizetti's opera generated ideas about historical causality and about what might inspire someone to join a revolution: ideas that had urgent application to Mazzini's political project in the mid-1830s.

The book's Paris section closes with a chapter that tries to imagine the kinds of musical performances and political conversations that went on in the salons frequented by the exiles, using as a starting point some cryptic allusions to a Bellini opera that are embedded within groups of parlor songs by Rossini and Mercadante. The poetry for these song collections was written by the exiled poet Count Carlo Pepoli, known mainly as the librettist for Bellini's last opera, *I puritani.* Both sets of songs contain lightly disguised allusions to *I puritani,* which was the operatic sensation of the moment, as well as to a raft of surprisingly stereotypical images of exoticized Italians—captured in such musical and poetic topoi as a Venetian barcarolle, a Neapolitan tarantella, and a seductive Tyrolienne. The similarities between the two cycles and their shared references to the Bellini opera grant insight into a mode of conversation and cultural activity that is usually opaque to history—the kinds of parlor games and subtle allusions that characterized conversation in the salon, an important counterpart to the official operatic culture at stake in the rest of *Waiting for Verdi.*

The book's final section consists of a single chapter on Verdi's operas of the 1840s. My focus here is not the famous *Nabucco,* which—as mentioned earlier—has been too much argued over and for which little documentary evidence survives. Instead I focus on Verdi's next opera, *I Lombardi alla prima crociata* (1843), which was also his first work to treat a theme from Italian history: the participation of the Lombard forces in the First Crusade to the Holy Land. I discuss the reception of Verdi's opera in counterpoint with a group of influential literary and historical texts dealing with the Crusades and commentaries on the very successful paintings on national and historical subjects by Francesco Hayez. Whereas writers on literature and painting seem to have been free, despite press censorship, to comment on the latent topical resonances of the works they critiqued, reviews of the opera are completely silent on these matters. Like the marginalization of Rossini in favor of choreographer Viganò before 1820, this bracketing of opera from political debates suggests that opera continued to occupy a special position in Italian cultural discourse, both central to and insulated from mainstream issues and opinion. While Italian music criticism had been fundamentally remade—invented, some might argue—in the years between Rossini's *Otello* or *La gazza ladra* and *I Lombardi,* the contrast between the receptions of Verdi and Hayez in the 1840s shows that opera maintained a veneer of otherness, of disconnection from worldly representation, which had come to embody both its uniqueness as a form of cultural representation and its animating power.

At the conference "Verdi's Third Century," held at New York University to mark the bicentenary of Verdi's birth in November 2013, "Va pensiero" was heard three times, far outpolling any other bit of music by the birthday boy. Each occurrence was charged with intense emotion but also intellectual unease, and the performances themselves displayed a pronounced estrangement from the original operatic context and voicing, as well as from the political-interpretive frames that were for so long inescapable whenever "Va pensiero" was heard or discussed. The famous chorus was first heard in a paper about the Lega Nord's use of Verdi's iconic chorus in a performance that featured Zuleika Morsut, the winner of a beauty contest run by the northern Italian separatist party, who led the crowd in singing "Va pensiero" at a 2009 rally in the Lombard city of Pontida. Morsut's untrained voice is badly miked, the recorded accompaniment distorted by feedback, and the crowd sings along at a leaden pace while throwing clouds of green confetti and waving banners bearing the symbols of the Lega.[41] Despite its low musical and visual production values, however, this performance conveys a convincing enthusiasm and populism. The next day "Va pensiero" was heard again in a paper on the uses of Verdi's music by Austrian military bands. In a nice twist of irony, this arrangement of the chorus, made for military band in 1846, was based on an arrangement prepared by Joseph Tutsch, an Austrian resident of Milan who had also led the stage band at the première of *Nabucco.* The significance of the discovery that Austrian musicians almost certainly performed in the première of *Nabucco* was somewhat diminished by the speaker's evident discomfort, his apparent (and unfounded) fear that these revelations would provoke angry and defensive responses.[42]

The chorus's third outing at the conference was live and unscripted—a sentimental, participatory singing of the chorus during dinner at one of the old Italian social clubs in Greenwich Village, joined with varying degrees of enthusiasm and expertise by all in attendance. This impromptu rendition of the chorus was intended as a sort of gift to Verdi, ignoring (of course) the fact that the chorus had earlier that day been implicated with racist and anti-immigrant policies of the Lega Nord. This sentimental performance by a group of well-informed historians of opera (joined by some theater people and opera lovers) reminds us how difficult it is to clear away the layers of historical and cultural significance that have accrued to Verdi, and to "Va pensiero," over the past 150 years. Essentially, in 2013, as in 1913 (and today), if you're going to sing a bit of Verdi, it pretty much has to be "Va pensiero." This was demonstrated again and again in Italy during the 150th anniversary of Unification in 2011, as when Riccardo Muti protested government cuts to the arts by leading the audience at the Rome Opera in a participatory encore of the chorus. In a brief speech from the podium Muti warned that "if we slay the culture on which the history of Italy is founded, truly our country will be beautiful and lost" (the last few words a loose quote from the chorus), then began an encore of the famous choral lament for a lost homeland, proposing that "we all sing along together." As the sing-along rendition reached its climax, leaflets fluttered from the galleries in a powerful (and probably deliberate) echo of the opera-house protest that opens Luchino Visconti's 1954 film *Senso*. Muti's canny use of this music points to the fact that we need two parallel (or asymptotic?) histories: one of the uses to which "Va pensiero" has been put since its first explicitly political outings around 1859; and another, to track and evaluate the broader claims for the political uses and resonances of opera—including but not limited to Verdi—in the period during which Italy was first formulating its national voices.

TWO

Accidental Affinities

GIOACHINO ROSSINI AND SALVATORE VIGANÒ

TEXTS AND ACTS, MILAN 1816 AND 1817

When Madame de Staël ranted in the *Biblioteca italiana* in 1816 that "sitting for five hours every evening listening to what passes for words in Italian opera must dull the intellect of the nation, for want of exercise," one might expect that Italian intellectuals, impresarios, librettists, or playwrights would have responded with spirited defenses of their theatrical pursuits, or proposed some more intellectually robust alternatives, or both.[1] What happened in response to the translation of Mme. de Staël's polemic looked more like retrenchment: scholars and journalists leapt to the defense of existing Italian ways of reading and writing in spirited attempts at rehabilitating classics of the Italian past, reframing the poetry and epic of Dante, Ariosto, and Boccaccio as newly relevant to post-Napoleonic realities. Twenty years later Giuseppe Mazzini's essay on the "Filosofia della musica" (1836) would finally insert opera into the national debate, although the essay's impact was both delayed and limited by the circumstances of its initial publication. By the mid-1840s, Verdi and his librettists would begin to adapt the works by Schiller and Shakespeare that Mme. de Staël had championed, providing Italy at long last with "serious" theatrical entertainments that were capable of nurturing a lively public discourse. The long gaps between these influential interventions can lull the historian into a sense that style and aesthetics advanced in sudden lurches, with audiences and critics patiently biding their time in between—waiting for Verdi, in a sense, or for the promotion of opera to a main strand in a braided discourse of politics, culture, and identity that took shape around the time of Verdi's early successes at La Scala.

Of course, the Milanese writers who participated in the debates sparked by Mme. de Staël did not recognize any such void in their theatrical existence. What we know about the reach of opera at the time suggests that most of these writers frequented La Scala regularly and were familiar with the new works of Rossini as they arrived in Milan, although they barely alluded to these sonic encounters in print. But neither did they consider La Scala derelict in the project of shoring up Italian public culture, and some of them discovered within its walls a surprising figure for lionization: the choreographer Salvatore Viganò. Viganò's cryptic and erudite ballets attracted all of the probing exegesis and aesthetic prestige that seemed to elude Rossini in this early phase of his reception, so much so that reactions to Viganò's works conditioned the reception of Rossini. This chapter revisits some of the key texts of the romantic debates sparked by Mme. de Staël, not to dwell on their disagreements about the Aristotelian unities or the achievements of Italian writers of the past, but to consider instead the theatrical experiences of the debates' main actors and the ways their encounters with dance and opera in performance inflected their theoretical stances.

In the process, we glimpse the emergence of a new mentality that could appreciate artworks for breaking the rules, for departing from the ideals of beauty and decorum, and for daring to depict characters and subjects less edifying than they were gripping or disturbing. These newly adventurous narrative forms—still frowned upon by many—brought Italian works into conversation with northern European trends and allowed them to interact more closely with the concrete realities of the surrounding world. While Carl Schmitt famously dismissed romanticism as abdicating realistic analysis of the world in favor of fantasy and individualism, the performances and criticism surveyed in this chapter suggest the opposite: that the narrative disruptions of romanticism promoted absorption and emotional engagement, building a public sphere in which art could inflect the real attitudes and actions of spectators.[2] As Adrian Lyttelton has put it, romanticism in Italy enabled "the formation of a new structure of expectations through which contemporary reality [could] be viewed, and amplified."[3] In this broad sense, as well as in the narrower realm of operatic reception, the years around 1816 served as a fulcrum. Art in general began to matter differently to Italian audiences, and at the same time responses to Rossini's operas evolved from the fanatical but rarefied excitement of the melomaniac to a discourse in which the encounter with opera could yield truths about experience, identity, and history. Attention to these debates and performances, then, is also a first step in understanding how opera came to matter to Italy and to Italians as more than escapist entertainment.

ROSSINI'S SILENT OTHER

Reading the volleys back and forth in the pamphlet war that followed the translation of Mme. de Staël's essay, one would conclude that the world of Italian letters was cautious at best, cleaving anxiously to a canon of established authors and a set of antiquated rules for the design of dramatic works. Leafing through the reviews in the Milanese press during those same years creates a completely different impression. While the academic authorities who held sway in the pages of the *Biblioteca italiana* and *Il conciliatore* deliberate at length before—just possibly—granting permission for the action of theatrical works to stretch across more than twenty-four hours or beyond a single physical location, audiences at La Scala and other leading theaters were regularly exposed to spectacles whose challenges to classical restraint went far beyond these tame conditions. As these vignettes from works performed at La Scala show, grotesquerie, erotic innuendo, and magical extensions of time and space were common coin:

> A young married couple lose their way on a hunting trip, and find themselves beneath an enchanted walnut tree. The bride is abducted by a witch, who imprisons her inside the entrails of a deer, where she is seduced, in turn, by allegorical embodiments of the three ages of man while her husband looks on with the aid of a magical periscope.
>
> A servant girl is imprisoned and sentenced to death for stealing from her employers. While she awaits sentencing in her jail cell, the town magistrate visits her, offers to barter her freedom for sexual favors and then begins an attempted rape, interrupted only when he is summoned to preside at her trial.
>
> In a ballet set in ancient Egypt, one tableau arranged four "comico-balletic" actors in a straight line, two kneeling and two upright, balanced on the shoulders of the other two in a pyramid formation copied from Egyptian sacerdotal symbols in which four statues represented the four primitive elements. The lower kneeling figures stood for water and earth, and the two balanced above symbolized the elements that looked to the heavens, but at the same time are found at the core of every living being, air and fire.[4]

Some will recognize the second of these scenes as an episode from Rossini's *La gazza ladra*. The more supernaturally and mystically inflected passages describe episodes from the ballets of Viganò, *Il noce di Benevento* (1802, but revived at La Scala in 1812) and *Psammi, Re d'Egitto,* premièred at La Scala a few months after *La gazza ladra* in 1817.

Although he was regularly hailed as a genius during his lifetime, Viganò's name is now invoked most often in connection with his fleeting association with Beethoven. It was for a ballet by Viganò that Beethoven composed his music for *The Creatures of Prometheus* in 1801, but since both the libretto that contained a synopsis of the ballet's action and its choreography have been lost, the collaboration survives mainly in the gawky theme that Beethoven reused in the last movement of the *Eroica* and in his *Eroica* variations.[5] In Vienna, Venice, and Milan over the first two decades of the nineteenth century, Viganò and his dancers were celebrated, their every move tracked and interpreted.

The rage for Viganò had elements of a fad and a cult of personality, but the choreographer's works also consistently received serious scrutiny in literary circles. Where Rossini's name is completely absent from the thousands of words spilled in the post-Staël polemics, Viganò figures prominently. He appears at the center of an imagined debate between a "classicist" and a "romantic" in one chapter of Ermes Visconti's "Elementary Principles of Romantic Poetry." The argument turns on the relative virtues of Viganò's ballet *Mirra* and its source in Alfieri's play of the same name, and rather surprisingly, it is the classicist in Visconti's dialogue who advocates for Viganò.[6] Visconti declares pantomimic ballet to be superior to spoken poetry for the speed with which it can depict successive moods and gestures and for uniting abstract ideas with the nobility of dance; similarly, he places it above painting in his hierarchy of the arts for its ability to link successive actions in an unbroken flow. Only as an afterthought does Visconti think to compare ballet to its sister art, opera. In a footnote he acknowledges that he has "contrasted the language of gestures in pantomimic ballet with the recitation of poetry, leaving aside the genre of opera *so as not to complicate matters too much.*"[7] The muteness of ballet comes into play in distinguishing Viganò's danced version of *Mirra* from Alfieri's play. As the classicist puts it, "When we are dealing with characters who move to the beat and gesticulate instead of speaking, one is transported into a different mode and one is primed to go along with even the most fanciful inventions, without reflecting as one normally would."[8]

When a composer does make an appearance in the romantic debates, it is not Rossini but the recently deceased Giovanni Paisiello. Writing again in *Il conciliatore* just a few months after the publication of the "Elementary Principles," Visconti places Viganò and Paisiello—or fictional surrogates for them—face-to-face, as two of the four interlocutors in an imaginary dialogue about the importance of the unities.[9] The premise for this imagined conversation is the "irregular" form of Viganò's ballet *Prometeo,* which provoked a feuilletonistic scandal after its 1813 première at La Scala by flagrantly ignoring the unities even while setting the mythological tale of Prometheus. Visconti's 1819 "Dialogue on the Dramatic Unities of Time and Place" can be counted as a belated contribution to the pamphlet war around *Prometeo.* Proceeding from the challenge posed by Viganò's sprawling ballet, Visconti stages a debate between two primary interlocutors: liberal philosopher Giuseppe Romagnosi, who serves as Visconti's mouthpiece, and the classicist Luigi Lamberti, with Viganò and Paisiello assigned slim supporting roles.[10]

Visconti gives Paisiello little to say except jocular interjections designed to elicit replies from the two main antagonists. In an exchange that points toward the true subject of Visconti's essay, Romagnosi asks first Paisiello, then Viganò whether they identify with their characters: "You, Paisiello, when you write a duet at the keyboard, you don't believe that you *are* the two lovers who are singing together. Nevertheless, you feel yourself empathizing with their passions, feeling joy, sadness, terror, hopes. Wouldn't you call that state of mind inspiration, enthusiasm, illusion?" Paisiello laconically responds, *"Sì: ebbene?"* (Yes, and so?). When asked the same question, Viganò resists a little. He insists that his connection to the emotions of his characters is tempered by a concern with form, with selecting and rejecting poses and groupings. As Paisiello retreats to the margins of the staged conversation, Visconti (via his avatar, Romagnosi) heads for his clinching argument: that the classical unities are at odds with the first rule of art, which is to imitate nature. Loosening the unities of time and place will unleash unconventional narrative strategies, which in turn will allow the artwork to represent the world more fully and promote the absorption of the spectator into theatrical illusion. For Romagnosi/Visconti such absorption is desirable for both the creative artist and the theatrical spectator. In the grip of inspiration, he argues, artists become oblivious to their concrete surroundings in the same way that spectators at the theater can, under the right conditions, be swallowed up in theatrical illusion, blinded to "the real objects around us, to attend instead to illusory things, which we nevertheless come to regard as fully real and true."

Among the many contemporary commentaries on the unities, both pro and contra, Visconti's is unusual in its frankness about what is at stake. The unities should be discarded because they diminish the impact and "truth" of dramatic spectacles; the kind of intense and immersive spectatorial experience Visconti espouses will both require and produce a theater that is more urgent, more relevant, more connected to the experiences and problems that spectators encounter off the stage and away from the opera house. Viganò plays a central role in this conversation because the surreal qualities in his ballets unseat the unities and promote absorption. Yet ballet—and specifically Viganò's work—is central to this shift in aesthetic perspective also because choreography grants a central place to formal balance and symmetry, and thinkers like Visconti seem to have been acutely conscious of those highly visible formal features. The most popular operas of the period—whether by Paisiello or Mayr or Rossini—were constructed with at least equal attention to convention, balance, formal planning; but critics write as if they are oblivious to that dimension of the operatic experience, instead figuring the operatic art (and especially the Neapolitan tradition represented by Paisiello) as a free and natural outpouring of song, unmediated by conscious creative decisions. Far from a predictable clash between values of classical preservation and romantic disruption, as they are usually seen, these fiercely argued polemics return cyclically to absorption and to the impact of theater on the spectator.

The obscure language of many of the romantic polemics notwithstanding, it is far easier to assess Viganò's critical reception than it is to form an accurate image of what actually happened on the stage during one of his ballets, or to grasp exactly what it was that critics saw and heard that made them react with such excitement. Since the genre of pantomimic ballet disappeared soon after Viganò's death in 1821, considerable archaeological work is required to recover a sense of what a spectator might have seen and heard at a performance of a Viganò ballet. Detailed information about the choreography, music, or scenic effects is scant. Besides the small handful of scenarios and vocal scores that survive, the best source is a detailed biography of the man and his works by Carlo Ritorni, published almost two decades after the choreographer's death in 1821.[11] It is worth taking time to visualize the images and feelings evoked by Viganò's ballets, not only because these forgotten works made such a splash at the time but because understanding something of their texture can tell us something about the elements of romanticism that most appealed to Milanese audiences.

One thing that quickly becomes clear is that the image of Viganò as arch-romantic, shattering the unities and erecting new structures in their place, is only half the story. The choreographer's influence probably resided at least partly in his ability to strike a canny balance between classicism and innovative effects, onstage and also discursively, in the prefaces to his libretti. Subject matter was often mythological, as with Viganò's two settings of the Prometheus myth and his later ballet based on the mythological Titans, or from elevated sources such as Alfieri's *Mirra*. Viganò also drew from the northern authors championed by Mme. de Staël, but in at least one such case he used a preface to mount a cautious defensive maneuver. In the preface to the libretto for his *Giovanna d'Arco*, based on Schiller's *Jüngfrau von Orleans,* he announces the "improvements" he has wrought on the sprawling drama and proclaims his respect for the classical unities, an allegiance that is baldly contradicted by the disjointed and roaming action of other Viganò works, such as *Prometeo* and *I Titani.*

Lacking words, beyond the fairly brief synopses in the printed libretti, the meanings of pantomimic ballet were always enticingly up for grabs. Whether critics responded with enthusiasm or resistance, the formidable hermeneutic invitation the ballets issued to audiences and critics was a crucial component of Viganò's appeal. The anonymous reviewer of *Psammi, Re d'Egitto* for the *Corriere delle dame* was happy enough to consult several books on customs and rituals of ancient Egypt to untangle the symbolism of the pyramid formation struck at one point in the evening by a group of four dancers. Rossini enthusiast Giuseppe Carpani, on the other hand, sarcastically lamented that one did not dare attend the theater without a copy of Cesare Ripa's sixteenth-century manual of iconography in hand to help decipher the centuries-old secret language of visual art upon which Viganò drew.[12]

Some aspects of Viganò's approach to choreography seem to anticipate innovations that would burst onto the operatic stage beginning in the mid-1830s. For example, at a time when Rossini was making tentative forays into Scottish and Venetian *couleur locale* (in *La donna del lago* and *Bianca e Falliero,* respectively), a typical Viganò ballet featured extensive character dancing for the corps de ballet, often in a style that was perceived as exotic or authentically ethnic. Viganò also mixed tragic and comic styles freely, with the comic or "grotesque" interludes often named among critics' favorite moments. Giovanni Gherardini, who would provide the libretto for Rossini's *La gazza ladra* five years later, especially praised the mixing of genres, free approach to the unities, and blending of mythological sources with elements of comedy when he reviewed two Viganò ballets in the *Giornale di Milano* in 1812.[13] Observers also commented on the individuality Viganò brought to the group scenes, in which each dancer was endowed with a unique set of gestures and a sharply chiseled personality, and the corps de ballet could appear as made up of twenty or thirty unique and differentiated characters. As the French dance master Michel Saint-Léon put it in 1852,

> Viganò understood the mistakes made by his predecessors [in choreographing large groups of dancers in a too-regular, almost militaristic style]; he saw the bad effect produced by 50 or 60 people all making the same gesture at the same time, and he was the first who moved pantomime away from this near-ridiculous uniformity and knew enough to distribute his corps de ballet in such a way that each dancer had a role and movements that corresponded to the character he or she was portraying.[14]

The placement of dancers onstage was also designed to highlight affective intensity and individual passions. One favorite technique was to place a solitary emoting character—usually male, and usually suffering from unrequited love—in relief against the background of an otherwise festive group scene.

Other features suggest a more simultaneous evolution of ballet and opera, or even an influence flowing from opera to dance. Like Rossini, Viganò commonly built key scenes around the opposition between individual and group, a juxtaposition often realized in terms of troubled interiority set against communal revelry. In the first act of *Giovanna d'Arco* (1821), Joan of Arc's rejected suitor skulks morosely around the edges of the stage as the entire village of Domrémy celebrates a French military victory. The scene is typical of Viganò in showcasing a confrontation between a frozen or unattainable woman, whose face shows her to suffer great interior turmoil but who remains physically and gesturally distant, and a more sentimental male lead, who is given copious opportunity to emote openly in just the way that is denied to the heroine. The plot of *La vestale* (1818), with its vestal virgin shaken by a transgressive love, was ideally suited to represent this relationship, but similar gender dynamics turn up in several other ballets. Whereas the plot synopses are rarely very communicative about specific gestures or emotions, they often go to great lengths to convey the distress of these spurned lovers. Yet there is nothing Byronic about these heroes of Viganò's; if anything, it is his women who are rebels and social outsiders. Obviously descendants of Goethe's Werther and Foscolo's Jacopo Ortis, the men perhaps have more in common with some of Rossini's trousered male leads than with the tenors who took their place a few years later.

Such comparisons, of course, contain a substantial fraction of conjecture, given the silence of the sources on many of the things we might most like to know about a danced performance of the early nineteenth century. In both opera and ballet the music is an essential source for expression and characterization, and some insights can be gleaned from consulting the selections of musical numbers from the ballets that were published in piano-vocal form by Ricordi in conjunction with performances at La Scala.[15] These volumes are conceived like the selections of popular operatic numbers, gathering together usually about six musical highlights from the ballet. These sequences of short, disconnected numbers raise as many questions as they answer about how these works sounded and looked in performance, since they give only intermittent indications of where each bit of music fell in the action and even sparser hints—just the very occasional stage direction printed above the stave—about how the music and choreography might have fit together. Still, some suppositions can be drawn about the interaction between music and drama, music and movement, as we shall see in a discussion of a scene from Viganò's *Otello*. Also puzzling is the almost unanimously positive reception of the musical component of the ballets, considering that very little of the music was newly composed, but rather borrowed—and often from fairly undistinguished sources.

The scores were constructed as pastiche, combining short movements from Italian operas of the moment (including Rossini) with a surprising amount of music from Viennese sources, much of which was completely unknown in Milan. Excerpts of borrowed music by composers such as Pacini and Weigl mingled with newly composed numbers by Viganò's long-term collaborators Peter Lichtenthal and Paolo Brambilla, with the occasional piece by Viganò himself thrown in (he had studied composition as a boy in Naples with his uncle, Luigi Boccherini, and had even penned a juvenile opera himself, *La creduta vedova*).[16] In this sense, Viganò was an important—and completely overlooked—vector for the dissemination of Viennese style in Italy. As Martin Deasy has shown, the years after the Congress of Vienna saw great shifts in musical taste in Milan. In 1816, just as the literary journals were beginning to beat their breasts about the need to import more German and French culture to Italy, La Scala staged productions of operas by the Viennese favorites Peter Winter (*Maometto*) and Joseph Weigl (*La famiglia svizzera*). Viganò could be seen as a partial answer to the demand for translations of northern romantic texts, with a career that had been established in Vienna and many professional ties maintained from that period. One of the most important of those was the Milanese correspondent for the Leipzig-based *Allegemeine musikalische Zeitung,* Peter Lichtenthal, who both contributed music to Viganò's scores and reviewed his works favorably in the journal. Reporting on the Milanese scene in the *AMZ,* Lichtenthal crowed (perhaps wishfully) that Milanese taste had begun to shift decisively, so much so that beautiful melodies without complex accompaniment had begun to sound vulgar to the Milanese.[17] And reviewing Viganò's *Prometeo* in 1813, Lichtenthal called the ballet "a triumph of German music on Italian soil," and claimed that many people had expressed a desire to experience the ballet as a form of absolute music, "shut in their boxes without seeing."[18]

Viganò's appropriation of Rossini is especially intriguing, since the same melody could elicit very different critical reactions when sung in its original context in an opera and when abstracted as instrumental accompaniment for scenes from Viganò's choreography. As is well known, Rossini was routinely taken to task by critics for composing music that was oblivious to the poetic text, as well as for reusing his own melodies with minimal concern for the altered dramatic context. The borrowed music by various composers in Viganò's pastiche scores, on the other hand, was often described as passionate and appropriate for the situation.

Critics' acceptance of borrowed music as perfectly suited to the new choreographic context in part reflects a mentality that heralded Viganò as a solitary and unfettered genius, almost a creator of proto-*Gesamtkunstwerk.*[19] Whereas reviews of Rossini premières tend to become catalogues of virtues and defects of the principal singers, whose power over the composer was sometimes lamented, Viganò's star ballerina Antonia Pallerini received comparatively little attention. Dancers' performances are downplayed to make room for analysis of the works themselves and for speculation about what the choreographer may have intended with some of his more esoteric effects— the very type of interpretive intensity that is missing from contemporary responses to Rossini. Nor did Viganò's dancers—with the partial exception of Pallerini—become celebrities in the way that singers of the time did, inspiring odes in the *Corriere delle dame* and a constant stream of little items about their travels or the terms of their latest contracts in that journal's "Termometro politico" section. Where Viganò's mute, pantomimic bodies were seen as sublimely eloquent and obedient to his controlling artistic vision, the voices on which Rossini relied for the realization of his operas were at once celebrated and demeaned as too willful, egocentric, and surface oriented. Writ large, the subtraction of the voice from Viganò's spectacles also enabled modes of criticism that slipped free of the moralistic aesthetics that governed contemporary Italian writing about music. The fascination— and mute eloquence—of Viganò's pantomimic ballets bypassed the prevailing anxiety that music would overwhelm sung words and thus evoke a listening pleasure that was not grounded in some sort of edification, opening the way for more varied modes of responding to operatic music.

We can begin to visualize the ways the music lined up with Viganò's choreography—as well as to understand more about the interdependence of Rossini and Viganò—by looking closely at a single example: Viganò's reuse of one of Rossini's most famous melodies, Desdemona's "Canzone del salice," or Willow Song, from *Otello*, for his own ballet about the jealous Moor. Although Viganò's plot in general stays closer to Shakespeare than does Rossini's (indeed, it might be difficult *not* to be more faithful than librettist Francesco Maria Berio di Salsa is in the first two acts of his libretto for Rossini!), ballet and opera converge in their final acts. In both works, Otello enters Desdemona's chamber, they engage in a short dialogue in which she protests her innocence, and Otello murders her. Oddly, given the extensive musical quotation from Rossini, Viganò's action for the last act of his ballet includes no semblance of soliloquy or solo dance for Desdemona. After a brief stage direction indicating that the curtain rises on Desdemona sleeping in an alcove of her bedchamber, the *programma* for the final act indicates that Otello should enter immediately: *"Dopo alcun intervallo di silenzio entra Otello."*

Since the printed score contains no descriptive titles or stage directions, the exact correspondence between music and stage action must rely on informed guesswork. But the position of the Willow Song as the fourth of six musical numbers in Viganò's last act suggests that this music accompanied the sequence of actions immediately preceding the murder, described thus in the libretto:

Desdemona, barefoot, gets out of bed and approaches him, asking him submissively why he is using such strange language. . . . She denies having given the handkerchief to Cassio, and swears to her innocence under heaven. But Otello, in his delirium, calls her a liar, promises to avenge himself with the blood of the traitor, and carried away by rage [*con trasporto di rabbia*] closes the curtains of the alcove. Desdemona collapses into distraught weeping;

Otello understands her distress to be caused by the threats he has made against Cassio: this idea stokes his rage to the breaking point, and the brutal man surges forward to murder her.

One can perhaps see a vague reflection of the strophic structure of Rossini's Willow Song here, with Otello's accusations intervening between repeating "verses" that would correspond to Desdemona's protestations of innocence. But how can Otello's *"trasporto di rabbia"* have been conveyed satisfactorily against the musical background of the melancholy and introspective Willow Song?

Far from creating musical space for mimesis of Otello's raging voice, the few alterations Viganò imposed on his Rossinian source tend to emphasize those inarticulate bodily gestures already implied in the music and to strip away the sense of a singing voice altogether.[20] Viganò's arrangement first departs from literal quotation at measure 14, where the ballet music repeats the previous four bars rather than building on the shorter cadential motive used by Rossini (see example 1). Starting from the repeated cadences that close Desdemona's first strophe (mm.14–17), Viganò's music moves in a new direction, elaborating on the broken chords that for Rossini facilitate a quick modulation back to G minor, stretching the broken-chord pattern out over six measures and passing through several keys (see especially mm.18–24 of Viganò's completion). In terms of melodic contour and phrase structure, the ballet music comes back into step with its model as the second strophe begins. However, Viganò here omits Rossini's increasingly florid second and third strophes and instead jumps straight to the final verse of the operatic Willow Song, in which Desdemona— spent and hopeless—relinquishes all vocal decoration in favor of a stark, prayer-like declamatory style. Besides cutting back the amount of ornamentation, Viganò's decision to use only Rossini's first and fourth strophes has the effect of emphasizing the chains of sigh figures, sliding down chromatically from E♭ to F, that are spun out in Rossini's final strophe (example 1, mm.33–36). Although these sigh figures are certainly vocal in conception, their elaboration here foregrounds repetition and chromatic play to the point that its vocal origins are disguised: what is left, each time, is the sense of a repetitive physical gesture that halts and undermines the logic of melody. By skipping over the middle two strophes of the operatic Willow Song, Viganò throws into the foreground the ruptures and the bodily tremors encoded in this music, pushing melodic continuity and vocal ornament into the background.

Viganò's idiosyncratic approach to matching gesture to music is high-lighted if we compare his choreography of the Willow Song to the analogous scene in Rossini's opera. The orchestral music that accompanies Otello's entrance in the opera's last act, immediately preceding the lovers' final dialogue and Desdemona's murder, is one of Rossini's rare moments of bodily mimesis (see example 2). All of the orchestral music in this scene is based on a single motivic pattern, treated sequentially, recombined, and broken up into fragments of different lengths. The descending dotted figure, first heard as Otello enters (mm.5–8), choreographs Otello's heavy and surreptitious tread. When this pattern recurs, in the midst of Otello's recitative, its gestural content is made explicit by a stage direction: *"piano piano si avvicinia al letto, ed apre le tendine, nel massimo tumulte del cuore"* (very slowly he approaches the bed and opens the curtains, with the greatest tumult in his heart). A variation on this treading figure, itself treated sequentially and outlining an utterly conventional (almost reassuring?) cadence in C major, is heard first at measures 11–15 of the prelude, then returns to accompany Otello's second cautious approach to the sleeping Desdemona (indicated with the stage direction *"avvincinandosi di nuovo al letto"*).

PERIOD SEMIOTICS

The example of the Willow Song shows that Viganò's practice of musical pastiche was not quite as parasitical as originally suggested. Far from cynically appropriating Rossini's aria, Viganò (or more likely his musical consultant) trimmed and reshaped the music to exploit its association with embodied emotion—sighs and tremors of grief—and to minimize the original aria's association with a folk tradition of strophic elaboration and bardic storytelling. Yet this case does not quite justify the views of those critics who applauded the "perfectly appropriate" mood of the music for Viganò's ballets. The use of *this* music to accompany choreography for both Desdemona's desperate pleas and Otello's enraged accusations flouts the conflict-laden dramatic context just as gravely as any of the famous moments of disregard for words or dramatic context in Rossini's operas.

And the disjunction between musical affect and dramatic situation here is anything but an anomaly. A bright waltz from *La gazza ladra* becomes the underpinning for a tense dialogue between clandestine lovers in Viganò's *La*

EXAMPLE I. Viganò, *Otello*, No. 23 (Andante).

No. 24

EXAMPLE I. *Continued*

EXAMPLE 2. Rossini, *Otello,* Act 3, Preghiera.

EXAMPLE 2. *Continued*

giun-to in-os-ser-vato,   e   so-lo   nel-la stan-za fa - tal-e

vestale; a melody from Beethoven's *Pastoral* Symphony becomes a virile dance in *Gli Ussiti sotto Naumburgo.* In the only recent attempt to consider this question, dance scholar Rossana Dalmonte attributes the apparent disjunctions to a historical shift in perceptions of musical affect: "These famous pages were perceived differently in their time than today: that which we hear as 'brilliant' must have seemed 'nervous' and music that strikes us as representing 'the supreme pleasure of nature' seemed more adapted for a dance by soldiers and shepherds."[21] It could also be that the novelty and pleasurable difficulty of Viganò's style simply persuaded spectators that what they were seeing and hearing *must* be well matched, with the impression of correspondence reinforced by the evident seriousness of the artistic project. Whatever the case, critics operated with a double standard. Listeners seemed to find opera—with its distortions, repetitions, and drowning of words by the orchestra—at least as slippery as Viganò's creations in its meanings and in its relationship to real life, nature, and morality. But what in one art form gave satisfaction, in the other provoked unease and opprobrium. That disapproval can be detected behind the light tone of an 1819 article in the *Corriere delle dame* entitled "Rules for Composing Fashionable Music," which instructed aspiring opera composers to treat the words as a mere accessory and allow them to be drowned out by the brass, piccolos, and drums, and to assign the principal parts not to the voices but to the orchestra—a key criterion for sounding modern. Another one of the rules made the association with Rossini impossible to ignore: "Take three operas by Rossini and cannibalize them to generate your entire repertoire."[22]

Complaining about Rossini's offenses against dramatic truth and defending him against such charges was almost a sport for Italian critics in the teens and twenties. Those complaints often led to broad pronouncements about the expressive capabilities of music and the limits of what music could express. Writing in *Lo spettatore* in 1818, one anonymous author begins to sound truly terrified of music, which he characterizes as "undetermined, vague, bizarre, an uncanny beauty that has nothing solid about it, nothing truly beautiful or meaningful."[23] The obscurity that gave such satisfaction in Viganò's works, perhaps because it *could* ultimately be deciphered, became frightening when projected onto music, like a ghost or a beautiful woman. Like many other contemporary commentators, *Lo spettatore*'s journalist thought the solution was to constrain and control operatic music, grounding melody firmly in words and urging composers to represent the true sense of the sung words in their music. The fear behind this kind of anxious aesthetic positioning is gendered; voices like these seem conscious that women constituted a large proportion both of their readership and of the operagoing public. The reiterated fear that music could bypass the intellect and work directly on the soul was often framed explicitly in terms of the moral damage that could result for women from allowing oneself to be ravished by music.[24]

At the far opposite end of the spectrum, a passionate champion like Giuseppe Carpani, eagerly embracing the frivolous, materialist pleasures offered by Rossini, argued against the idea that music should be edifying or morally acceptable. Carpani tried to put a positive spin on music's lack of specificity, contrasting music with other arts that possess secure semiotic systems. He rated the legibility of pantomimic ballet below poetry or painting but far above music, which he believed lacked a system of conventional signs for ideas and emotions:

> We have an oratorical art, a poetic art, a pictorial art, and in principle we almost have a pantomimic art; that is, even though our dancers are not capable of representing dramatic events in gestures nor of weaving panegyrics, or expressing events, like the Roscii of ancient Rome, they nevertheless do possess a series of conventional signs, by which, without a whisper of speech,

events, sentiments, and emotions are made manifest to the observer and are understood. This is not true of music.[25]

Carpani was a passionate *Rossiniste,* and his reasoning stretches almost to the breaking point here in this rather desperate attempt to rescue Rossini from charges of cynical, antidramatic recycling of old melodies. According to Carpani's theory, Rossini could not be faulted for matching a scene in one mood to a melody that seemed to project another, because music simply lacked the specificity to capture or convey emotional states through widely comprehensible conventions. While the journalist writing in *Lo spettatore* is a representative of what Carlida Steffan has termed the neoclassical position, clinging to a moralistic and word-bound conception of music inherited from an earlier era, Carpani (like his contemporary Stendhal) outlines a sensualist aesthetics, which allows a role for pleasure and physical sensation in listening. Although commonly cast as opposite poles in the early-nineteenth-century aesthetics of music, both parties agreed that music was indefinite in what it could communicate, and this near-unanimous agreement on music's semiotic and expressive vagueness was *the* key reason that allowed Viganò and panto-mimic ballet to usurp the position opera might have occupied in this early phase of the romantic debates.[26]

ADMIRABLE LIGHTNESS, MONARCHIC BADINAGE

All this anxious positioning may seem quaint in the current musicological climate, in which Rossini's style has been embraced precisely for its energetic embodiment and its indulgence of sensation, unfettered by the semantic or prosodic strictures of the poetic text. Moments from the comic finales such as the famous dissolution into nonsense syllables and sound effects in the first-act finale of *L'italiana in Algeri* have been celebrated as a salvation from the tyranny of Germanic notions of meaning, interiorized expression, and musical depth. Historian James Johnson zeroed in on this moment as an example of the antimimetic noisiness and disregard for semantic meaning that he believes served as a gateway to ease Parisian listeners into the appre-ciation of absolute music such as Beethoven symphonies. For Richard Taruskin (drawing on a formulation from Julian Budden) the same passage became a central exhibit in a mobilization of Rossini as a leader in the nineteenth-century battle between *"Geist und Sinnlichkeit"*: the "mechanical grotesquery" of this number, Taruskin writes, in which the characters are "transformed by emotion into puppets," works as a necessary and welcome alternative to the German spiral into the depths of the soul. The onomatopoeic effects of this finale represented one end of the spectrum in Melina Esse's account of the scientific/medical assumptions—ranging from moralism to sensationalism—that informed Italian music criticism, and are figured as a (meaningful, intentional) topos for chaos in Emily Dolan's history of timbre as sonic material.[27]

These approaches engage in a kind of historiographical alchemy. Beginning from critiques focused on the music's *absence* of meaning, they transmute Rossini's "nonsense" into a positive statement, almost a proposition, and the music itself is treated as a readable cultural artifact. Such interpretations are founded on the near-universal popularity of the music: the fanatical enthusiasm it aroused early in the nineteenth century underwrites a belief that its aesthetic was embraced, unchallenged, by a majority of listeners. While the nonimitative approach to text-setting and the subject matter distance the operas from the lived reality of early-nineteenth-century Italy, Emanuele Senici sketches a connection by way of that meaninglessness, suggesting that Rossini's exuberant and affectively unmoored music may have served a cathartic function for a public suffering from post-traumatic stress in the wake of the Napoleonic invasion and the political reorganization of the peninsula after the Congress of Vienna.[28]

Even through the most intense period of Rossini-mania, however, critics continued to measure the music by the concepts of musical imitation and word-music correspondence, which suggests that Italian listeners of the time—whatever their experiences of war and occupation—continued to believe that music *could* have verbal, emotional, and dramatic meaning, and that there was sufficient consensus about these matters that Rossini could be judged against some conventional standards of expression. There may only have been a single voice who discarded any notion of meaning without hesitation or regret; but it is one that has projected far better across time than those of the more earnest critics who labored to situate Rossini within existing theories of representation and expression. That penetrating voice belonged to Stendhal, who adored Rossini and devoted an entire book—plus scores of additional scattered observations—to commentary on the operas and their place in the age. In almost any chapter of his *Vie de Rossini* (published in 1823) one can find forceful articulations of what might be called a "pro-nonsense" position.

Stendhal anointed *L'italiana in Algeri*, for example, as "perfection in *opera buffa*" and argued that the music's supremacy was possible only thanks to the utter absurdity of the plot. Half facetiously, he counseled operagoers to ignore libretti as much as possible: a quick skim of the text to get a sense of the main plot events was permitted, but listeners should ignore any specific poetic lines and instead simply invent words of their own for arias and ensembles.[29] This notion of (nearly) wordless listening was designed to prop up Stendhal's conviction that music—*all* music, not just Rossini's—was powerful precisely because it was completely detached from reality, able to carry listeners away on flights of imagination and to free them from the fetters of everyday existence. Stendhal's commitment to what he termed "idealism" and his unconcern for word-music correspondence places him at odds with the moralistic mainstream of operatic criticism, and some of his more extreme formulations seem to be devised with the aim of flouting that establishment. In a flight of idealist metaphor, he compares music to "the sheen of the rainbow ... [containing] nothing of the real," so "delicate and evanescent" that "it takes no more than some involuntary association of disagreeable ideas to ruin forever the effect of a masterpiece for an audience."[30] When those disagreeable ideas do intrude, Stendhal can be ruthless in his condemnation. And because his usual tone is so rhapsodic, his admiration for Rossini verging on the frivolous, he becomes most valuable as a cultural critic and a historical barometer when he writes about those few Rossini operas he dislikes.[31] He maligned *Cenerentola* as coarse and vulgar, redolent of "the stockrooms of the shops in the rue Saint-Denis" and "the fat businessman drunk on gold, who drives me away whenever he enters a *salon*."[32] And although its music ultimately redeemed the experience of *La gazza ladra* for him, Stendhal also found that opera's plot distastefully close to the representation of everyday realities—and to middle-class taste.

The resistance that *La gazza ladra* aroused for Stendhal lay not only in the grim elements of the plot—the story of a servant girl sentenced to death for the theft of silver cutlery that was actually stolen by a magpie—but also in the libretto's derivation from a popular Parisian *mélodrame*, Caigniez's *La pie voleuse* (Théâtre Porte-Saint-Martin, 1815), and in the rumor that the events dramatized in the play had actually happened. It did not help that the drama softened the tale somewhat: in real life, the servant was executed; in the play and opera, she is spared at the last minute.[33] Caigniez's melodrama found its way onto the Italian stage by way of the libretto competition that La Scala mounted in 1816.[34] The libretto—which did not win the competition but was nevertheless selected for staging—was penned by the prominent journalist and lexicographer Giovanni Gherardini, who also wrote the scenario for Viganò's *Mirra*. *Mirra* and *La gazza ladra* were unveiled at La Scala within a fortnight of each other in May 1817, prompting direct comparisons between the two creators in the press. A few years later, Stendhal claimed to have seen the two works performed at La Scala on the same evening, with *Mirra* as an intermezzo for *La gazza ladra,* where he found that Viganò's ballet about father-daughter incest lightened the scathing realism of the Rossini: "The mythological ideas seemed truly delicious after the *too realistic* horrors of the judge of Palaiseau and his soldiers."[35]

Stendhal's encounter with *La gazza ladra* prompted him to articulate his idealist philosophy of opera more clearly than it is laid out anywhere else in the *Vie de Rossini,* and the particular strategy he adopted for defending Rossini's sensitivity to words and dramatic atmosphere—rather surprisingly focusing on the opera's use of "waltz" meters—was taken up in later writing on Rossini, rippling out in works by Gaetano Barbieri and Giacinto Amati. In an opening salvo that clarifies both his reservations about *La gazza ladra* and his general insouciance about the need for any connection between words and music, Stendhal contrasts imagined German and French reactions to this plot:

> Germans, for whom the world is an unsolved problem ... would be thrilled with the degree of darkness that *reality* adds to the sad drama of *La Pie voleuse.* ... The French man of taste says to himself: the world is such a villainous place, it is just self-indulgent to dwell on the idiocy of He who made it; let's escape this sad reality. And he demands from the arts the *beau ideal* that will allow him quickly and for the longest time possible to forget this sordid world.[36]

In the end, however, no amount of willed ignorance could insulate Stendhal from the socially relevant aspects of *La gazza ladra,* and as we shall discover, his analysis repeatedly veers into political opinion and social criticism. The opera's unfamiliar tone and genre—a foray into the amorphous mixed genre of *semiseria*—was troubling to many early critics.[37] Reviewing the opera's première in the *Gazzetta di Milano,* an anonymous critic was reticent but clearly disturbed by the mismatch between lurid events and light tone in certain scenes: "The composer frequently sacrificed a natural tone [*la convenevolezza*] in favor of brilliance, and the situation and the phrases of the characters were not always painted with the appropriate tints."[38] Viganò's chronicler Ritorni, too, registered disapproval of the "weak *semiserio* genre." Among the weaknesses he enumerates are the ambivalent character of the Podestà (or village magistrate), who oscillates between the stances of buffo and tyrant; the "extravagant ornament" of the choruses, who are meant to sing in a peasant style; and the court of justice set up in a village. Rossini's response to these weighty themes, Ritorni complains, is typically flippant: "He laughs one of his festive and ironic laughs, and says 'No problem!' If I have enough freedom, it will all work out."[39] Ritorni here jumps on the bandwagon of complaint about the music slipping away from the words and the drama as he asks rhetorically how the performers can embody their roles convincingly "when the forms of the drama, and the harmonic measures on which those forms are based contradict the dramatic action?"[40]

Stendhal himself tackles the question of words and music from the surprising angle of the waltz. He relates that during the first run of performances of *La gazza ladra,* two camps were formed, protesting or defending the use of rollicking, dancelike melodies (mostly but not only waltzes) in the midst of the trial and sentencing to death of the unjustly accused servant Ninetta. Although no specific numbers are mentioned—Stendhal refers only to "the many waltzes that appear in the second act of *La gazza ladra"*—the surrounding context indicates that he may have had in mind two triple-meter movements from the Act 2 quintet (which encompasses the trial and sentencing), as well as the more obvious waltzes in the cabaletta of the aria for the Podestà and the *tempo d'attacco* of the duet for Ninetta and Pippo, both of which feature prominently in the opera's famous overture.

> I must at this point bring up a point in Rossini's favor: that the waltz tempo captures the terrible and inevitable speed of the hammer-blows of fate. The worst thing about the feelings of a person condemned to death who knows he will be executed within three-quarters of an hour is the sensation of speed. It is not the fault of the music that we have taken up the habit of dancing waltzes; this fashion will pass in thirty years or so, but Rossini's way of depicting the speed of the advancing clock will always be valid.[41]

Here Stendhal already seems to force the issue somewhat by insisting on a one-to-one correspondence between musical topos and dramatic mood: waltz meters can be appropriate even in tragic situations since they embody the inexorability of fate, the sense of time flying away. Then, half contradicting himself, he invokes a compensatory logic in which waltzes mask or render palatable the unbearable dramatic situations: "Rossini's supporters (for there were two camps, sharply distinguished one from the other) maintained that we ought to be grateful to him for having disguised the atrocious brutality of the subject with the lightness of his cantilenas."[42]

The contradiction in itself is trivial. As we've already seen, consistency and accuracy are insignificant for Stendhal, and across the book as a whole the state of "idealism" in which music transcends words and renders them irrelevant is far more important than any stray attachment to correspondence between music and word. But the conflicted logic of Stendhal's defense of *La gazza ladra*'s waltzes takes us to the core of an issue that resonates insistently throughout the *Vie de Rossini*. Almost every chapter of the book contains some strong opinion about pacing or tempo, as if Stendhal implicitly situates the success of Rossini's music in his treatment of time. Thus, tempo emerges as essential to the impact of *La gazza ladra:* Stendhal is scathing in his valuation of the performances at the Théâtre-Italien, in which "the orchestra's leader . . . had altered the tempo of nearly every one of Rossini's numbers," slowing the music down in a way that made the opera unbearably sentimental.[43] Striking a balance between the quick succession of musical ideas and repetition is equally crucial, and Stendhal often wishes that Rossini had eschewed novelty and change in favor of dwelling longer on a phrase or idea. Most often he chides the composer for rushing ahead for fear of boring the audience, but in the opening scene of *La gazza ladra* he finds one of the rare moments in which Rossini allows his musical ideas to breathe: "We see that the composer had the courage to face up to the challenge of boring his audience, and to neglect little entertaining gestures; thus he attains the truly grandiose."[44]

The central waltz number in the second act of *La gazza ladra* exploits this sense of the passage of time to a remarkable degree. The waltz crops up in the cabaletta of the aria for the Podestà, the predatory basso buffo who desires Ninetta and has no scruples about using power as a weapon. With Ninetta about to be sentenced to death, he sees an opportunity to barter freedom for her virtue. His sleazy delineation of this plan takes the form of a double aria, launched by a falsely ingratiating slow movement whose subsequent sections become more and more overtly violent, until the magistrate is interrupted by a trumpet signal that announces the beginning of the trial at which he must preside (see example 3). In a broad dramaturgical sense, the Podestà is late—he has almost missed the trial because of his thwarted erotic dalliance with Ninetta; but the words he sings during the cabaletta shift attention to an imagined scenario in which *she* is too late. Dropping the elegant and antiquated pretenses he had affected in the slow movement (*"Si, per voi pupille amate"*), the Podestà delivers a threatening prediction entirely in the future tense. Ninetta has not yielded to his demands and, he warns, she will soon be begging him to intervene to save her life:

> *Udrai la sentenza,*
> *perdon chiederai;*
> *ma invan pregherai,*
> *ma tardi sarà.*

(You will hear the sentence, you will ask for my pardon; but you will plead in vain; but you will be too late.)

The waltz theme itself is heard between the two statements of the Podestà's cabaletta, a section usually reserved for kinetic music loaded with conventional signifiers of transition. It is common for markers of the "real" world, beyond the intense emotions of the characters, to feature in these transitional sections, as they also do in the *tempo di mezzo* that bridges the slow movement and cabaletta in a double aria complex. Trumpet fanfares are typical signals of offstage action, recalling the characters from their plunge into solipsistic emotion and vocalization to take account of the (usually grim) fate that is about to strike them or their loved ones. This transition is announced conventionally, with the chorus directing us to listen to a signal from offstage: *"Udiste? è questo l'avviso"* (Listen? that is the signal).[45] Rossini elevates the trumpets and drums to central elements of the musical texture, layering the conventional active music of the transition over a timbrally and harmonically luxurious waltz melody, the effect promoted by the richly dissonant thirds falling on the downbeats.

The entire cabaletta is in quick triple meter, but the waltz pattern emerges gradually; the number's force and momentum derive from the gradual removal of metrical barriers to the waltz. The rhythms of the vocal line are often at cross-purposes with the steady tapping of the accompaniment: unruly top Cs and Ds pop out on second beats, inserting accents that unbalance the forward motion of the orchestra. These accents fall mainly on the last line of the quatrain, with its hint at the dark consequences of being too late. It is of course the magistrate who is really too late at this moment, although the atmosphere of time rushing forward—as Stendhal notes—also encompasses Ninetta, who senses an unjust death in her near future. The words of the second quatrain are more static and more conventional, shifting to the contemplation of an emotional state: *"In odio e furore / cangiato è*

EXAMPLE 3. Rossini, *La gazza ladra,* Act 2, Aria (Podestà).

(In questo punto s'ode da lontano il suono de' tamburi con cul
s'annunzia al Popolo che s'apre la sessione del Tribunale)
*(At this point the sound of far-off drums is heard, announcing
to the populace that the hearing has begun)*

EXAMPLE 3. *Continued*

l'amore / pieta nel mio petto / più luogo non ha" (My love has changed into hatred and rage; pity no longer has a place in my heart). This is where the waltz asserts itself, the topos established mainly by the orchestra—the ornaments emphasizing downbeats in the violins, with each second and third beat supplied by the woodwinds in a near-caricature of the standard waltz accompaniment. The simultaneous exuberance and foreboding created by the combination of the waltz and military topoi mingle two distinct dramatic planes, the excited pleasure of the waltz textured and destabilized by the indexical force and realism injected by the trumpets and drums.[46]

Although Stendhal is largely silent about this aria, beyond his general defense of the opera's waltzes, the character of the Podestà elicits from him a rare and revealing political rant.[47] Without wavering outwardly from his commitment to musical idealism and complete disregard for words and plot, contemplation of the Podestà's venality causes Stendhal to veer into an incensed commentary on the state of the Italian judicial system. The magistrate, he claims, is an entirely "faithful portrait" of the judges, appointed by the church, that Rossini would have encountered in his youth in the Romagna.[48] Under this regime, before the improvements wrought by Napoleon, chambermaids could be condemned for eating chicken on Fridays. "It is true that this admirable lightness, this charming and positively *monarchic badinage,* has often been noted in recent years, among judges, members of the highest social circles, who have pronounced death sentences against enemies of those in power while playing, or rather without interrupting the games of their pleasant, insouciant lives."[49] Although Stendhal's official position is that opera and theater should have nothing to do with external reality, his stance of perfect idealism and detachment slips here. Counterintuitively, it is the most melodramatic elements of Rossini's *opera semiseria* that compel Stendhal to draw connections between stage action and lived reality. The threatened miscarriage of justice at the center of the second act seems simultaneously to trouble and thrill him, and perhaps that is the response invited by Rossini's music. The bifurcated texture of the waltz interlude in the Podestà's aria seems to achieve the feat of transporting the listener, mimicking the mechanism by which the spectator is at once conscious of being in the theater and also transported to a fictional realm.

The effect recalls a passage from the four-way conversation about the unities penned by Ermes Visconti for *Il conciliatore* in 1819. Just before he interrogates Paisiello and Viganò about their level of identification with their characters, Visconti's interlocutor Romagnosi envisions a theatrical experience in which once or twice during each act, for just "two or three beats of the pulse," the spectator would come to believe that he is *really* seeing Brutus stab Caesar, taking the scene to actually *be* Rome, momentarily oblivious to the rest of the audience, orchestra, lighting, and proscenium, even forgetting that he is in a theater or in Milan.[50] Perhaps it is the measurement of the experience in pulse beats that invites a connection to Rossini's waltzes; but could this be the kind of reaction promoted by the Podestà's waltz? Stendhal argues almost precisely the opposite—that the waltz distracts us from the "atrocious brutality" of the plot, defuses the dread of the imminent death sentence—but he was clearly engaged in special pleading, and of a not particularly convincing sort. Considering Stendhal's reaction to these moments in *La gazza ladra* together with Visconti's model of theatrical illusion highlights the gulf between the endeavor of the thinkers who were trying to theorize romanticism in Italy and the Brechtian legacy that now shapes our perceptions of theater: that for an audience to engage actively with a dramatic performance spectators must be detached, aware of the proscenium, cognizant of the fictionality of the characters and events. The theatrical experience imagined by Visconti, and felt by Stendhal as he listened to *La gazza ladra,* is the opposite. For a few rare moments the spectator is swept up into the fiction and loses conscious awareness of her surroundings, and such moments of immersion were what enabled a political engagement with artistic performances. What counted as a "political" work of art would once have been an allegorical cantata or a play like Giovanni Battista Niccolini's 1819 *Nabucco,* in which the dramatis personae equated each character with a contemporary political figure (for example, Nabucco = Napoleon); the rise of absorption, theatrical illusion, and indirect meaning facilitated the emergence of a variety of political art based on more slippery but also more intense, more personal modes of signification.

MUTENESS ENVY

The role of orchestral noise has been explored with great imagination in recent musicological writing on Rossini, but amid the attention to timbre and to instrumental technologies it is sometimes forgotten that "noise" and orchestral complexity also had a simpler meaning for early-nineteenth-century Italians, as the negation of the feature long believed to define Italian opera: voice. The endless references to noise in this criticism are essentially always about voice—and thus about the Italian tradition, stemming from the fear that the pure, hallowed Neapolitan vocal style that is ritually traced back to Paisiello and Cimarosa might be erased by too much orchestral noise. Even the worries about inappropriate intrusions of the waltz and about metrical travesties of tragic scenes may devolve into fundamental concerns about voice: critics fear that purely instrumental or purely "musical" logic such as rhythm or meter may wash away the more familiar, more direct, and more human expressive lexicon of the voice.

These fears of excess cascade through the musical criticism of two writers known primarily as journalists and translators, though each of them dipped into music criticism as well. Michele Leoni, author of some of the earliest Italian translations of Shakespeare, did not share Stendhal's unflappable attitude to the occasional mismatches between words and music and the proliferation of characteristic musical styles in this music.[51] Writing in 1821, Leoni sounds panicked in the face of Rossini's busy surfaces:

> The mob [*folla*] of so-called characteristic passages, the storm of notes which do not leave you a moment to breathe, the timpani, the penny-whistles [*pifferi*], the trumpets, the horns, and all the rest of those noisy families of instruments, assault you, they seduce you, they confound you, they seduce you once again, they deafen you, they transport you, they confuse, they agitate, they inebriate; and they make you dance the *allemande* when the singer is shedding tears of anguish, or impel a *minuet* at moments of the greatest desperation, transmuting a species of tragedy into a bacchanale and a house of sorrow into a jousting match.[52]

If panic threatens here, it is certainly mixed with pleasure. Leoni's direct address rhetorically shifts the aesthetic problem from the music to the listener, who feels impelled to dance even in moments of anguish and desperation. Where the emphasis for Stendhal falls on meter and tempo, in Leoni's account of being overwhelmed by Rossini it is the brash instrumental colors—the pennywhistles, the noisy families of instruments—that claim attention, dwarfing any apparent mismatches of meter or tempo.

Serving as an accidental foil for Leoni, journalist and translator Gaetano Barbieri took both a more positive and a more politically purposeful view of Rossini's excesses of timbre and volume. Even more prominent on the Milanese cultural scene than Leoni, Barbieri was a cofounder and editor of several leading theatrical papers and was responsible for the introduction of Walter Scott's novels into Italy, beginning with his translation of *Kenilworth* in 1821.[53] In a pamphlet devoted to Rossini that was published anonymously in 1827, Barbieri praised the use of the French horn in the orchestral intro-duction to the title character's cavatina in *Tancredi* (*"Tu che accendi questo core"* / *"Di tanti palpiti"*), which he found evocative yet subordinate to the supreme expressive role of the voice. Perhaps thinking like a translator (and deriving inspiration as well as many actual turns of phrase from Stendhal), Barbieri equated such extended passages of instrumental music with the way description might be used by the author of a novel to "adorn a scene of dia-logue and fill in the silences necessary in speech," without ever interrupting or drowning out that speech.[54]

But Barbieri was also alarmed by what he believed to be the moral dangers of an overdeveloped orchestra. Always teetering on the edge of excess, Rossini (in Barbieri's estimation) just manages to "measure the moral instruments of the human voice against the mechanical instruments" and to rein in display so that florid passages sound natural and can express more than just "the mastery of a builder of bassoons or clarinets." For Barbieri the preeminence of voice is linked to the Neapolitan tradition, and the proper cultivation of vocal melody is thus also a sign of both Italian primacy in opera and a broader, atemporal notion of Italian superiority. On a deeper level, voice is also the carrier of humanity, subjectivity, and identity, as Barbieri recognizes in a footnote that differentiates human from mechanical instruments: "a perfect bassoon is always a bassoon, a violin is always a violin; but Colbran is not Bassi, David is not Tacchinardi."[55]

The rhetoric of writers like Barbieri and Leoni shows how the Italian eleva-tion of voice—and attendant mistrust of orchestral effects—was becoming a constraint on both criticism and creativity, somewhat akin to the prison house enclosed around the spoken theater by the unities. Therein lay perhaps one of the attractions of Viganò—as an example of an expressive and absorptive music-theatrical experience that could dispense with the conventional con-straints on voice and the word. Viganò's early biographer Carlo Ritorni pur-sued this logic a few years later when he invoked the deceased choreographer as a model of how operatic composers and dramatists might temper the excesses of vocal display and orchestral development, and revivify the fusion of voice and gesture of the classical theater.[56] The corrective, the path to reinte-gration of the dispersed arts, according to Ritorni, lay in expressive gesture, as indicated in details of the musical score and as executed by dramatically sophisticated singers such as Giuditta Pasta and Henriette Méric-Lalande.[57]

In general Ritorni was against beginning arias with long orchestral intro-ductions, which he compared to introducing a character by having her

shadow walk onstage ahead of her. Yet he was impressed by the instrumental prelude to the final scene of Bellini's *Il pirata,* especially as rendered by soprano Henriette Méric-Lalande as Imogene. Almost like Viganò's star ballerina Pallerini, Lalande was able here to use her body to give meaning to what otherwise would have been empty, abstract harmonies, miming "the blindness with which [the insane Imogene] believed herself to be stricken, completely following all of the unfolding of the instrumental accompaniment."[58] What Ritorni does *not* say is that the orchestral prelude from *Il pirata* represented a new musical style and function, one almost nonexistent in Rossini. Rossini, of course, wrote virtuosically for orchestra and routinely prefaced his most important scenes and arias with extended instrumental preludes. But those introductions tend to depict either a static landscape in picturesque terms or a single emotion experienced by the character in that setting, without much trace of human presence or movement. Orchestral motives with embodied associations like those we saw in the final scene of

EXAMPLE 4b. Rossini, *Tancredi,* Act 2, Scena e Cavatina (Amenaide).

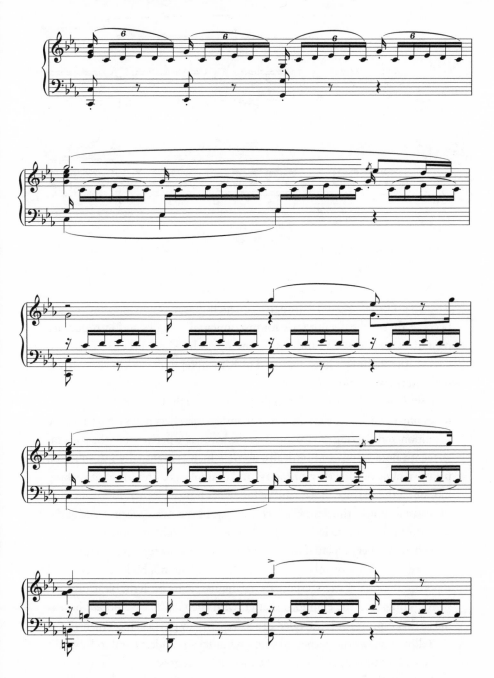

Rossini's *Otello,* treated through sequencing and fragmentation, would become almost the default style for instrumental preludes and introductory recitatives by the 1840s and 1850s; any opera by Verdi bristles with such effects. The Bellini prelude discussed by Ritorni represents a kind of halfway point in this evolution.

If we look back at the *Tancredi* prelude that caught Gaetano Barbieri's ear, for example, we can see that the music's considerable effect flows from the cyclic repetition and layering of two motives, the barcarolle pattern and the pastoral sixteenth-note woodwind birdcalls, above which is eventually introduced a plaintive oboe melody (beginning at m. 5, example 4a). The constant rocking motion in the clarinet, violas, and cellos denies human agency, foregrounding instead a feeling of timelessness or continuity. In the Act 2 prison scene of the same opera, an oboe melody wracked by quasi-vocal sighs and moans is underpinned by another perpetual-motion figure, repeating sextuplets for strings (see example 4b). Here Rossini's orchestra evokes voice but not body: conventional topoi of emotional distress (especially sigh figures) paint both the bleak physical surroundings and the emotions that go with them. What we do *not* hear is music that captures or is intended to accompany any physical movement.

Bellini eschews the perpetual-motion figures so fundamental to Rossini's orchestral writing and structures the melody in progressively shorter phrases with progressively more interruptions (see example 5). As the stage directions

EXAMPLE 5. Bellini, *Il pirata,* Act 2, Scena ed Aria finale (Imogene).

instruct Imogene to enter, weeping and confused, holding her young son by the hand, the English horn plays four measures of a melody in F minor. The recurring D♭-C sobbing figure moves into the foreground at measure 6 as the melody both fragments and stretches its range, corresponding to jerky stage directions that instruct Imogene to shift gestures and emotions every two measures ("appear to search for something in the air in front of her," "signs of contentment," "falls back into sorrow.") Later in the scene when Imogene takes "irregular steps" as bystanders try to comfort her, a melodic arc building to a cadence is interrupted in nearly every measure by some kind of melodic hiccup—brief silences or sudden chromatic tones. Imogene's erratic feelings and delusions are shown as shaping the music we hear and also what we see, moment by moment.

The emerging aesthetic that privileged musical access to the depths of a character may have rippled out to affect the narratives and paratexts that purported to document the creative process. This is suggested, at least, by the vast difference between accounts of Rossini's compositional process (rushed and cynical) and Bellini's (halting, tortured, and deeply personal). The shift is best illustrated by a widely disseminated letter that Bellini supposedly sent to his friend Agostino Gallo in 1829. That the letter was eventually discovered to be a midcentury forgery hardly matters, since the aesthetic priorities it advertises only become more significant if they are the preoccupations of opera fans and critics rather than of the composer himself. In the Gallo letter "Bellini" describes his compositional process as a solitary experience, a retreat into the depths of self, and a communion with the poetic word:

> Shut up in my room, I begin by declaiming each character's lines with all the heat of passion, and I closely observe the inflections of my voice, the speeding up and slowing down of the declamation in each situation, the overall accent and the expressive tone that characterizes a man in the grip of passion, and I find the motives and the general rhythmic character best suited to demonstrate them and infuse them with new life by means of harmony. Then I throw them onto paper, try them out on the piano, and when I myself feel the corresponding emotion, I judge that I have succeeded.[59]

This seems a remarkably modern notion, even for 1843 when the letter was probably really penned—almost Stanislavskian. In order to craft his distinctive melodic style, Bellini had to feel the characters' emotions himself, to fall into the rhythms of their movements, and even to ventriloquize their speech. The Gallo letter recalls the fleeting exchange in Visconti's 1819 dialogue on the unities, in which the avatars for Paisiello and Viganò in turn proclaim that they can experience creative inspiration without losing themselves in their characters. The stand-in for Viganò in the dialogue both allows for this kind of inspiration and hastens to assert that a concern with form is a constant, and a desirable one. When Viganò's ballets allowed the writers of *Il conciliatore* and other journals to begin to theorize a uniquely Italian romanticism, rather than one modeled on imported literature, they may also have set in motion a cultural process by which new models of selfhood—selves perhaps riskier, less governed by religious observance, and less neatly integrated with civic and social expectations—could be depicted onstage and discussed in the public sphere.[60]

It may be with this not so surprising realization that the outlines of early Rossini criticism connect back to reactions to Viganò's ballets; but this criticism also points us forward toward what will within a decade or so become mobilizing connections between artistic romanticism, political activism, and Italian identity. It may be that it was no more and no less than their differing relationships with that powerful signifier—voice—that set Viganò and Rossini on such different trajectories of reception. Perhaps Viganò was conceded the right to be challenging and romantic because his art form escaped the aesthetic confines and the indigenous traditions of voice. If so, this is a distinction that has consequences for more than formal features of the two arts. In the defensive and preservationist climate of early-nineteenth-century writing about music, to silence the voice was also to glimpse a means of escape from old notions about what it meant to be human and from the moral connections between the singing voice and the human heart that thrum through the era's musical criticism.

THREE

Elizabeth I, Mary Stuart, and the Limits of Allegory

MORPHOLOGY OF A MONARCH

Chapter 2 began from a narrow focus—on a single city and a single theater, and on one quirky choreographer whose works became a wedge for new modes of representation and perception. Viganò's ballets created a space in which Milanese audiences could enjoy storytelling that broke with the classical unities and admitted alternatives to the consistent, unadorned lyrical voice as the seat of character, paving the way for a spectatorial experience based in sympathy and inquiry. In this chapter the focus falls on an operatic fad whose popularity extended throughout the Italian peninsula and internationally, over more than two decades. Between 1815 and about 1850 Italian stages saw more than a dozen operas set at the Tudor court, the most successful of them focusing on Queen Elizabeth I. Rather than narrating any specific sequence of historical events, these operas explore a type of character—the female absolute monarch—and the nature of her authority, the lapses and cracks in that authority, and the mechanisms that went into producing it. Composers and librettists were attracted by the mix of power, female rivalry, and betrayal in these plots but also by the modest exoticism of the setting—safely removed from any resemblance to or actual kinship with current Italian rulers—and by the *frisson* that surrounded the political and romantic vicissitudes of a female monarch.

Stories about the Tudor queens had been popular in England and France since the late seventeenth century, but the Italian career of these characters began in Naples in connection with ceremonial occasions, where the queen on stage in some ways stood for the king, newly restored to the throne after the Napoleonic interregnum.[1] Tudor plots quickly became popular beyond

Naples, with the representation of the queen's struggles with rivals and with her court taking on new associations in each urban milieu and political regime. So where chapter 2 took a laser view of a single set of polemical publications and the performances that shaped their writers' opinions about the power and potential of theatrical expression, the geographical purview of this chapter is wider, extending from Naples to Milan, dallying briefly also with Tudor operas premièred in Paris and London.

Although the Tudor trend is often linked to the popularity of Walter Scott (whose novels *Kenilworth* and *The Abbot* feature Elizabeth I and Mary Stuart), the surge of interest in Tudor subjects predates Scott's arrival in Italy.[2] Where Scott's popularity is usually seen as part of a broader romantic appetite for exoticism, *couleur locale,* and historicism, the Tudor plots are distinguished by their urban settings and their concern with the delicate nuances and manipulations of communication at court. Dramatic treatments of the Tudor queens and their power struggles often lay closer to allegory than to vicarious tourism. Following the Tudor works through to midcentury offers a new angle both on the evolution of historicist consciousness in Italy and on the gradual eclipse of occasional works and political allegory in favor of a darker depiction of monarchy and life at court. Of course, monarchy never really went away in nineteenth-century Italy—when the peninsula was unified in 1861 it was under the scepter of a constitutional monarch, Vittorio Emanuele—but the forms it took morphed drastically with the time and the place.

The eclipse of allegory by new representational and spectacular mechanisms emerges most clearly through a pair of scenic archetypes that recur in one Tudor opera after another. The first of these is also the most transparently allegorical: scenes that dramatize the uneasy split between public control and private emotion that characterizes the female monarch. The bifurcation of private and public selves that underpins these scenes maps easily onto the conventional slow/fast, interior/exterior divisions of double aria. The clear changes of tempo, texture, and mood in the double aria dramatize the tension between the monarch's public persona and the roiling emotions below the surface, as her exterior control is disturbed by unruly erotic attractions and often by jealousy of a female rival.

In what follows I shall be interested both in the sheer replication of the double aria structure as a mode of introducing queens and in the inflections the form acquires when sung by different queens in operas conceived for different cities and audiences. The same is true for the second archetypal scene this chapter will address, a juridical moment when the queen signs a death warrant for a character accused of treason. The earlier Tudor operas end with an opera seria-like display of clemency by the monarch, pardoning traitors and giving the man she secretly loves permission to marry her rival. But by about 1830, as tragic endings became more common in Italy, the operas typically end with an elaborate aria for the character facing death. The death scene is usually preceded by a scene of convoluted political maneuvering that shows the queen hesitating to give the order for execution, torn between affection and power and often manipulated by unscrupulous ministers. The emphasis on the document through which the death sentence is handed down makes this new ending almost a direct negation of the acts of mercy popular a decade earlier. The queen is shown to act at a remove, her impact on her subjects now mediated by scheming ministers and the paper decree.

Because reviews of these works contain only hints of the political resonances early spectators may have seen or heard in this material, much of the evidence in this chapter comes instead from libretti and scores of the works themselves. Adapting an approach akin to Franco Moretti's "distant reading," in which meaning is generated from clusters of related texts more than from close reading of any individual passages, I shall at times treat the Tudor operas as a single collective work, looking for patterns in the kinds of scenes, emotions, and ideas that were most compelling for librettists, composers, and audiences.[3] The nine years and 130 miles that separate (for example) the premières of Mercadante's *Maria Stuarda* (Bologna, 1821) and Donizetti's *Anna Bolena* (La Scala, 1830) might momentarily shrink to near-invisibility, as will the half century and countless shifts of political power that elapsed between the historical events the two operas portray, in favor of attention to situations shared between the two.

THE DREAM OF PARTENOPE: NAPLES AFTER 1815

It was no accident that the operatic history of the Tudors began in Naples rather than in Milan, where the high-flown debates about Viganò and romanticism played out. There had been isolated Tudor works before 1815; but the subject really took hold with the successful première at the Teatro San Carlo of Rossini's *Elisabetta, regina d'Inghilterra* in 1815, and solidified with Donizetti's emulation of Rossini's model fifteen years later in *Elisabetta al castello di Kenilworth*, also premièred at the San Carlo. (See table 1 for a list

TABLE 1 Works on Tudor subjects read and performed in Italy, 1809–1845

Title	Composer/author	Librettist	Place, date	Characters, setting	Literary source(s)
Maria Stuarda	Vittorio Alfieri	PLAY	Milan, Pietro Agnelli, 1809		
Maria Stuarda	Pietro Casella	Francesco Gonella	Florence, 1812	Mary Stuart at Dunbar	Camillo Federici, *Il trionfo dei Carbonari*, Padua, 1812
Elisabetta, regina d'Inghilterra	Rossini	Giovanni Schmidt	Naples, San Carlo, 1815	Elizabeth I, Leicester, Amy Robsart	Sophia Lee, *The Recess*, 1783
Maria Stuarda, regina di Scozia	Luigi Carlini	Francesco Gonella	Palermo, Carolino, 1817–18	Mary Stuart at Dunbar	
Elisabetta in Derbyshire, ossia il castello di Fotheringay	Carafa	Antonio Peracchi	Venice, Le Fenice, 1818		
The Abbott	Walter Scott	NOVEL	1820; translated as *L'Abate* (Milan, Ferrario, 1823)	Mary Stuart at Lochleven	
Kenilworth	Walter Scott	NOVEL	1821; translated as *Il castello di Kenilworth* (Milan, Ferrario, 1821)	Elizabeth, Leicester, Amy Robsart	
Maria Stuarda, regina di Scozia	Mercadante	Gaetano Rossi	Bologna, Teatro Comunale, 1821	Mary Stuart at Dunbar Castle (Scotland)	
Le tragiche avventure di Maria Stuarda regina di Francia, d'Inghilterra e di Scozia	?	NOVEL/HISTORY(?): *"Opera postuma di un elegante scrittore"*	Milan, A.S. Brambilla, 1822		
Maria Stuarda	Agostino Pendola	PLAY; *"tragedia"*	Turin, Chirio e Mina, 1822		
Leicester, ou le chateau de Kenilworth	Auber	Eugène Scribe	Paris, Opéra Comique, 1823	Elizabeth, Leicester, Amy Robsart	Boirie and Lemaire, *Le Château de Kenilworth*, Théâtre de la Porte-St-Martin, 1822
Maria Stuart regina di Scozia	Carlo Coccia	Pietro Giannone	London, Haymarket, 1827	Mary Stuart at Fotheringay	Schiller, *Maria Stuart*

(continued)

TABLE 1 Continued

Title	Composer/author	Librettist	Place, date	Characters, setting	Literary source(s)
Maria Stuarda	Giovanni Galzerani (choreographer)	BALLET	Venice, Le Fenice, 1827		
Elisabetta al castello di Kenilworth	Donizetti	Andrea Tottola	Naples, San Carlo, 1829	Elizabeth, Leicester, Amy Robsart	Scott, *Kenilworth*, via Hugo and Scribe; and Hugo/Foucher, *Amy Robsart*, 1822/1828
Maria Stuarda a Dombar	?	PLAY; "*dramma in cinque atti*"	Milan, Visaj, 1829		
Maria Stuarda	Lorenzo Barichella	PLAY; "*tragedia*"	Vicenza, Piero Picutti, 1829		
Anna Bolena	Donizetti	Felice Romani	Milan, Scala, 1830	Henry VIII, Anne Boleyn, Jane Seymour	Alessandro Pepoli, *Anna Bolena*, 1788; Marie-Joseph Chenier, *Henry VIII*, 1791, reworked by Pindelmonte as *Enrico VIII, ossia Anna Bolena*, 1816
Il conte d'Essex	Mercadante	Felice Romani	Milan, Scala, 1833	Elizabeth and Essex	Ancelot, *Elisabeth d'Angleterre*, 1829; Italian translation, 1838 (Milan)
Maria Stuarda	Donizetti	Felice Romani	Milan, Scala, 1835	Mary Stuart at Fotheringay	Schiller, *Maria Stuart*, translated by Pompeo Ferrario, 1819 (Milan, Pirotta); Andrea Maffei, 1829 (Milan, Annali universali); and Eduice De Battisti di s. Giorgio, 1829 (Verona, Libanti)
Roberto Devereux	Donizetti	Salvadore Cammarano	Naples, San Carlo, 1838	Elizabeth and Essex	Ancelot, *Elisabeth d'Angleterre*, 1829; and Romani, *Conte d'Essex*
Maria regina d'Inghilterra	Pacini	Leopoldo Tarantini	Palermo, 1843	Love triangle with Mary Tudor, Clotilde Talbot, and Fennimoore; London (Tower)	Hugo, *Marie Tudor*; translated by Luigi Marchionni, 1838
Elisabetta d'Inghilterra	Giuseppe Checchetelli	PLAY; "*tragedia*"	Rome, C. Puccinelli, 1845		

of theatrical works on Tudor subjects performed in Italy in the first half of the nineteenth century.) More than in any other Italian city, opera in Naples was economically, institutionally, and physically tied to the Bourbon monarchy from the eighteenth century until and beyond Donizetti's frustrated departure from his position as director of the royal theaters in 1838.[4]

The court clung to these continuities in the face of material change. The close entwinement of absolutist monarch and operatic spectacle was gradually overtaken by a theatrical system whose economic and aesthetic choices were controlled mostly by the forces of the free market, enabling a less direct, potentially more subversive relationship between dramatic performance and official power. Hand in hand with the economic shift went an aesthetic evolution, from a theatrical style based in ceremonial enactment and allegorical symbolization to a tentative embrace of certain forms of dramatic realism, beginning with the geographical specificity of *couleur locale* and—in the realm of character—a gothic attraction to dark interiors and abnormal psychology. This chapter traces one aspect of that transition, following the progress of an operatic topos and an archetypal character that began as a late manifestation of Neapolitan pomp and allegory but then traveled up the Italian peninsula to regions with very different configurations of power and display.

John Rosselli has shown that at least until the Napoleonic occupation beginning in 1808, King Ferdinand had personal control not only over the subject matter of new operas but also over such practical details as the assignment of boxes in the San Carlo, construction materials for new seats, how to deal with a disappointing tenor, and which artists should be granted galas or benefits.[5] These practical connections between court and opera house were overlaid by the less tangible matter of courtly theatricality, the exploitation of a quasi-operatic variety of spectacle in projecting the public face of the monarchy.[6] The Napoleonic occupation severed these ties temporarily from 1808; but the restoration of the Bourbons after the Congress of Vienna flamboyantly reasserted the theatricality of the ruling class while also promoting a rhetoric of continuity and stasis, a pretense that the Napoleonic period had been no more than a hiccup in the city's unchanging reality.[7] When the long-reigning King Ferdinand IV was restored to the throne in 1815, he choreographed a triumphal return to the city on horseback, greeted by jubilant crowds waving green branches and colored handkerchiefs. Upon his first appearance in his box at the San Carlo about a week later, his bust was placed on stage and the public cheered for more than half an hour.[8] Over the next several months reports in the official paper, the *Giornale del Regno delle Due Sicilie,* ritually credited the king himself with the renewal of culture and religion in the city: "The generous gifts from his hand in recent days are proof of the more than paternal solicitude with which he seeks to make good the disgraces of the unfortunate victims of the recent events."[9]

The Teatro San Carlo was a crucial piece of this propaganda campaign. Celebrated as the most sumptuous theater in the Italian peninsula, the San Carlo followed the neoclassical design typical of Italian opera houses: a façade organized into rows of evenly spaced white pillars and arched porticoes and the ascending tiers of boxes inside the theater that gave concrete expression to the social stratification of the audience. When Ferdinand had been back on the throne for only nine months, on the evening of 12 February 1816, a stray lantern set fire to the theater, which was destroyed down to its external walls. Since the theater was connected to the royal palace, the crown prince Francesco himself went out into the streets to calm residents of the quarter during the blaze. The king's stature and credibility with his subjects were decisively shored up when the theater was rebuilt in less than a year, in a style almost slavishly faithful to the original 1737 plans of architect Giovanni Antonio Medrano. In reality, much of what was being preserved was in the mind—and perhaps the most important element for the self-image of the city was simply that the wealth of the fittings continued to be recognized as the most lavish in the peninsula. The façade had already been modified by Antonio Niccolini in the early nineteenth century, and several new elements were introduced during reconstruction, including retouched interior decorations and a new ceiling. While public discussion of the reconstruction militated against any sense of loss by emphasizing continuity with the past, the *Giornale del Regno delle Due Sicilie* announced that the curve of the boxes would be modified to improve sight lines from the boxes to the stage and, intriguingly, that an obstructing "sconce" on the old stage would be removed so that singers would no longer have to leave the center of the action and move up to the edge of the orchestra pit to deliver their arias.[10]

The reconstructed theater was inaugurated with great pomp on 12 January 1817, with a performance of Giovanni Simone Mayr's allegorical cantata *Il sogno di Partenope,* staged as a gala to mark the birthday of the newly restored king, now designated as Ferdinand I under the new Restoration regime. The cantata was paired with the première of *La virtù premiata,* a ballet on the story of Cinderella that had been in rehearsal when the fire broke out.[11] Galas were frequent at the San Carlo, promiscuously marking birthdays of members of the royal family and visits by foreign dignitaries, usually marked by festive illumination of the theater's exterior, the performance of a cantata composed for the occasion, and attendance by the royal family, whose reactions to the performance were often noted in the papers the next day. Birthdays and marriages involving members of the Neapolitan royal family usually merited newly composed works, of which Donizetti composed several, including his own treatment of the Partenope myth to celebrate the birth of a new child to Queen Maria Carolina in August 1838.[12]

Mayr's *Partenope* cantata is a particularly transparent example of the suture between stage spectacle and royal reputation. A preface to the libretto by Urbano Lampredi explains that the cantata's action dramatizes a dream of the siren Partenope (symbol of the city), who witnesses the fire but then awakes to find the theater untouched, resplendent.[13] The cantata was performed before sets designed by Antonio Niccolini, who had supervised the theater's reconstruction, and its main setting was a backdrop depicting the neoclassical Temple of the Muses, identified in the libretto as standing in for the Teatro San Carlo. The cantata's first act concerns the burning of the temple/theater by the evil Poliflegonte, and the second act opens with a strophic aria for Partenope and her sister muses, who weep before a "view of the destroyed theater."[14] Once the inconsolable siren falls asleep, Mercury summons Time and asks him to reverse history, to return to the time before the fire. The cantata ends with a double aria for Isabella Colbran as Partenope, who praises Apollo (a thinly disguised King Ferdinand) as benevolent ruler and beloved father, while she, as allegory of the city, is garlanded with lilies, the flower depicted on the Bourbon coat of arms.[15]

The most insightful commentary on this performance came from a source who was not even present at the San Carlo that evening. Amid the "diary" entries published as *Rome, Naples, et Florence*, Stendhal pieced together an account of the evening that leaves no doubt about the importance of the San Carlo as a mirror for king and state. In Naples, he implies, opera was far more influential than any government document or decree could ever be:

> This hall, rebuilt in three hundred days, is a *coup d'état:* it connects the populace to the king more than the constitution granted to Sicily, which they would also like to have in Naples....
> The splendor of the *San Carlo* reflects adoration onto King Ferdinand: he can be seen in his box *sharing* the audience's enthusiasm: this word *sharing* causes us to forget many things.[16]

Stendhal's barbed mention of "sharing" ironizes the notion that the theater creates a sense of community and of equality between royalty and the people. The "many things" that opera can efface, he goes on to spell out, include the inequality and the miseries he had witnessed in the villages around Naples.[17]

Theater was a crucial tool of self-representation and nation-building for the restored Bourbons; but the restored monarchy also relied on more straightforward cultural products to represent the dynasty as au courant, populist and accessible, and more firmly in power than ever before. One of the first tasks was to generate a new bank of imagery advertising both the modernity of the Bourbons and their secure control over the Neapolitan territory, and the portraits commissioned during these first few years speak of a regime that knew it needed to update itself, giving the lie to the rhetoric of continuity promoted by the official papers. The first official portraits of Ferdinand after his restoration cannily adopt the French neoclassical iconography popular under the Napoleonic regime, even employing the same painters favored by Joachim Murat. The silver-wigged Ferdinand of eighteenth-century portraits such as Angelica Kaufmann's of 1782–83, in which the king wore vaguely medieval armor and held a small scepter, is unceremoniously dismissed, replaced with a monarch in a more relaxed full-figure pose and to be more in tune with the surrounding landscape.[18] The portrait painted in 1815 by Giuseppe Cammarano (father of librettist Salvadore), for example, depicts the monarch in a frock coat bedecked with military decorations, positioned between a classical statue and a window opening out onto a view of Vesuvius and the Bay of Naples, the landscape denoting his control of his realm (see figure 1).[19] The family portraits are equally revealing, with the post-Napoleonic iconography intriguingly suggesting an embrace of allegory and theatricality. The most famous image is Kaufmann's, painted in 1782, showing the royal family gracefully arrayed in a classical outdoor setting, with hunting dogs in the foreground and a harp and classical vase as props symbolizing the family's patronage of the arts.[20] By 1820, Cammarano paints the family of Ferdinand's son Francis I, who will assume power in 1825, outdoors with the inescapable Vesuvius in the background, arrayed around a bust of the father and reigning king (see figure 2). These new scenarios relinquish the trappings of visible power, connecting the royal family more closely to the local landscape and projecting a more approachable monarch.

These portraits combine techniques of allegory and of romantic portraiture—showing the subject(s) as melding with the surrounding landscape but also surrounded with objects that stand for abstract ideas, sending

FIGURE 1. Giuseppe Cammarano, *Portrait of Ferdinand I,* 1815, Palazzo Reale, Caserta.

a clear message about the meaning of the monarchy.[21] The Tudor operas of Rossini, Donizetti, and others operate within this same space between allegory and romantic subjectivity, and much of their power for contemporary audiences may have come from the way they balanced the two modes of representation. Seen as aesthetically flat and too deferential to patrons and power, allegory commanded little prestige in the nineteenth century; but literary theorist Barbara Johnson has shown that the allegorical mode held a continuing force because it functioned as a form of public speech whose signification is based in distance and indirection. Because decoding an allegory always requires the viewer to substitute one term for another ("justice" for a robed woman holding a scale, for example), allegory has a special ability to reveal and dramatize the conflicts that are constitutive of the public sphere

FIGURE 2. Cammarano, *Portrait of Family of Francesco I of Two Sicilies*, 1820, Museo di Capodimonte.

but habitually concealed beneath a shiny surface.[22] In other words, where romantic painting depended on an impression of seamless, inevitable connection among the various aspects of a representation, allegory foregrounds the representational effort that goes into the construction of meaning.

Although the deconstructive theory that undergirds Johnson's reading of allegory might seem alien to the pictorial and operatic styles of early-nineteenth-century Naples, the reminder that reading, seeing, and listening always involve a slight gap for interpretation (or translation) may provide a valuable perspective from which to listen to Rossini and Donizetti. The disconnect between words and music, and between dramatic situation and musical style, that troubled early critics of Rossini is a much greater problem if we assume, with the romantics, that successful art must communicate as an indissoluble expressive unity, its components blended naturally and without effort. Johnson's critical stance offers much more than just a recuperation of allegory itself; her appreciation of the labored connection between signifier and signified in allegory shows a way to hear Italian opera as partaking of romantic techniques and images, while also preserving a representational aesthetics that allows for a work built from discrete components that could be combined in various ways but would never meld completely.

Seen this way, the differing reception of Viganò's ballets and Rossini's operas makes a different kind of sense. Viganò's pantomimic ballets were easier for the early-nineteenth-century Milanese intellectuals to love, and to write about, because they combined two elements with fairly weak traditions of signification (untexted music and the dancing body), while Rossini's operas upended the traditional treatment of poetry and vocal music, both of which had much stronger and more historically fraught meanings for Italian readers and listeners. A similar bifocal aesthetic enabled the creation and reception of the operatic portraits of the Tudor queens, from Rossini's 1815 Elizabeth to Donizetti's Mary Stuart in 1835, which drew equally on existing traditions of allegory and a looser, more subjective romantic symbolism. When the dreaming Partenope stands for a Naples made whole again after the rebuilding of the Teatro San Carlo—or when Queen Elizabeth in an opera by Rossini or Donizetti stands for the newly approachable, defeudalized, humanized Ferdinand I—the representation gains force from the *distance* between signifier and signified, the slight hiccup that occurs perceptually when mythical creature and metropolis, or past and present monarchs, are linked in the mind.

THE QUEEN'S TWO BODIES

Before pursuing the implications of this view of allegory, two more basic questions demand attention. One is a question that presents itself about any fashion or fad, and can be simply stated: What made this subject so interesting to audiences? Where did its appeal lie? But with the Tudor operas there is also the question of how and why the subject could be attractive or even acceptable to kings, to theater administrators, and to impresarios anxious to please their superiors. The idea of creating an opera with a historical monarch as protagonist would have been an easy selling point, but what happened in the private chambers of the palace, or in the royal box, when the patrons realized that the monarch was a woman and that the opera's plot revolved around her rejection by her lover, the agonies of jealousy and abandonment she suffers, and the machinations she undertakes to secure the devotion of a man who loves someone else?

As the first new opera heard at the San Carlo after Ferdinand's restoration and a commission for a royal gala, Rossini's *Elisabetta, regina d'Inghilterra* played nearly as important a role in the ceremonial life of the city and was charged with almost as much allegorical weight as the Partenope cantata. Yet the story of Elizabeth's unreciprocated love for the Earl of Leicester hardly seems a natural choice for a royal gala, unlikely to flatter the king or offer a pleasing portrait of absolutist rule. The subject was a vivid (if mostly fictional) episode in the life of Queen Elizabeth I, chosen by the impresario Domenico Barbaja probably with some degree of royal consultation. On the most obvious level, Elizabeth must have been meant to stand in for King Ferdinand, her successes in statesmanship and empire-building gesturing optimistically toward an expanded role for Naples on the European stage. Yet the substitution of Ferdinand with a female head of state introduces a startling new dimension. It is a central feature of almost all the Tudor operas that Elizabeth is depicted as divided, torn between the command she masters in her public role and the uncertainties of her emotional and romantic life, and she is depicted also as softened, compromised, by her gender. Accounts of the image making and control of rhetoric surrounding Elizabeth in her own time suggest that her gender was perceived—and strategically employed—as at once liability and asset, and the perceived conflict between femininity and statecraft was only more heavily emphasized in later historical and fictional portraits of the queen. This split self is captured in the words that the historical Elizabeth is supposed to have spoken to her troops prior to the Armada: "I know I have the body of a weak and feeble woman, but I have the heart and stomach of a king, and a king of England too."[23] In a kind of inversion of Ernst Kantorowicz's famous notion of "the king's two bodies," in which elaborate rituals ensure that the monarch's governing power survives beyond the death of the physical body, this ritualized performance of self is based on an almost opposite principle: the queen is softened, her femininity played up, as if to humanize the monarch and perhaps place her more on par with her subjects, both on and off the stage.[24]

Perhaps the best way to see how the ambivalent gender identity and affective persona of the queen projected across the proscenium of the San Carlo is to consider Rossini's 1815 *Elisabetta* together with Donizetti's revisiting of the same plot and characters fifteen years later, in his *Elisabetta al castello di Kenilworth* of 1829. Both operas were unveiled on royal occasions—Rossini's to honor the birthday of Ferdinand I's son Francis, and Donizetti's for a gala performance on the birthday of Queen Maria Isabella in 1829. Both place the queen's divided self center stage, and both supply the queen with a docile and vulnerable double in the form of her rival. Although based on different literary sources—Rossini's libretto drawn from a dramatization of an episode in Sophia Lee's 1783 novel *The Recess,* Donizetti's from Scott's *Kenilworth*—the operas tell essentially the same story: that of Elizabeth's connection to Robert Dudley, the Earl of Leicester, who reputedly married in secret and hid his wife away from the eyes of the court in order to preserve his status as Elizabeth's favorite.[25] The opening acts of both works grant a prominent place to pageantry and royal celebrations, against which the queen's conflict between love and duty is explored. Rossini's *Elisabetta* stages the queen's entrance in the midst of celebrations of Leicester's victory over the Scots, while Donizetti's first act concludes with her arrival at Kenilworth on horseback, heralded by trumpets, cannons, and rows of massed spectators "calling out joyfully."[26]

The two operas also converge to a remarkable degree in their treatment of Elizabeth's less admirable qualities. Both feature ensemble scenes based on deception and dissimulation, in which Elizabeth sadistically uses her knowledge of the secret marriage, which the young couple believe they have concealed. Rossini casts this component of the plot in memorably public form, as the centerpiece of the first-act finale. With the court assembled to celebrate Leicester's military victories, Elizabeth presents him with a scepter and, thus, the expectation that he will rule as her consort. Knowing that his secret wife, Matilda, is disguised in the crowd, she takes visible pleasure in the anguished reactions of the secret lovers and their fear of discovery. A very similar exchange in Donizetti and Tottola takes place in private, as part of a duet between Elizabeth and Leicester in the third act. Near their midpoints both operas digress into conspiracy scenes that seem to have more to do with contemporary Italy and an appetite for all-male cloak-and-dagger choruses than with history or with the characterization of royalty.

The acts of clemency that conclude each opera cement the image of Elizabeth as benevolent ruler on the opera seria model. Rossini's final scene is not only more convincingly motivated than Donizetti's but contains a surplus of gestures toward the division between the queen and common woman. To visit Leicester and Matilda in prison, Elizabeth dons commoners' garb. When the Duke of Norfolk pulls a dagger, Matilda shields the queen, foiling the attempted assassination. Out of gratitude, Elizabeth blesses the couple's union and commutes their death sentences, announcing, "Your queen approves the sentence, but Elizabeth cannot." The *rondò finale* in which she reacts to this decision hammers home the schizophrenic-monarch message once more: "It is not the queen who is here now, but Elizabeth." The treatment of this episode by Donizetti and his librettist, Andrea Leone Tottola, is untroubled by causality. The plot provides no trigger for Elizabeth's lifting of the death sentence; she simply seems to recall her better nature, expressing affection and joy for the married couple in a *rondò finale*.

All of these similarities notwithstanding, Donizetti's *Elisabetta al castello di Kenilworth* projects a very different mood and attitude to the monarch than does Rossini's opera. The main difference is one of focus. Queen Elizabeth is simply on stage less of the time in Donizetti's opera, garnering less emotional and musical attention. Tottola's is a more private story, more focused on the queen's girlish foil Amelia, through whose eyes the audience often perceives Elizabeth.[27] This larger role for the queen's rival is linked to an overtly romantic sensibility derived from Walter Scott (and thus absent from the Rossini). The character of Amelia is a magnet for the opera's gothic thrills, threats, and visual cues. Much of the first act centers on Leicester's plan to hide Amelia away in a *"stanza erma"* (isolated room) during Elizabeth's visit to Kenilworth, and it is through that captivity that she comes under the influence of the predatory Warney, who alternately desires, threatens, and conspires against her with evil glee.

The ceremonial scenes in which the queen is introduced, though, are remarkably similar, suggesting either conscious modeling by Donizetti or strong convention. Both center on triumphal entrances for Elizabeth, heralded by fanfares and a chorus of adoring courtiers, leading to entrance arias that dramatize the queen's split self. Reversing the usual role of the slow movement in a double aria of granting access to interior feelings, both of these arias devote the slow movement to public address, in which the queen thanks the courtiers for their affection and loyalty; in the cabaletta of each, Elizabeth peeks secretly at her feelings, enjoying a ripple of anticipation at the idea of seeing Leicester again and (in Donizetti) a twinge of fear at the prospect of discovery.[28]

But the kinship between these two Elizabeths lies not only in the ways that their arias operate the hinge between public and private, slow movement and cabaletta. Both also introduce the queen in her slow movement with a stentorian section that is open-ended, declamatory, and highly ornamented, evocative of a call to arms or call to order, before introducing what will become the movement's main melodic figure. Rossini often begins lyric movements with such a block of declamation and ornament; one familiar example is the music Angiolina sings when she arrives at the ball in the Act I finale of *La Cenerentola,* in which the grandiose tone serves to advertise the maid's altered status, as she (ironically) speaks of her disdain for riches and polished surfaces. In Rossini's *Elisabetta,* the vocal style situates the queen firmly in the public eye; she speaks of sweetness and gratitude, but it is a satisfaction that comes from seeing her subjects celebrate:

> *Quant'è grato all'alma mia*
> *il comun dolce contento!*
> *giunse alfin il bel momento*
> *che c'invita a respirar.*

(How pleasing it is to my soul / This sweet collective contentment! / Soon the beautiful moment will arrive / When I will be able to breathe.)

The queen's authority is conveyed through an unpredictable declamatory flow of sustained notes, pauses, athletic ascending leaps, and ornaments that impel the melodic line forcefully forward (see example 6). The music perhaps offers a few glimpses of vulnerability—in the sustained top note A on the second syllable of *"momento"* at m.11, perhaps, and in the lyricism of the melodic repetition at m.12—but overall the relationship between text and music is distant, the thirty-second note scale turns and fragments are distributed according to structural rather than semantic logic.

Writing for *his* Elisabetta, in a nearly identical dramatic situation, Donizetti expands but also softens the effect. The expansion is, first of all, an effect of the libretto: Tottola's text for Donizetti extends to ten lines, compared to Schmidt's single quatrain. Yet Tottola's poetry comes across as more monochromatic than Schmidt's concision.[29] Where Schmidt allows Elisabetta a glimmer of interiority as she looks forward to the moment when she might be able to "breathe" and think private thoughts, Tottola places her in a sequence of stiff public stances. She first thanks her subjects for their praise and honor, then visualizes the benefits that the English nation could enjoy if peace were to be achieved, and concludes by imagining the happiness she would feel as queen if this should come to pass. Even as Elizabeth moves through these wooden stances, Donizetti's music mimics the melodic gestures we expect from a lovelorn soprano. After an initial phase (see example 7, mm.1–7) peppered with ornaments and fermatas that feel both highly formal and slavishly Rossinian, the movement shifts (from m.8) into the

EXAMPLE 6. Rossini, *Elisabetta, regina d'Inghilterra,* Act 1, Coro e Cavatina (Elisabetta).

EXAMPLE 6. *Continued*

men 6 to, che c'in - vi - ta, che c'in vi ta a re - spi rar,

che c'in vi - ta_____

a re - spi - rar.

EXAMPLE 7. Donizetti, *Elisabetta al castello di Kenilworth,* Act 1, Coro, Cavatina, e Finale.

EXAMPLE 7. *Continued*

2

repeating, lyrical melodic phrases more typical of Donizetti's slow movements, the music belatedly granting Donizetti's Elizabeth the interiority and
vulnerability that Rossini's seems to lack.

But the slow movement is only one half of the introductory scene for the
queen, and the cabalettas for the two queens' entrance arias show these characters in a far more conventional light. Donizetti's Elizabeth expresses joy at
the thought of her beloved Leicester in balanced phrases and memorable
melodic motives, with a predictably expressive turn to the minor as guilt and
unease briefly surface; here Elizabeth could almost be mistaken for the still-
sane Lucia di Lammermoor looking forward to seeing Edgardo in the cabaletta of that opera's first-act aria for the lead soprano ("Quando rapito in
estasi"). And Rossini's cabaletta has a very familiar ring. An early case of
Rossini's notorious practice of self-borrowing, the music had appeared first
in an aria conceived for the castrato Giovanni Battista Velluti in *Aureliano
in Palmira* (La Scala, 1813), before being reworked for Elisabetta. A year after
the première of *Elisabetta,* the cabaletta surfaced again, in *Il barbiere di
Siviglia* (Rome, 1816), as the closing section of "Una voce poco fa."

The translation of music intended for a queen into the mouth of a head-
strong young woman is hardly a surprise, given Rossini's habit of repurposing
his music in radically different contexts. To call on the principles of portraiture once more, this is not an instance of the central character blending completely into a setting, but rather of distinct characters slotted into surroundings that are mostly fixed in advance. Not that the cabaletta was repeated
note for note in each of the three operas; Rossini made many small changes,

some perhaps reflecting the character or dramatic situation but more of them probably prompted by the change of performer or simply by momentary inspiration. In the reworking of the cabaletta for Rosina, one alteration in particular works to transform royal authority into coquetry.

Both Elisabetta's and Rosina's versions of the cabaletta are based on a split at the number's center and on an unveiling in the third line of the quatrain of the "real" woman behind the public façade. "Una voce poco fa" is famously subdivided by the word *"ma"* (but), which ushers in Rosina's account of what she is like when crossed: not sweet and obedient but *"una vipera."*[30] The turn in *Elisabetta* is a classic flip from public to private, as the queen contemplates her love in an aside:

> *Questo cor ben lo comprende,*
> *palpitante dal diletto.*
> *(Rivedrò quel caro oggetto*
> *che d'amor mi fa brillar.)*

(This heart understands it, / trembling with pleasure. / [Now I will see that dear one who inflames me with love.])

The setting of the first two lines is nearly identical in the two versions, except that the ornamental flourishes fall for Elisabetta on the pleasure- and body-oriented words *"palpitante"* (trembling) and *"diletto"* (pleasure), whereas the text-music match seems looser (or perhaps more ironic?) when Rosina delivers these slightly shrewish embellishments on the words *"obbediente"* and *"amorosa"* (obedient, loving).

The only real change comes in the number's second half, beginning just after that teasing "but" in "Una voce poco fa." The comic version made famous in recitals and compilation recordings proceeds with a motive that rocks between B and C♯. Where Rosina begins each phrase with this oscillation and then dissipates its energy into jaunty repeated notes and later a scalar pattern, Elisabetta clings to the two-note pattern, delivering it over and over in rapid fire, cranking up tension with each of its ten iterations (see example 8). This is a minuscule difference, one that can almost vanish with inflections and spontaneous ornamentation of a particular performance; but the translation of Rosina's flexible phrasings into Elisabetta's more propulsive energy hints at the kinds of musical identity markers that could distinguish middle-class *Volkston* from absolutist authority.

The substitution of Rosina for Elisabetta, with the music altered only in tiny details, reminds us how much of what we see and hear in nineteenth-century

Italian opera was conceived for immediate, visceral effect, short-circuiting any patterns of symbolic or political interpretation. Let us turn then to examining what we can discern of those effects as they may be captured in published reviews of the Tudor operas. Although the critics (as always) comment on only a narrow band of issues and effects, and certainly cannot be read as access to the visceral impact of these operas, certain themes and concerns run through reviews of all the Tudor operas that can tell us something about how these fictional queens were viewed and how they were believed to relate to the singers who impersonated them.

HAIR PULLING, FISHING NETS, AND OTHER LAPSES OF ROYAL DECORUM

Although allegorical opera may have had an especially long and robust history in Naples, the aesthetic issues that shape the presentation of Queen Elizabeth in these entrance arias are not specific to Naples. The archetype of the Tudor plot resonated across and beyond Italy, although reactions to specific themes or scenes varied according to the experiences and sensitivities of local audiences. As the archetype migrated from one opera to another, and as individual operas traveled through the peninsula, new meanings and associations emerged. Donizetti's *Maria Stuarda* is an especially interesting case because of its difficult and peripatetic genesis. Conceived and composed in Naples, where Donizetti had succeeded Rossini as the composer for the royal theaters, this adaptation of Schiller's play *Maria Stuart* was withdrawn from the docket of the San Carlo by royal decree after the dress rehearsal had already taken place.[31] Donizetti and his librettist Emanuele Bardare quickly prepared a travesty that purged the characters and events that might have offended the censors, and the new work—entitled *Buondelmonte*—received a few unsuccessful performances at the San Carlo in the fall of 1834. A year later composer and librettist tried again at Milan's Teatro alla Scala with Maria Malibran in the title role, but the material was judged too incendiary there as well and the opera was pulled after a single performance. The offending passage that made the opera unacceptable in Milan occurred during the climactic encounter between the two queens, when Mary vilifies Elizabeth as *"figlia impure di Bolena"* (impure daughter of Boleyn) and even *"vil bastarda."*

Unlike Naples, Milan was not exactly a monarchy: at the Congress of Vienna, the city had been granted to the Austro-Hungarian empire, and so it was formally ruled by another Ferdinand, the Hapsburg emperor Ferdinand I (based in Vienna); but day-to-day decision-making was in the hands of an Austrian viceroy. Equally important, print journalism and the craft of music criticism burgeoned in Milan in the 1830s, so while the première of Rossini's *Elisabetta* had barely been mentioned in the press other than to chronicle the attendance of the royal family, Donizetti's Tudor operas stimulated lively commentary among critics.[32] Not that those northern Italian critics were obliging enough to offer any direct observations about the opera's depiction of Elizabeth as monarch or any critiques of absolutist power; they were probably restrained both by censorship and by the lack of a critical tradition that regarded opera as relevant to political discourse. The critics instead looked at absolutism from an oblique angle, returning again and again to questions of impersonation and dramatic authority.

This interpretive thread runs straight through from Stendhal, who in 1824 equated Isabella Colbran with the Bourbon Ferdinand I, to the Neapolitan journalists a decade later who obsessively retold the story of the fight that broke out between the two sopranos rehearsing Donizetti's *Maria Stuarda*. Where Stendhal rhetorically conflates singer with queen to make a political point, the chronicler of the dress rehearsal gone awry seems far more guileless—perhaps actually convinced that the singers lost themselves in their roles and absorbed the enmity of their dramatic characters. Writing about Rossini's *Elisabetta* in Naples, Stendhal delivers a death blow to Ferdinand and the Bourbon monarchy by way of an elaborate backhanded compliment to Colbran. According to Stendhal, Colbran had begun to lose her voice and to sing hideously out of tune by 1815; but had maintained her supreme position in the Neapolitan operatic world through one of the strategies that crops up so often in diva narratives—a sexual liaison with the impresario Barbaja. Yet Stendhal concedes that Colbran made a wonderful Elisabetta, a feat she achieved by leveraging her own habits of imperious whim (and perhaps her somewhat wooden dramatic presence?) to capture the customary demeanor of the absolute monarch. In a lengthy description of her performance in the role, Stendhal casts Colbran as an imperious diva but reverses the typical portrait of the diva as overwrought and physically demonstrative:

> Signorina Colbran, as Elizabeth, used no gestures, did nothing theatrical, nothing of what are vulgarly called *poses or tragic movements*. Her immense power, the weight of the events that a single word from her lips could call into being, all this was conveyed by her Spanish eyes, so beautiful and at times so terrible. It was the glance of a queen whose fury is restrained only by a vestige of pride; it was the stance of a woman who is still beautiful, and

who has long been accustomed to seeing her first hint of a whim followed by the swiftest obedience. Seeing Signorina Colbran speaking with [her rival] Matilde, it was not to feel that for twenty years this proud woman had been a queen whose authority was absolute. It was the timelessness [*ancienneté*] of the habits that absolute power demands, the lack of any doubt about the devotion that her slightest caprice would inspire, that was the main feature of the acting of this great artist: all these things could be read into the tranquility of the movements of the queen. The few movements she did make were stirred by the violent clash of passions that tore at her soul, not by the desire to be obeyed. Our greatest tragic actors, even Talma himself, can rarely resist strong and imperious gestures in the roles of tyrants. Perhaps these imperious gestures, these tragic overstatements [*gasçonnades*] are one of the demands of the parterre of bad taste, those spectators who decide the fate of our tragedies: but those gestures are no less absurd for being applauded. An absolute monarch is the man of all the world who makes the fewest gestures; they are no use to him: he has long been accustomed to seeing his slightest sign followed, like lightning, by the execution of his wishes.[33]

In his distaste for absolutism at least, Stendhal is consistent. His unease at feeling seduced into sharing the feelings of Ferdinand when he beheld the rebuilt Teatro San Carlo, and even maneuvered into admiring the king, is echoed here by his twinned suspicion of Colbran and the monarchs she resembles. There is a dazzling symmetry to Stendhal's paired sketches of diva and queen. The diva playing a queen, he suggests, effortlessly mimics the monarch in her immobility, her quiet confidence that she will be obeyed; and at the same time the monarch resembles the diva in the caprice and selfishness of her wishes and her commands. This is far from the usual picture of the diva indulging in scenes and tantrums; and Stendhal's characterization raises the question of whether kings and queens are scarce in opera partly because their behavior is in fact *not* theatrically rewarding.

Stendhal's strong voice and the relative freedom he enjoyed by publishing in an opinionated and whimsical biography set his comments on *Elisabetta* apart from journalistic reactions, which tended to be less fanciful, more diffuse, and less politically pointed. Forever after, critics always seemed to doubt whether the prima donna was equal to the challenge of embodying a real, historical queen. Even stars like Giuditta Pasta and Maria Malibran could be dismissed as too lightweight; and since the Tudor operas always set the queen against a kinder, gentler rival, critics rarely resisted the temptation to play the two principal women in an opera off against each other.

The consistent focus on the regal authority of the prima donna may be one facet of the public relations aspect of theatrical journalism. It seems counter-intuitive that critics would obsess over whether a prima donna could convincingly inhabit the role of a queen, when so many of the biographical essays and pamphlets devoted to singers depict them as queenly and unassailably powerful, not unlike the way Stendhal describes Colbran.[34] But that very focus ensures that this would be one element that readers would be prepared to think about and perhaps could easily visualize; anyone taking on the role of Elizabeth after 1815 would be in the shadow of Colbran and the other *prime donne* who had gone before. When a diva *manquée* took on the role, as Giacinta Puzzi-Toso did in both Carlo Coccia's and Donizetti's *Maria Stuarda* (London, 1827; Milan, 1835), the question of presence and charisma became especially urgent. Reviewing the première of Coccia's opera in London, the *New Monthly Magazine* complained that Giuditta Pasta as Maria lacked "the softness which we could have desired," approaching "the energy of Madame Pasta's Semiramide and Medea." Pasta's unseemly force as the victimized Scottish queen was exacerbated by the musical and dramatic weakness of her counterpart: although Puzzi-Toso's singing had improved, the critic opined that "there is a total absence of dignity and nerve in her performance; she is inanimate and apparently a stranger to the feelings which such a part ought to inspire."[35]

Reviews of Donizetti's *Elisabetta* in Naples are typical of the public relations mode. Critics consistently devoted space to oohing and aahing over the illumination of the theater in honor of the queen's birthday, to noting the reactions of the royal family, who attended the second performance, and to feeding the rivalry between sopranos Adelaide Tosi and Luigia Boccabadati, who sang the roles of Elisabetta and Amelia. Because Boccabadati's career had been built mostly in comic roles, the question was whether she could command enough presence and authority as Amelia to balance the force of Tosi's Elisabetta. In contrast to Stendhal's minority view that a less histrionic portrayal translated into greater credibility for an operatic queen, the Neapolitan journalists seem to be looking for overt temperament and gestural flair rather than stillness and control. The *Giornale del Regno delle Due Sicilie* allowed itself to doubt whether Boccabadati possessed the "majesty of form and of bearing, as well as the art of gesture and the corresponding vocal force" to succeed in heroic roles in the leading theaters.[36] Other papers opined that the role of Amelia was too passive and that Donizetti had not given her enough arias, and that "Signora Tosi, representing the queen of England, was the queen of this score."[37] Luigi Prividali went too far for some when he attributed the opera's *entire* success to the Elisabetta, Adelaide Tosi, prompting a sharp retort from one of the local papers.[38]

Prividali is one of those critics whose voice cuts through the published reactions to these operas. Together with Gaetano Barbieri, the pioneer translator of Walter Scott whom we encountered in chapter 2, Prividali typifies one of the possible paths taken by the intellectuals and scribblers who shaped reactions to opera. The early years of Prividali's career moved in loose parallel with the transalpine itinerary traced by Carpani and Viganò. He briefly worked as a court poet in Vienna, where his duties included the authorship of libretti for two cantatas that were sung at private occasions by the Empress Maria Theresa herself and where he twice collaborated with Viganò.[39] Back in Venice around 1810, Prividali worked as a translator, journalist (for the *Osservatore veneziano*), librettist (most notably writing the text for Rossini's *L'Occasione fa il ladro*, 1812), and briefly as a theater impresario in Trieste. But Prividali probably attained the height of his influence when he settled in Milan, where in 1829 he founded the *Censore universale dei teatri,* whose content he generated almost single-handedly.[40]

Amid the critical reactions to Donizetti's *Anna Bolena* (La Scala, 1830), it was again Prividali who voiced the strongest and most vivid reactions to the opera, enumerating several ways in which Giuditta Pasta's performance as Anne Boleyn fell short of the tragic intensity he hoped for. The subject matter of *Anna Bolena* puts a new spin on the theme of royal authority, since the title character is a queen but not one who was born to the throne or enjoyed the divine right to rule that could be claimed by both Elizabeth and Mary. Prividali was scandalized that Pasta allowed herself to appear with bare arms in the final scene, a wardrobe malfunction that symbolized for Prividali a broader lapse of royal decorum.[41] He complained that her delirium in Anna Bolena's final scene was too reminiscent of Giovanni Paisiello's deranged *semiseria* heroine Nina (from *Nina, ossia la pazza per amore*), making it impossible for Romani's more tragic scene to be truly moving.[42] But Prividali, who never seems to have published a review that didn't contain contradictions, inaccuracies, or inconsistencies, ultimately thought that the greater problem was the haughty tone that Pasta's Anna took with her rival Jane Seymour. At one point, he notes, Pasta threw her rival a look of disdain that would have been suitable only if Anne Boleyn had herself been "born a queen."

The theme of dueling sopranos reached an apotheosis a few years later, when the comparison of the *prime donne* depicting Elizabeth I and Mary Stuart became the *whole* story, completely supplanting any actual hearing of the work. This happened, again, in Naples, when Donizetti's *Maria Stuarda* was famously withdrawn from the docket of the San Carlo by royal decree after the dress rehearsal had already taken place. The skeletal journalistic record contains no discussion of either dress rehearsal or censorship. The only published discussions of events appeared in the Bolognese *Teatri, arte, e letteratura,* which reported with prurient enjoyment on the face-off between the two women:

> You know the story of Mary Stuart and of Elizabeth: you know to what point the queen detested the beautiful queen of Scotland.
>
> After two hundred years, the hatred of Elizabeth has been reawakened. Elizabeth grabbed Mary Stuart by the hair, and the poor queen of Scotland, who got the worst of the fight, had to take to her bed for 15 days. . . .
>
> Now, it happens that these two women had long harbored a rivalry. The impresario had gambled on this reciprocal dislike, casting them in the parts of two enemies; without a doubt he was saying to himself that they would invest their performances with real hatred, the illusion would be all the more vivid, and the opera would be a wild success.[43]

Unlike the reviews cited earlier, this one has received more than its fair share of scholarly attention. Federico Fornoni calls it "more than an anecdote," taking the report of the scuffle—which may of course be apocryphal—as a symptom of a new form of dramaturgy, one that could cause deep identification between singers and their roles. Anselm Gerhard agrees, taking the clash of sopranos as an indication that Donizetti's drama, and especially its central encounter between the queens, was so powerful that the two women's dramatic roles melded with their offstage selves.[44] Whether or not the catfight actually happened is less important than the discursive shift signaled by this journalistic meme. The attention garnered by the absorption of the two singers into their historical roles announces the passage of Tudor operas from allegory into mimesis: Elizabeth no longer stands in for a sitting monarch but now undergoes feelings of rivalry and indecision that depict her as a passionate woman (who just happens to be a queen). Writers such as Fornoni and Gerhard credit the new register of *Maria Stuarda* entirely to Donizetti, whose musical and dramaturgical language made it not only possible but almost inevitable that both singers and spectators would lose themselves somewhat in the drama, identifying with the condemned Mary Stuart.

Donizetti's *Maria Stuarda* does certainly confront the listener with a more believable, less allegorically cardboard kind of queen. But the significance of this anecdote surely lies also in the discursive work it did to obscure the *real* chain of events in Naples. The articles in *Teatri, arte, e letteratura* show that the situation was blurry and confused: the opera's title was altered more than once in attempts to appease the censors, and the date of the eagerly awaited première repeatedly delayed.[45] In a sense, the singers and their reputations were sacrificed in order to have something to report about a situation that was of great interest to the public, and as so often happens in the annals of nineteenth-century opera, the immoderate emotions of a pair of competitive or ambitious women served (opportunely or by design) to mask the limits on expression imposed by the Bourbon monarchy.[46]

When *Maria Stuarda* made it, very briefly, to Milan late in 1835, even the incomparable Maria Malibran was measured by the yardstick of royal decorum and found wanting. In a long and unusually probing review, Prividali articulated one of the reasons people may have cared about queenly presence so much. Setting himself as a *portavoce* for Schiller, whose underwhelmed reactions to Bardare's libretto he imagines at some length, Prividali asserts that "[Schiller] would not have framed this great catastrophe as a family drama about a woman who sacrifices her rival in the hope of regaining her lover."[47] And in a tortured effort to laud Malibran while dismissing the production as cheap and mundane, Prividali rhetorically interrogates the singer about her choices of costume and gesture: "Why, rather than as Maria, present yourself as a disobedient and recalcitrant girl kneeling before her father? Why wander around the park with that veil and that saddle-drapery? why ascend the scaffold with that fishing net?"

The issue was greater than just the gravitas of the female protagonist as queen. In the modern legislative landscape of Milan, there was none of the concern that had haunted the Neapolitan criticism that the stature of real queens might be slighted through inadequate dramatic impersonation. Donizetti's queens needed to be impressive—terrifying, even—so that the operas did not descend into mere sentimentality and so that opera in general could lay claim to a dramatic clout that, if not quite matching Schiller, would ennoble Italian theater and allay concerns that audiences were wasting their time on trivial entertainments. When he defended Schiller against Bardare and wished the libretto possessed greater tragic weight, Prividali spoke not as an apologist for Austro-German aesthetics but as a modernizer whose tastes and values were in tune with those in the *Biblioteca italiana* and *Il conciliatore*.

BUREAUCRATIC MONARCHY

Lurking behind Prividali's deference to Schiller's authority are some unspoken assumptions about adaptation: that an opera should endeavor to capture the dramatic style and emphasis of its source play, but also that operas generally fall short of the moral seriousness of the plays that inspire them. What Prividali did not mention were the profound and specific ways in which Bardare's libretto for Donizetti's *Maria Stuarda* departed from Schiller, sculpting the story of Mary and Elizabeth according to Italian preferences and preoccupations. Bardare and Donizetti focused the drama around the Catholic Mary as object of sympathy and around her execution as a spectacle of martyrdom. Where Schiller's play set up a scrupulous symmetry between the two queens, Italian texts tended to grant Maria far more expressive space than Elisabetta, culminating in cathartic and redemptive portrayals of her final confession and execution.[48]

Such glorification of Mary stretches back at least to William Robertson, whose popular six-volume *History of Scotland during the Reign of Queen Mary and James VI* (originally published in 1759) served as a source for Schiller and went through at least four Italian editions between 1784 and 1830. Robertson repeatedly describes Elizabeth as austere, rigid, and unbending, while casting Mary as gentle, forgiving, gracious, and courageous. His text is larded with admiring references to the "sublime spirit of the Scottish queen, not defeated by the misery she suffered" and "the perfect composure of her spirit."[49] After Robertson, the story of Mary and Elizabeth was disseminated in Italy in equal part through translations and adaptations of Schiller.[50] A fairly loose adaptation by Pierre Lebrun was taken up in 1821 by the Compagnia Reale Sarda in an Italian version by Gaetano Barbieri that would in turn become an important source for Coccia's 1827 opera and for Donizetti and Bardare.[51] As Barbieri explained in a translator's note, the tailoring of Schiller's text to French taste meant that the character of Mary had to be bleached of all guilt or eroticism: thus the elimination of the scene in which Mortimer declares his love for the Scottish queen, as well as of her dying admission of her guilt in the Babington plot to assassinate Elizabeth.[52] While confessional difference and the idea of Catholic religious observance were highlighted in these texts, the concrete elements of actual Catholic ritual (crucifix, communion host and chalice) that punctuate Mary's dialogue with her confessor in Schiller were stripped away on Italian stages in deference to the widespread laws against enacting religious acts in the theater.

Endings, as I hinted earlier, are a crucial point of articulation in the collective entity that is "the Tudor operas." While the dramatic articulation of "the queen's two bodies" through a split-personality double aria remained a constant across three decades, endings shifted dramatically. In 1829 Donizetti and Andrea Tottola were nostalgic when they followed Rossini's lead in closing their *Elisabetta al castello di Kenilworth* with an act of clemency: such scenes had long been out of style. Just a few years later *Roberto Devereux* would end with an execution for treason, as does *Maria Stuarda*.[53] The evolution from operas that end happily, often under duress from censors or patrons, to the acceptance of tragic dénouements is a familiar milestone in the story of romanticism's incursion in Italian opera. But the transformation in the ways the Tudor operas end is about more than the substitution of a tragic for a happy ending. The mechanism by which the death sentence is handed down in the later works, via a paper decree that needs to be signed—visibly, reluctantly—by Elizabeth, makes this new ending almost a direct negation of the acts of mercy popular a decade earlier.[54] Rather than appearing to mingle with her subjects in a symbolic union ennobled by music, Elizabeth acts at a remove, her impact on her subjects now mediated by scheming ministers and the paper decree.

The force of this change becomes tangible when we compare the music Rossini composed for Elizabeth's act of mercy in 1815 to the last strains we hear of Elizabeth's voice in Donizetti's *Maria Stuarda*. As we have seen, the entrance arias that showcased the queen's two bodies leaned toward the rhetorical rather than the lyrical, addressed to a group of adoring subjects and structured as declamatory orations. The final arias in the clemency scenes are instead expansively melodic, luxuriating in melodic variations and emphatically conjuring the physical presence of both the queen and the prima donna impersonating her. In the *rondò finale* of Rossini's *Elisabetta,* the queen wishes eternal happiness for the lovers (Leicester and his secret wife, Matilde), calling them to embrace her (*"a questo sen venite"*). She dispatches the entire four lines of text in just eight measures of songlike simplicity, before launching into a pattern of repeating ornaments on the dominant (see example 9, mm.10–13). When Leicester and Matilde fall to their knees, exclaiming, "Oh great one!" Elizabeth replies *"Sorgete!"* and this little ballet of courtly homage and noblesse oblige becomes the occasion for a small cadenza (mm.14–15). As Elisabetta begins to repeat the opening melody, now embellished, the aria acquires yet another facet of presence and embodiment. Although the embellishments here are written out, the variation principle calls forth a topos of improvisation, drawing attention to the technique and inventive genius of the singer.

Scenes that hinge on the signing of a death warrant occur prominently in at least five Italian Tudor operas.[55] The staging of these conflicted, momentous, almost surreptitious actions is starkly opposite to the grandeur that marks the beginnings of these operas. The signing of the warrant happens in seclusion, with the queen alone or in collusion with one or two ministers of her inner circle. Arguably it is at these moments that we most closely approach the queen's true interior, in physical and metaphorical senses. The emphasis on the signature, threatened, then withheld, then affixed to the fatal document, dramatizes the speed and capriciousness of royal will in a way that is completely at odds with the ceremonies that feature so often in first acts.[56]

The prominence of the parchment prop originated with Schiller's *Maria Stuart.* Schiller leaves Elizabeth alone with the decree during a tortured monologue, in which she shifts rapidly between imagining the freedom and surge of power she will feel once Mary is dead and nervously anticipating the public protests that will follow the execution. Her uncertainty is captured concisely in the stage direction at the moment when she signs the warrant: "She signs, quickly and firmly, then drops the pen and recoils with a frightened expression."[57] Moments later, about to hand the warrant over to the minister who will actually set the execution in motion, she prevaricates,

EXAMPLE 9. Rossini, *Elisabetta, regina d'Inghilterra,* Act 2, Finale secondo.

EXAMPLE 9. *Continued*

insisting that it is his decision whether and how rapidly to enact the decree and taking refuge behind the mediating distance provided by the document and the signature: "I was asked to sign this. I have done so. But a piece of paper decides nothing. Names don't kill."

The execution takes place, of course, as Elizabeth knows and hopes it will. But the sophistic separation she has enforced between the paper decree and the action it orders enables the play's final scene, a legislative postscript in which Elizabeth sheds all responsibility for the execution. Claiming that her signature was not equivalent to her will ("The mob were pressing me to sign it: I followed their will, and signed, under duress"), Elizabeth distributes the blame between Davison, who delivered the decree to Burleigh for enactment, and Burleigh himself, disingenuously insisting that they should have known to await a further order before acting on the decree in the document.[58] This deferral of responsibility to ministerial middlemen and the documentary paraphernalia of government is a powerful statement about how life-or-death decisions are made, the integrity of leaders, and what constitutes action in government. The transfer of responsibility from queen to a parchment that can go anywhere, carried by many different hands and differently envoiced by each intermediary, is a concrete instance of the devolution of both government and poetic invention to a class of professional civil servants that was characterized by Friedrich Engels as the "bureaucratic monarchy," and by Carl Schmitt as the "civil servant monarchy."[59]

If the events of Schiller's play destabilize the traditional, allegorical view of the absolutist state as identical with the quasi-divine person of the monarch herself, Donizetti's opera conveys yet another vision of the relation between the queen and the state. Elizabeth's long, schizophrenic soliloquy before signing the death warrant falls away in the libretto, as does Schiller's closing scene of ministerial wrangling and hairsplitting. The opera concludes instead with a double scene featuring Mary—first her conversation with her confessor, Melville, and then the grand execution scene, cast as a double aria with a frame of lamenting chorus. Of course, operas conventionally end with arias and with grand scenic effects like executions and heroic last words, not with diplomatic squabbles and ironic barbs from the author. The glorification of Maria at the opera's end satisfied operatic *convenienze* while also catering to an emerging taste for martyrs, both religious and political.[60]

But the soliloquy does not disappear without a trace. Elizabeth's moment of indecision and her eventual action are cast instead as an orchestral introduction early in the third act, during which she sits at her desk, sunk in thought, followed by a brief and tempestuous duet with Lord Robert Cecil, one of Mary's chief opponents. Elisabetta moves to sign the decree at the end of her recitative dialogue with Cecil, then finally does sign in an abrupt and underplayed movement, when Leicester bursts into the room unexpectedly. The scene is unusually dense, saturated with semitone- and tritone-based motives that twist, layer, and modulate in a style of motivic working that reminds us of the Viennese training of Donizetti's teacher, Mayr. Donizetti marks the moment of Elisabetta's initial decision to sign with a strong burst of gestural music consisting of three swirls of sixteenth notes, sequencing down through an E♭ triad (see example 10, mm.56–57). The music for Elisabetta's arrested impulse is taken up a few moments later as the main motive of the duet's first lyric section, in which Elisabetta replays the conflict, first reminding herself how much she would like to see Maria dead and then recalling how her heart stopped her hand from acting (*"ma la mano il cor s'arresta"*) (see example 11, m.65). The music for the actual affixing of the signature a few minutes later is dissociated from physical movement, characterized instead by a dissonant, circular motive, with no audible mark for the moment when the paper is signed (see example 12, mm.147–48, 151–52). This music makes it clear that lyricism is no longer the province of Queen Elizabeth at this point in the opera or, really, anywhere in *Maria Stuarda*. Allegorical drama and the glorification of the monarch have become obsolete. Vocal and melodic luxuriance is entrusted to Maria and to Leicester when he is with her or singing about her. And indeed, Leicester reintroduces lyricism almost as soon as he begins to sing in this scene, turning the tonality back to the flat keys and compound meters that have been associated with Maria and her attachment to nature, as he delivers a paean to her innocence (*"Deh! per pietà sospendi"*), and eventually dragging Elisabetta and Cecil along with him (see example 13).

The juxtaposition of styles here suggests that deferral and mediation—musical and expressive, as well as legislative—have supplanted presence. The unusual tangle of chromatic motives that frames this scene seems like a diametric opposite to the ceremonial and allegorical poetics of the typical opening scenes of the Tudor operas. Indirection and deferral trump spectacle, ceremony, and overt statements of intent and affect; expressive as well as legislative power have been transferred away from the queen's body and into a shifting, unstable, elusive *idea* of will, a mute paper object, and a network of functionaries who follow orders (but whose orders can also be changed or falsified).

Allegory perhaps does not dissolve completely in *Maria Stuarda,* but its force is weakened and diffused, so that what is represented is a corrupt, indecisive monarch, pragmatic to a fault. Friedrich Dürrenmatt once characterized Schiller's *Maria Stuart* as a depiction of a political world in which state power was still clearly dominated by the gaze, whereas modern power had lost that visibility, becoming anonymous and bureaucratic.[61] But in fact both Schiller's and Donizetti/Bardare's dramas seem to "know" that true power evades the gaze and operates invisibly.

Recent commentaries on *Maria Stuarda* have emphasized the novelty of the character of Maria, who disregards status and protocol, communicates her feelings frankly and openly, and communes with nature in the manner

EXAMPLE 10. Donizetti, *Maria Stuarda,* Act 2, Scena e Terzetto.

Elizabeth picks up the pen to sign the document, then stops indecisively and rises.

EXAMPLE 10. *Continued*

of the romantic heroine.[62] Had the opera enjoyed wider exposure in nineteenth-century Italy, the fusion of this romantic archetype with the thematics of Catholic martyrdom might have made Maria Stuarda into one of those sacrificial victims who populated midcentury fiction, both serious and popular, and whose example helped inspire young Italians to fight and to make sacrifices for the liberation and unification of the peninsula.[63] But the record of reception from the opera's short-lived Milanese outing in 1835 indicates that critics were more interested in Elisabetta and in the dynamic between the two women than in the virtues of Maria herself. *Maria Stuarda*—and, to some extent, later *Roberto Devereux*—stage a compromised, cynical, and reduced figure of the queen and of the absolutist state that seems to reflect the modernizing efforts of the Bourbons of Naples while also anticipating the instrumental role the Savoy kings would play in the construction of Italy's constitutional monarchy from 1848 on.[64] In this new political terrain, monarchs would continue to play a key role, but only when their power was mediated by mandarins and ministers and the mode of allegory was dissolved, or

EXAMPLE 11. Donizetti, *Maria Stuarda,* Act 2, Scena e Terzetto.

EXAMPLE 12. Donizetti, *Maria Stuarda,* Act 2, Scena e Terzetto.

EXAMPLE 13. Donizetti, *Maria Stuarda,* Act 2, Scena e Terzetto.

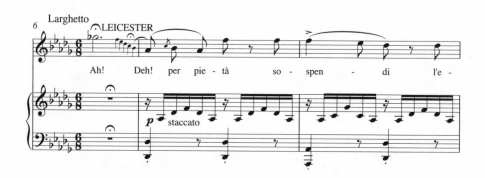

perhaps reformulated in a more self-conscious style. When *Maria Stuarda* at long last received its Neapolitan première in 1865, the words and gestures of both queens must have resonated in a new way for audiences who were slowly acclimating to their new identities as citizens of the Kingdom of Italy.

FOUR

Reading Mazzini's "Filosofia della musica" with Byron and Donizetti

Leave, instead. Get away for good, far from the life we've lived since birth. Settle in well-organized lands where everything really is possible. I had fled, in fact. Only to discover, in the decades to come, that I had been wrong, that it was a chain with larger and larger links: the neighborhood was connected to the city, the city to Italy, Italy to Europe, Europe to the whole planet.

ELENA FERRANTE,
Those Who Leave and Those Who Stay (2014)

THE CULTURAL POLITICS OF EXILE

When Donizetti's *Anna Bolena* received its first performances in 1830, the opera was presented not at La Scala but at the Teatro Carcano on the edge of the city, just beyond the Porta Romana. Reports of the première in the musical press could barely get around to giving an account of the wildly successful opera, so fixated were they on the logistical challenges of moving operagoers to the suburbs:

> The opening of the Teatro Carcano this year was another true festivity. In order to save the inconvenience of a long and uncomfortable trip to the theater, the administration has instituted three *Omnibus* to transport spectators to the theater. These three enormous carriages, adequately appointed, lighted internally and externally by lanterns, traverse the streets of the city center, greeted by popular exultation: their measured entry into our splendid avenues mixed with the racket made by the elegant coaches produced a bizarre bustle of to-ing and fro-ing that was a bit reminiscent of the lively joys of carnival. The magnificent Porta Romana offered a spectacle of frenetic activity that in some ways resembled the nighttime festivals on the Grand Canal in Venice when the illuminated gondolas carry the populace to the theaters.[1]

Another newspaper, reporting on the same performances, drew an analogy between the transplantation of opera to the periphery and a rich gentleman who tried to recreate "all the frills of the typical English garden—streams, a few Chinese pagodas, Swiss cottages, a few ruined castles, some ancient monuments," sparing no expense with the landscaping and engineering, and even creating an artificial lake on his parched land, only to find that no plants would grow in the desert-like terrain.[2] The actual distance between La Scala and the new theater could be traversed in a quarter hour on foot; but the shift in the geographic center of operatic life in the city felt significant enough that these writers needed to draw on analogies with distant locales and mores to capture the sensation of being carried in a public vehicle beyond the city's walls to hear an opera.

The uproar bespeaks the localism of Milanese operatic and social circles in the 1820s and 1830s and, in a larger sense, the ways "the city" as an entity (geographic, social, material) shapes histories of opera and politics during the period. In earlier chapters we sampled the lively conversations pursued—in person and in print—among Milanese personalities such as Giovanni Gherardini, Vincenzo Monti, Stendhal, and Peter Lichtenthal about theatrical aesthetics and sociability. The vitality of that conversation was possible partly because Austrian control of the city was displaced and obscured, channeled through a viceroy, and not much resisted or deplored by the Milanese until early in the 1840s. In Naples, in contrast, direct control of theater and the press by the Bourbon monarchy meant that allegorical theater persisted into the nineteenth century; romantic and gothic plot elements were forbidden; and the press worked more as a bulletin of official events than as an independent source. Each major city on the Italian peninsula had a distinct governmental structure—whether as part of the Papal States, under the Habsburgs, under the (originally Spanish) Bourbons, or as a separate principality. Some of these arrangements were new since the Congress of Vienna, others much older; but all municipalities had deep-rooted identities based in architecture, history, and tradition—so much so that suspicion of any bonds that were *not* local was an important obstacle for the nationalist project. But at the same time cities were important enabling structures for new modes of perception and communication, in Italy as elsewhere in the nineteenth century. The design of urban centers created spaces that encouraged forms of sociability rooted in a simultaneous perception of proximity and anonymity, bonds that flowed from common interests and pursuits rather than enduring ties of family and village. With new transportation networks and spaces for the display of consumer goods came new technologies and expectations for the display and presentation of the self and of cultural products.[3] In that sense, the urban center offers a powerful framework for thinking about how affect and aesthetic experience could be mobilized in service of the building of a new nation-state.[4]

In this chapter and the next, these functions of the city as a node of sociability and communication will come into focus through a displacement from the Italian centers, such as Milan and Naples, to Paris, where so many Italian artists and political leaders landed in the 1830s. For the composers in this story, the migration north was voluntary and short term: Rossini, Bellini, Donizetti, and eventually Verdi all spent time in Paris, tailoring new works for the Théâtre-Italien or the Opéra, drawn by generous fees, freedom from censorship, and sophisticated audiences. Rossini's arrival in 1823 had stoked the demand for new works by Italians, and the vogue reached a peak early in 1835, when both Bellini and Donizetti received their first commissions to compose new works for the Théâtre-Italien. Donizetti's *Marino Faliero* and Bellini's *I puritani* were premièred within six weeks of each other, the conjunction provoking a minor media frenzy. Italian singers were at least as much in demand, and stars such as Giulia Grisi, Luigi Lablache, Giovanni Rubini, and Antonio Tamburini (who together would become known as the "*Puritani* quartet") all made Paris and the Théâtre-Italien their home for part of each year.

While the northward movement of composers and singers from Italy to Paris followed an irregular but constant cycle dictated by fashion and, often, by increasing frustrations with political and artistic constraints in Italy, the concurrent migration of Italian political figures was spasmodic and often irrevocable, with a wave of expatriations following each failed uprising, cresting with the suppression of the revolutions in Romagna and Liguria in 1831.[5] Some rebels were officially exiled by Austrian authorities; many more slipped across the border to escape arrest and imprisonment. The French government officially welcomed these refugees and even gave them state subventions, to make up for the fact that France had stood by and allowed Austria to quell the rebellions, defying the "principle of nonintervention" adopted after the July Revolution.[6] The government assigned the new arrivals to specific cities and regions, while only the social and intellectual elites were allowed to settle in Paris.[7]

By the autumn of 1831, 1,524 Italians were drawing some form of subvention from the French government, constituting almost a fifth of the foreigners supported by the ministry of the interior. Among the new arrivals to Paris between 1831 and 1835 were Princess Cristina Trivulzio di Belgoioiso (prominent rebel, journalist, and hostess of the salon where Liszt and Thalberg would duel at the keyboard in 1837), publisher Niccolò Bettoni, actor Gustavo Modena, poet and Bolognese aristocrat Carlo Pepoli (who would write the libretto for Bellini's *I puritani*), Agostino Ruffini and his brother Giovanni (both of whom wrote libretti for Donizetti), and Niccolò Tommaseo (journalist and political essayist). As the theatrical publication *Vert-Vert* jested while reporting on the dress rehearsal for *I puritani*: "The severity of Austria, the banishments of Metternich, the obscurantism of the papal office appear to be good for France! Francis I and Louis XIV imported great artists and poets from Italy; today Italy sends them to us *gratis*. Let us just hope that Rome, Milan, and Naples will exile Lablache, Tamburini, Rubini, and company forever."[8] Investigating the connections among these two groups of Italians—the political exiles and the musicians capitalizing on the wealth and cosmopolitanism of the French capital—this chapter will ask how displacement from Italy colored discourse about independence from Austria and unification, and specifically how cultural events featuring Italians contributed to that conversation. To begin to answer these questions, I focus on a rather disappointing première at the Théâtre-Italien and on an influential essay on operatic aesthetics published in Paris around the same time.

Early in 1835, Bellini's *I puritani* was premièred at the Théâtre-Italien to wild acclaim, followed just over a month later by the less celebrated *Marino Faliero*, drawn from Byron's 1821 drama of the same name. Although Bellini had long enjoyed a reputation as the more innovative composer, it was Donizetti whom Giuseppe Mazzini singled out as pointing the way toward a properly social and morally informed "music of the future" in his 1836 essay "Filosofia della musica," which appeared in a journal published by the Italian émigrés in Paris. One of the central questions this chapter will investigate is why Mazzini might have selected *Marino Faliero* as exhibit A of his treatise on the current state of opera, and how much the libretto's themes of popular rebellion and martyrdom and its partial authorship by Mazzini's close associate Agostino Ruffini may have shaped that judgment.

AROUND THE RUE QUINCAMPOIX

The Italian community in Paris was tight-knit, although certainly not without factional divisions. Niccolò Tommaseo records in his journals that the émigrés went to great lengths to maintain certain habitual aspects of everyday life, seeking out Italian barbers and laundresses and frequenting restaurants owned by Italians.[9] Some of these establishments, including a restaurant in the place des Italiens called "Il Gobettino," came into the public eye late in 1835 during judiciary proceedings around the "Fieschi affair," a failed attempt by a Corsican immigrant to assassinate Louis-Philippe by detonating a bomb during a parade of the Garde nationale at the Tuileries.[10] Writing long after the fact, in 1902, historian Raffaele Barbiera visualized the exiles clustered in the old alleys of the Quartier latin and other dingy neighborhoods, many of which had been erased by Hausmannization by the time Barbiera tried to track them down:

> The wreckers' hammers have not yet destroyed the rue Quincampoix, near Boulevard Sébastopol, nor the long, narrow, shadowy, filthy rue de Vénise, that horrifying profanation of the name of the most artistic city in the world! ... This is the Paris of the Middle Ages: a fetid maze of twisted streets suffocated by tall, cramped houses and greenish oozing foam. Above the narrow doors hang old smoke-stained placards for inns where the guests pay by the night; and at night scrawny, hairless dogs that scrabble through the filth for bits of bone mix with the squalid shades of the old and equally malnourished prostitutes. . . .
>
> [The exiles] were young, full of hope and brio: they could even laugh at their own poverty. . . . The poorest among them received a small subvention from the French government. . . . They worked all day, studying, writing, and giving lessons, traversing kilometers across the immense metropolis, under the baking sun, under the belting rain, in the snow, in that city of huge distances. And in the evening . . . they all gathered at an Italian *traiteur*, a certain Paolo, in the rue Le Peletier near the Opéra: there they had a room reserved for them alone, on a mezzanine, with minimal prices and minimal repasts, washed down with water from the well, if not from the Seine. But isn't good cheer worth more than the most effervescent champagne? Celebrations, greetings, and patriotic cheers nourished these meals.[11]

Barbiera plays the idealism and fortitude of the exiles off against the squalid details of their everyday lives—greenish ooze, seedy hotels, and a local travesty of Venice—a sentimentality perhaps necessary a generation after Unification as Italians had begun to notice that modernization and economic advantage had not magically followed from the political reorganization of the peninsula.[12] But Barbiera's claim that "the unity of Italy was forged outside of Italy, by the exiles," is more than just overblown rhetoric. Forced beyond the confines and traditions of their home cities, the expatriates could articulate an Italian sensibility in new ways, less rivalrous and less constrained by the regional bonds known in Italy as *"campanalismo,"* or exaggerated dedication to the parish or town of origin.[13]

The expatriates tended to agree on a few central principles: that Austrian domination of Lombardy and the Veneto needed to come to an end, and that Italy deserved more support internationally, on a par perhaps with the naval support that France (and Great Britain and Russia) had provided for the rebels in the Greek War of Independence in 1827. But the community fractured when it came to the most effective means of liberating and uniting Italy. Followers of Giuseppe Mazzini and his "Giovine Italia" movement espoused a program of conspiracy and armed revolution very much like the 1831 operations that had led to the expulsions. The other main faction was centered on Vincenzo Gioberti, a cleric and political thinker who had served as chaplain at the court of King Carlo Alberto of the Savoy until he was abruptly accused of conspiracy and banished in 1833. Gioberti and Mazzini clashed in 1834 over Mazzini's failed plan to invade the Savoy with an army of exiles. Gioberti objected to the Savoy expedition because it risked alienating the pope and powerful princes who might otherwise support the Italian cause.[14] The confrontation between incendiary idealism and pragmatism would animate many more debates before Unification, especially where Mazzini was involved. The émigrés most closely connected to the opera world tended to be adherents of the Mazzinian position, although mostly not full-fledged members of Giovine Italia. The composers engaged by the Théâtre-Italien—themselves neither émigrés or exiles but more like celebrity visitors to the French capital—maintained a cautious distance from political movements and mostly avoided outright political statements. Librettists, singers, and journalists tended to be more outspoken. One of the most vocal was Agostino Ruffini, who with his brother Giovanni had been a schoolmate of Mazzini's. The three went into exile together in 1833.[15] Both Ruffinis would work with Donizetti in Paris—Agostino revising the libretto for *Marino Faliero,* and Giovanni writing the text for *Don Pasquale* (1843), as well as translating Donizetti's *Dom Sébastien* into Italian for its première at La Scala.[16]

The Ruffinis were introduced to Donizetti by Michele Accursi, a journalist and member of Giovine Italia whom Donizetti employed to handle his correspondence and business affairs in Paris. Accursi was long suspected of being a plant within the organization, spying for the papal states. By the mid-1840s, Accursi was using Donizetti's Paris address as a front for his correspondence with Mazzini, advising his friend to send letters to the Champs-Élysées address when the unsuspecting composer was away in Naples or Vienna.[17] Like all good plotters they had a secret sign: particularly important missives were addressed to the "*Stimatissimo*" Gaetano Donizetti, and the most sensitive material was written in lemon juice between the lines of the official correspondence.[18]

More hesitant about Mazzini's extremism was Carlo Pepoli, the Bolognese aristocrat who dabbled in libretto writing before crossing the channel to become professor of Italian at University College, London.[19] Chapter 5 will explore aspects of Pepoli's most successful libretto, for Bellini's *I puritani,* in tandem with his texts for songs on Italian themes by Rossini and Mercadante.

The Italian singers resident in Paris were also swept up in political debates, more so than were Rossini, Donizetti, or Bellini. At least three of the quartet of singers who created the main roles in *I puritani* and *Marino Faliero* were sympathetic to Mazzini and Giovine Italia, although their connections to the movement are documented beginning only around 1838. Luigi Lablache was apparently drawn into the movement first by his cook, and Giulia Grisi and her common-law husband, Mario de Candia, had become staunch contributors to Mazzini's causes (which also included the charitable support of Italian émigrés, distinct from political agendas) by the time they—and Mazzini—had settled in London in the late 1830s.[20] Grisi's vocal coach and close associate Marco Aurelio Marliani, with whom she had made the journey from Italy to Paris, was also a republican who would die in a clash with Austrian troops in Bologna in 1849.[21]

AGAINST ROMANTIC INDIVIDUALISM

Tracing the exiles' itineraries through the city and documenting their face-to-face encounters grants one kind of access to the experience of the Italians in Paris, lending an immediacy and a hard economic truth to the political dividends stimulated by this concentration of educated and progressive Italians within the narrow physical and social spaces of Paris. The solidity of these material traces can sometimes overshadow the discursive character of the community, especially the copious journalistic record which is inevitably marked by partisan agendas and subjective preoccupations.

The exiles themselves, however, regarded the printed word as central to their political activities, and they knew that words and stories published in

Paris could have real impact in Italy. Because French censorship standards were far more permissive than those within Italy, the exiles devoted their energy to establishing newspapers that they hoped would strengthen ties among the expatriate community and also be read in Italy, airing ideas that could not be stated overtly in Italian publications. During the 1830s two Italian periodicals appeared in succession in Paris, helmed by different editorial teams and with slightly different missions, but with an overlapping group of contributing authors. The first, *L'Esule,* was safe and uncontroversial, similar in content and format to literary journals published on Italian soil, mostly devoted to celebrating great Italian voices of the past, including discussions of and excerpts from Tasso, Ariosto, Dante, and Machiavelli.[22] *L'Esule* enjoyed a brief moment of notoriety in 1833, when its editors objected to an anti-Italian slur in Victor Hugo's *Marie Tudor* and challenged the playwright to a duel.[23] A confrontation was averted by a written apology from Hugo, in which the playwright averred that the defamatory phrases were pure fiction, uttered by his characters and not to be confused with his own opinions.[24] Hugo's insistence on the bright line between reality and fiction—a line of defense adopted by many a writer since—is hard to gainsay, yet at the same time it is not difficult to understand why the Italians objected. The clash reminds us of the stereotypes the Italians had to surmount when gathering support for the fight against Austria. Versions of these same stereotypes also influenced journalistic reactions to Italian opera in Paris—fueling, for example, the incessant emphasis on the speed with which Donizetti's works were composed and remarks about his reliance on familiar musical patterns, which the Parisian critics both craved and loved to dismiss as stale.

The newspaper that filled the gap when *L'Esule* ceased publication, *L'Italiano,* was explicitly intended to be exported back to Italy and to convey, under cover of literary criticism, political ideas that could not be openly stated in Italy.[25] Founded and edited by Michele Accursi, *L'Italiano* was supported financially by Mazzini, who also contributed seven articles across the paper's year-long run and authored the statement of objectives that appeared in the inaugural issue. That programmatic essay sketched the main tenets of Mazzini's philosophy of a socially engaged art, ideas that also undergirded his long essay on music, "Filosofia della musica," which was serialized across three issues of the journal. The most important themes, also featured in essays by other contributors to *L'Italiano,* were the conviction that the formal qualities of art could convey socially transformative ideas, and the need for new energy to regenerate the "exhausted age." Mazzini also confronted the egotism that he perceived at the heart of romanticism, declaring his intention to tap romantic individualism as a source of social energy and cohesion rather than allowing it to atomize or isolate individuals.[26]

Read alongside other essays in *L'Italiano* and Mazzini's other essays on the arts from the period, the "Filosofia" emerges clearly as an activist text rather than a narrowly focused pitch for operatic reform that anticipates the stylistic innovations of Meyerbeer, Verdi, and Wagner, as the essay has often been read in musicological circles.[27] Mazzini casts individualism as both villain and savior. "Individuality is sacred," the essay intones as a kind of refrain; but Mazzini complains that in the musical dramas of the moment individuality is restricted to melodies and used only to depict the passions, while ignoring the individuality of characters, of each member of a chorus, and of the age and place in which the drama is set.[28] Mazzini follows eighteenth-century aesthetics in equating melody with individualism and harmony with a collective social impulse.[29] His war on individualism began with the postrevolutionary glorification of liberty and human rights, which he believed had led to the cultivation of (romantic) individualism to the detriment of the far more important notion of human *responsibility* to others. Mazzini proposed to replace postrevolutionary "fraternity" with a regime of "association," a concept he took from Saint-Simon to mean that the rights of man must be complemented or extended by a recognition of the duties that men owed to each other and to society.[30]

In the contemporary operatic scene as visualized by Mazzini, Rossini was the "Napoleon" of operatic composition, the consummate individualist who broke all the rules—of musical imitation and of the dramatic unities. Mazzini concedes that Rossini's exercise of will "saved" music, by rendering it sovereign, not subordinate to word or idea. Even so, Rossini's music was not the culmination of a process of musical evolution, but the second in a three-stage evolution of musical style. Rather than blazing a truly new path, Rossini's achievement was to restore and reconsecrate existing patterns, raising the old conventions to the highest possible level. (In this sense, Rossini is aligned with the romantic movement, assigned a role analogous to that occupied by Byron in Mazzini's overview of contemporary literature.) Those who regard Rossini "as the head of a radical revolution in the tendencies and the fate of the arts . . . make the same error as those who want to find in literary romanticism a true faith, an organic theory, and a new synthesis and—worst of all—they are hanging onto the past while loudly proclaiming the advent of the future" (54).

As the language here suggests, Mazzini's model of historiography was a Hegelian one, although he arrived at it apparently without reading Hegel.[31] He visualized historical and artistic change in terms of progress and resurgence, and that progress was articulated in triads, with a first term corresponding to the past, a middle term capturing the (unsatisfactory) present state of affairs, and a third term that represents the culmination or synthesis to be wished for. Underpinning each three-stage process was a foundational structure: the evolution of political systems, in which monarchy was swept away by the French Revolution, and the values of the Revolution which has dominated for forty years next need to be superseded by a new social order. As with all synthesis, which can just be glimpsed in a utopian future, the third phase of operatic evolution has not yet been fully realized. Dismissing Bellini in a long footnote as merely a "transitional genius," Mazzini finds in Donizetti's music energy and "regenerative tendencies" that have the potential to transcend mere imitation of Rossini and forge a true individuality of style.[32] Here as well, the perception of an evolution over time is more important than the specific features of any single opera:

> From *Zoraide* to *Anna Bolena*, to *L'elisir d'amore*, to *Parisina*, and finally to *Marino Faliero*, to *Lucia di Lammermoor*, and to *Belisario*, is marked out a proportional scale which works like a thermometer to measure the degree of development Donizetti has achieved in each work—and perhaps an accurate examination of all these dramas would reveal in each a progress, a perfecting of each musical element. (69)

Besides *Marino Faliero*, only *Anna Bolena* is singled out for any commentary beyond the broadest terms of approval and optimism. What piques Mazzini's interest in *Anna Bolena* is the acute historical sensibility with which Donizetti depicts the tyranny of Henry VIII and his court. In particular, he praises the sharp differentiation of musical style between Henry and his victim Anne, and the "severe," "tyrannical," and "artificial" idioms Luigi Lablache adopted as Henry VIII. This attention to power dynamics—and to the musical embodiment of plot structures—will also be fundamental to Mazzini's appreciation of *Marino Faliero*.

On the surface, Mazzini's embrace of *Marino Faliero*—an opera he could never have heard in the theater and which enjoyed only modest success after its première at the Théâtre-Italien—might seem capricious. The Théâtre-Italien was hardly the most likely place to find an opera that would break new ground, musically or ideologically, nor did Donizetti have any reputation as politically articulate or committed. Agostino Ruffini must have had Donizetti in mind when he wrote to his mother shortly after the première of their opera, complaining that "there does not exist a composer who understands the mission of music: they are not logical: because one does not become a philosopher before becoming a composer we have nothing [from them] but pretty motives: we will never have a true musical idea."[33] Yet *Marino Faliero* gained a political force almost in spite of itself through a series of associations—with Ruffini as librettist, certainly, but also with Byron whose play it adapted, and with its setting in medieval Venice, which evoked a lost republican past, oligarchical oppression, and the city's present state of aestheticized decay all at once.[34] Each of these associations worked in distinct ways; but the global effect was to write *Marino Faliero* into a lively set of conversations about the role of cause and effect in historical events, about power and representation, and about the resonances of geographical setting.[35] From this perspective, Mazzini's approval of *Marino Faliero* may seem overdetermined: perhaps the real question is not why Mazzini anointed this particular opera as his ideal of what lyric art should become, but what led Donizetti to write exactly *this* kind of opera for his Parisian debut.

THE MAKING OF A REBEL

Over and above his friendship with librettist Ruffini, Mazzini's interest in *Marino Faliero* must have been stimulated by the opera's favorable depiction of a popular uprising and its debt to one of the writers Mazzini admired most, Byron. Not only does *Marino Faliero* depict a revolt against the Venetian oligarchy led by a doge who himself was not a patrician, but that rebellion is masterminded by a shipbuilder at Venice's Arsenale. The question of why a sitting doge would join an uprising against his own throne sparked lively debate and speculation among critics of the opera and its literary sources, Byron's *Marino Faliero* (1820) and Casimir Delavigne's eponymous play, staged at the Théâtre de la Porte-Saint-Martin in 1829.[36] New attempts to grapple with the causes of the French Revolution had thrown the problem of historical causality into relief, and the question of what causes a rebellion—and more specifically of what might inspire a powerful individual to join a revolutionary movement that challenged his own government—was a live concern for historians and casual readers alike in the 1830s. In Italy the question had special resonance among those who hoped to arouse broader support for the nationalist cause.[37]

The various dramatic retellings share one important element of backstory, which has roots in history. Before the stage action begins, a patrician has scribbled an insulting verse on the ducal throne in the midst of a carnival ball, insinuating that Faliero's young wife is unfaithful. Whereas Byron had depicted the wife as innocent, explaining in his preface to the play that he wanted to avoid the exhausted dramatic motif of jealousy, one of the biggest changes Delavigne made to the outlines of Byron's drama was to give her an adulterous love interest and, indeed, to raise the curtain on a scene in which she is dreaming about her lover, followed by an intimate scene for the two of them.[38] In both Byron and Delavigne, Faliero has demanded that the Council of Forty punish the vandal for his insult, and in both plays the first act is driven partly by Faliero's suspense about what that punishment will be, turning to rage when news arrives that the offender has been sentenced to only one month in prison. At the same time, offstage, the shipbuilder and navy veteran Israële Bertucci suffers a similarly public insult from a patrician (in Donizetti it is the *same* patrician, Michele Steno) who, impatient for the repairs on his gondola to be completed, contemptuously strikes Bertucci. Faliero and Bertucci, from high and low stations, are depicted as parallel before they have even met on stage, and their respective humiliations by the contemptuous patrician become personal incentives for Bertucci to plan and for Faliero to join the rebellion.[39]

This sequence of events establishes callous display of patrician power at the heart of the drama and presents a number of reasons for Faliero to join Bertucci's conspiracy. Subtle shifts of emphasis by a playwright or librettist could imply that the doge acted out of anger at the insult to his own honor represented by the graffito, out of a desire to avenge (and attest to) his wife's honor, out of personal ambition, or from blind jealousy and a suspicion that Elena might actually be unfaithful—and any of these could be compounded by genuine populist sentiment and concern for the living conditions of the city's plebeians.

Byron placed the issue of motivation front and center in his *Marino Faliero,* in an extended preface that weighed competing historical theories. Although one of his sources, Sismondi's *Histoire des républiques italiennes* (1807–8), had attributed Faliero's participation in the conspiracy to jealousy, Byron reaches back through the historical record to argue that the earliest accounts, such as Marino Sanuto's sixteenth-century chronicle (reproduced in an appendix to Byron's play) did not mention jealousy but instead stressed Faliero's desire to extend his own power.[40] In the preface Byron jabs at a certain "Dr. Moore," whose account in a 1781 guide to Italian manners was "full of stale jests about old men and young wives and wondering at so great an effect from so slight a cause." Byron drives his point home with a page-long list of major historical events provoked by trivial causes, all of which he claims should have been well known to Moore: "He knew that a basin of water spilled on Mrs. Masham's gown deprived the Duke of Marlborough of his command, and led to the inglorious peace of Utrecht . . . that Helen lost Troy . . . that a personal pique between Maria Antoinette and the Duke of Orleans precipitated the first expulsion of the Bourbons."[41] Byron concludes that it is natural and understandable that a man like Faliero, "used to command, who had served and swayed in the most important offices," should be offended and moved to action by a public affront such as the insinuating graffito.

When Casimir Delavigne's *Marino Faliero*—Donizetti's direct source for the opera's libretto—was premièred in Paris in 1829, the question of motivation was again central, and again hashed out over the body of a woman.[42] The contested purity of Faliero's wife, Elena, is a necessary premise for what was otherwise (to most viewers and readers) an inexplicable turn of plot: that someone in Faliero's position would join a populist movement, and ultimately be charged with treason and executed. In an extended review of the play, Charles Nodier took Byron's side, complaining that building the plot around marital infidelity dragged the play down to the level of a Molière farce about a cuckolded old man and diminished Faliero's dignity. Writing with an ambivalence that bespeaks the disavowed revolutionary sympathies of his youth, Nodier devoted most of his attention to diagnosing the play's position on liberty, romanticism, and political reform. He approved of Delavigne's assimilation of elements from the boulevard theater into what was nominally a tragedy, and found that the boulevard actor Gobert as Bertucci gave the most compelling performance. But for Nodier the play was too topical, its appeal to old-school revolutionary values and hatred of the nobility so strident that he compared the experience of watching it to receiving a letter announcing the marriage of a distant cousin just after you've attended his funeral.[43] He writes with more than a hint of regret about the advent of "the people" as a character:

For about forty years in France we have seen that there was a real entity—palpable, animated, intermittently dramatic—that has been overlooked by the theater, and it is called the people. And since the people has, for better or for worse, now entered into everything—into the vagaries of the State, into political emotion, into institutions, and above all into history—it is natural that this new character—uneasy, agitated, usurper of nature—has earned a place in tragedy.[44]

LISTENING WITH MAZZINI

In his comments on the opera in the "Filosofia della musica," Mazzini does not address Faliero's reasons for joining the conspiracy; nor will he mention Byron's *Marino Faliero* at all in his 1839 essay "Byron and Goethe." But the sense of a revolutionary mission and the conviction that artists and their fictional creations alike should be measured according to their commitment to social and political change is never far from the surface. Much as he admires Byron's commitment to liberty and equality, Mazzini is impatient with the Byronic hero, whom he finds egotistical, aimless, infatuated with an empty notion of liberty: "What can they do with the liberty so painfully won? On whom, on what, expend the exuberant vitality within them? *They are alone* . . . . . . they have no mission, no belief, no comprehension even of the world around them."[45]

In the "Filosofia della musica" the expectation for initiating change is projected onto operatic style itself, which should evolve to emphasize certain relational categories (empathy, collectivity, accurate depiction of the geographical other) and to downplay others (the individualism showcased in lyrical melody and vocal display). Characters and plots are almost invisible in Mazzini's vision of the future of opera; but it is probably not incidental that his discussion of *Marino Faliero* lingers longest on the scene in which Bertucci persuades Faliero to join the conspiracy. Here Mazzini exhaustively describes the careful moves through which Bertucci maneuvers Faliero into position. Within the essay's larger argument, this duet—and especially its through-composed, speech-like opening section—stands for what opera can and should become, how it can depict distinctive characters and emotional situations while downplaying the melodic beauty and vocal display that Mazzini saw as egotistical and self-serving.

The duet falls in the middle of the first act, just after Faliero has learned of the light sentence the council has handed down to the patrician Steno for defacing the throne and impugning Elena's virtue. Most of the scene's delicate psychological negotiation is carried out in an extended dialogic opening section (often labeled a *tempo d'attacco*) preceding a more conventional slow movement and cabaletta. Although Mazzini's account of the duet is selective, singling out just a few key passages and effects, it is worth pausing for a moment to consider this section as a whole, to examine how Donizetti and librettist Bidéra sketch the disparity of power between the two men and with the competing pull of public and private concerns on the doge. In parallel statements of a stolid, march-like melody, the two men momentarily switch roles: Faliero affects a position of impotence, declaring that any revenge against Steno would be impossible because he is backed by the entire council, while Bertucci boasts that he can marshal *"mille brandi e mille eroi"* (a thousand swords and a thousand heroes) to fight the patricians. The two feel each other out in progressively quicker exchanges, until Faliero pauses and invites Bertucci to speak freely. Employing the rhetoric of the ruler's two bodies so central to the Tudor operas, Bertucci asks whether he is speaking "to the Doge, or to Faliero," to which Faliero replies, *"Sparve il Doge"* (the Doge has vanished).

This assurance opens the way for Bertucci's campaign of persuasion, which begins by appealing to Faliero's social conscience. His melodic fragments entwining with an insistent, chromatic melody in the violins that knits together the entire exchange, Bertucci prods Faliero to address "the servitude of the common man, and the fear, sobs, and rancor of the plebeians" (see example 14). Twice in succession Faliero counters Bertucci's pleas, shifting to a remote key and replying that these crimes are not enough to justify overturning the government (*"sono tremende smanie / che sbranono ogni cor / ma per salvar Venezia / non bastanti ancor"*). It is only when he again brings up Steno's personal insult against Faliero, and when he moves from a melodic style to recitative, that Bertucci finally manages to win the doge to his side. Bertucci and Faliero occupy distinct tonal and melodic spaces during this exchange, their only common ground the jagged, constantly striving violin melody that runs through the background. They finally come together musically in the slow movement that follows ("Odio, sdegno"), although their words (completely delivered as asides) signal that they continue to observe each other covertly and suspiciously. From one perspective, the outlook for their shared project of rebellion looks bleak already at this point, since the two voices mingle only in a static, ornamental, highly nostalgic idiom that harks back to the static slow movements of Rossini's Neapolitan style.

EXAMPLE 14. Donizetti, *Marino Faliero,* Duetto (Israële, Faliero), Act 1, mm.73–88.

EXAMPLE 14. *Continued*

The section of Mazzini's "Filosofia" devoted to *Marino Faliero* runs for two full pages but is constructed as a single headlong sentence, punctuated with many dashes and commas. The breathless syntax echoes the pacing of the music Mazzini finds most exciting, scenes in which the action hurtles forward with the continuity of spoken drama and where the dialogue principle dominates. Mazzini packs into this one monumental, almost unreadable sentence the entirety of the opera, from the "shadow of old Venice" that looms over the drama to Bertucci's wrenching farewell to his sons before he is executed for treason in the final scenes. Along the way, Mazzini mentions almost every significant turn in the action and pauses to single out individual numbers for a few words of praise—such as the ball that ends the first act, which he declares "truly of the times," or Fernando's cavatina "Di mia patria, o bel soggiorno," which he says only an exile can understand. Although the discussion of *Marino Faliero* reads a bit like casual jottings hastily transposed into print, the choice of sentence structure may be deliberate, underwriting Mazzini's preference for a speech-like style of declamation, for forms that embed action into set pieces, and for melodic pacing that musically encodes the idea of progress.[46]

Nearly half of the passage on *Marino Faliero* is devoted to a discussion of Bertucci and Faliero's Act 1 duet—focusing on its dialogic opening section alone, which Mazzini admires for its fluid treatment of form and of psychology. Besides the confrontation it stages between the popular principle and aristocratic privilege, Mazzini praises the scene's treatment of the psychology and physiology of manipulation, persuasion, and decision-making

> that admirable mastery at once of musical science and of the science of human physiology, mastery of Israele's increasing insistence, and of Faliero's increasing agitation: I would call it a blade inserted by Israele into the Doge's chest, one that penetrates, penetrates, and then, when the cry of a mistreated people is not enough, and Israele throws onto the scales "l'onta del Doge," which he implants in the Doge's heart,—and that rapid announcement of his victory "Bertucci Venezia avrà il brando di Falier," which rises to the stars . . .[47]

The two quoted phrases in Mazzini's account of the duet are drawn from the libretto, but their placement in the description creates an accelerated sense of the scene's unfolding. The first phrase (*"l'onta del Doge"*—the shame of the doge) comes from the recitative just before the slow movement begins; Mazzini perceives this as the exact moment when Faliero decides to join Bertucci's movement. The phrase *"Venezia avrà il brando di Falier"* (the sword of Faliero shall fight for Venice) comes from the transition between the slow movement and the cabaletta, where Israële finally clinches Faliero's participation in the conspiracy, so that Mazzini's account of the duet—detailed as it is—creates the impression of an unrelenting dramatic forward motion, skipping over and effectively erasing the conventional moments of static contemplation in slow movement and cabaletta that actually make up the bulk of the duet. Mazzini's recourse to quotations from the libretto here—and to conversational phrases drawn from the midst of a scene rather than aria or ensemble incipits—harks back to the historical accounts of Faliero's downfall by Sanuto and Sismondi, both of which quote imagined (or reconstructed) dialogue for this moment alone, as if this interview in which the doge was coaxed into articulating his shame and colluding with the rebels has a special presence and immediacy for historians.[48]

More than any other passage in the "Filosofia," the discussion of Bertucci and Faliero's tête-à-tête makes clear what Mazzini meant by "progressive" style in opera, and what he heard and liked in Donizetti. When he argues for music that highlights dramatic action and psychological insight or that subordinates voice to orchestra, Mazzini can sound much like other operatic reformers. What is particular to Mazzini's vision is his deep-rooted belief that the specific choices composers made about the musical and dramatic structures could affect experience outside of the opera house, and could even perhaps alter social realities. Even though he held opera to have an urgent, immediate relevance to contemporary political life, he had little interest in narrative or in the allegorical resonances that a plot about an uprising, or about one national group dominating another, might have for Italian audiences. Nor was form important: questions like whether a composer dispensed with the expected cabaletta in a double aria, for example, were of little interest compared to the small-scale effects of pacing that he understood to mirror states of mind and body.

WE ASCEND THE SCAFFOLD SMILING

Despite its broad reach and breathless tone, Mazzini's discussion of *Marino Faliero* is full of fleeting musical details—notations of a cello obbligato here, a string of low baritone notes, or a high E♭ "on which the entire aria hangs" there.[49] Yet the essay was written while Mazzini was living in hiding near Geneva, and he never traveled to Paris, the only place where the opera had yet been staged. Mazzini read music well and sometimes requested that friends and family mail him music that he could play on the guitar, so he likely had a copy of the piano-vocal score at hand while writing, possibly sent by Ruffini.[50] Ruffini must also have been an important informant about the opera's plot and musical style, and perhaps also for some of the essay's larger ideas.

The evidence for the younger Ruffini brother as an important source for the "Filosofia della musica" mounts when we dip into the opinions expressed in the long and confessional letters he wrote to his mother at home in a village near Genoa. It is hard to know for sure in which direction the ideas were flowing—perhaps back and forth equally—but the presentiments of the ideas that would shape Mazzini's "Filosofia" are very pronounced in Agostino's letters around the time of *Marino Faliero*'s première. Writing in January 1835 about his discovery of Weber and of German music in general, he connects the pleasure and directness of the style to Alpine music, building up a metaphor of a vibration that flows straight from nature to the listener's body:

> These are not those fugitive sounds that tickle the ear in passing: this is not the laughing, capricious, decorated music of Italian composers . . . this is something religious that purifies the soul, that feeds all the fibers of the being, which retain it long after the sounds have ceased. . . . Rossini, Bellini, Meyerbeer never wrote anything as beautiful [as Weber's *Dernière pensée musicale*]. I will send you some other pieces of music, music of the heart, mountain music, sounds that are found only in the atmosphere of the mountains, chords that emanate as if from the immense keyboard of nature. Far from the music of the theater. My opinions about music have changed a great deal.[51]

Not only does Ruffini's range of musical reference here coincide with Mazzini's, who had invoked Weber's *Dernière pensée* on the first page of the "Filosofia" and invoked Meyerbeer with admiration; but the casting of music as "something religious that purifies the soul" clearly corresponds to Mazzini's musical aesthetics.[52] Ruffini's comments on *Marino Faliero,* too, adumbrate the observations Mazzini would include in his philosophical essay nine months later. Describing the première to his mother in March 1835, Agostino zeroes in on the same duet that attracted Mazzini's notice, which he singles out because it transcends the hegemony of Rossinian style:

> I have heard very little music more beautiful or more grandiose. This is no longer the *sensation* of *Rossinisme,* it is the *idea* that dominates this score. There is a duo between the Doge, who has been offended by the patrician Steno, and the plebian conspirator Bertucci that is simply a masterpiece of art and of logic. One's soul by turns weeps, trembles, and clenches.[53]

Ruffini goes on to tell his mother about "a long article" he has written under the inspiration of this powerful music. Because it says some negative things about Rossini, he has been warned that it may be difficult to publish, since *"Rossini est un grand nom."* The article is never mentioned again in Agostino's letters, which suggests that it probably was not published—at least not under his own name.[54] Mazzini recorded the stages of his work on the "Filosofia" in his own correspondence, making it unlikely that the essay was actually ghostwritten by Ruffini.[55] What is more plausible is a reciprocal conversation (in person or via letters that have been lost) in which Mazzini and Ruffini hashed out shared ideas about opera's potential as a form of political communication, which then shaped both of their writings. Indeed, there are aspects of Ruffini's work on the libretto for *Marino Faliero* that support the notion of Mazzini as a sort of ghostwriter of that text, indirectly shaping the presentation of Bertucci's character, the way the chorus is used, and the scene just before the rebels are executed for treason, where their triumphant cries from the scaffold have almost the ring of propaganda.

Ruffini's most important contribution to the revised libretto was to supply a completely new opening scene, cutting a narration of Bertucci's clash with Steno and replacing it with a busy scene among shipbuilders at the Arsenal that climaxes in their confrontation.[56] This change not only emphasized the imbalance of power in Venetian society but created space for Ruffini and Donizetti to showcase a chorus with (to invoke Mazzini's terms once again) "an independent, spontaneous life of its own, like the populace for which it is the born spokesman" ("Filosofia," 64). The opera's first sounds and images show laborers hefting boats and equipment on the docks, singing snatches of stylized work songs: *"Issa, issa, issa là . . . Bada, tira, tira, là"* (roughly: "Heave-ho" and "Haul away"). Work gives way to gossip, the workers eagerly trading information about the latest rumors. Their insinuations about the doge, his wife's virtue, and the accusation written on the throne are cast as melodic fragments tossed back and forth between the two *divisi* groups, harmonized "as questions and replies, charged with the variety of sensations, comparisons, emotions, and desires that normally vibrate through a crowd" (64). The tense, excitable exchange of rumor as currency underlines the exclusion of the workers from the main flow of information, showing them as at once connected and peripheral to the power center of the palace.[57]

Many of Ruffini's minor changes to the libretto nudge the libretto toward a more aggressive confrontation with power, employing elements of the vocabulary identified by historian Alberto Banti as constituting a discourse of national identity in the literature of the period.[58] Words like "liberty" and "oppression" are highlighted, replacing the less confrontational synonyms preferred by Bidéra (and most other librettists of the time). Bidéra's phrase *"salvar Venezia"* in the duet for Bertucci and Faliero is rewritten by Ruffini as *"sollevar la patria"* (*"save* the nation" becoming "incite the nation to rebellion"). Faliero's imprecation *"contro i Dieci, contro i re"* becomes *"contro i perfidi oppressor,"* the doge's adversaries redefined from the specific Council of Ten to the broader (and more pejorative) "perfidious oppressors." And after his nephew Fernando dies at the end of Act 2, Ruffini has Faliero seize his sword and swear *"distruggiamo questa stirpe maledetta"* (we shall destroy this cursed race), replacing the much vaguer cry of *"sia Venezia maledetta"* (let Venice be cursed) in Bidéra's text. Taking advantage of permissive censorship policies in Paris, these changes refocus the libretto, emphasizing incendiary concepts such as "tyranny" and "oppression" that could easily be lifted out of context to apply to the current Italian situation.[59]

In the opera's last act, Ruffini subtly alters the stance of the condemned rebels as they face execution, replacing Bidéra's grim meditation on death with defiant hope. In both versions, the opera actually concludes with a duet for Faliero and his wife, in which she (finally) confesses her infidelity and he absolves her. The need to resolve this personal conflict—and to do so in a conventional prayer-like idiom—tempers the political aspect of the dénouement, leaving us with a Faliero who is more betrayed husband than idealist or defender of honor. By the final scene, the operatic Faliero is no longer the kind of character who could deliver the bitter prophecy that Byron's doge lets loose at this point, darkly predicting Venice's decline into "a province for an empire, petty town / in lieu of capital," beset by vice and oppression.[60] However, the opera does not sacrifice the political dénouement altogether: the statement about continuing defiance and defense of revolutionary values is displaced from Faliero to Bertucci, for whom Bidéra fashioned (and Ruffini substantially revised) an extended multipart aria, with a prominent role for the chorus of condemned men. This scene has no antecedents in either Byron or Delavigne, both of whom dispatch Bertucci and his band without ceremony. At the aria's center is Bertucci's poignant farewell to his two sons; but the scene also includes an opening chorus in which the rebels curse the temporal world they are about to depart (*"Sia maledetta . . . "*), a slow movement punctuated with ruthless cries of *"A morte"* (Put him to death!) from the council, and a cabaletta that ends with a full-throated statement for the rebels.

Although the idea for the aria—as well as the idea of supplying Bertucci with two sons, and a sentimental tableau of farewell to them—originated with Bidéra, Ruffini's substantial revisions to the text strike a starkly different tone, more optimistic and more oriented toward their legacy for the future. The cabaletta that in Bidéra's libretto had begun, *"Noi dispergiam la morte, le scure, e le ritorte, gli strazi ed i supplizii"* (We disdain death, the shadows, the chains, the trials and tortures), is remolded by Ruffini into these manically affirmative lines:

Il palco è a noi trionfo,
e l'ascendiam ridenti:
ma il sangue dei valenti
perduto non sarà.
Verran seguaci a noi
i martiri e gli eroi:
e s'anche avverso ed empio
il fato a lor sarà,
lasciamo ancor esempio
com'a morir si va.

(For us the scaffold is a triumph, and we ascend it smiling: but the blood of the valiant will not be squandered. We shall have disciples, martyrs and heroes: and if their fate includes misfortune and evil, at least we leave them an example of how to meet death.)

Where Bidéra's proposed text suggested an affinity with the lugubrious, cultish tones of the *Cavalieri della morte* in Verdi's *La battaglia di Legnano* (1849), Ruffini's lines emphasize the legions of future disciples who will carry on the fight. The music Donizetti fashioned for this cabaletta bears a vague family resemblance to the patriotic hymns tossed off by the dozens in the years leading up to the 1848 revolutions: plenty of dotted rhythms, triplet trumpet tattoos, woodwind doubling, all punctuated by fervent shouts from the chorus (see example 15).

And although "Il palco è a noi trionfo" was not destined for a new surge of popularity in 1848, the vision of martyrdom it promotes became increasingly important among champions of unification and independence in the 1840s and 1850s.[61] The doggedly cheerful tone of defiance that permeates Bertucci's aria gives the impression that Donizetti and Ruffini aimed to write a new patriotic anthem but slightly missed the mark—either because even this cheerful approach to the scaffold was too fatalistic to meet the recruitment and morale-boosting needs of the movement, or (more likely) because the opera as a whole was a bit too earnest and never became quite popular enough for any of its tunes to make it into the revolutionary hit parade.

Reviews of the première of *Marino Faliero* suggest that the critics reacted with reserve partly because they found the opera to be a little too French. By far the most common criticisms, cropping up in nearly every review, were that Fernando (sung by Giovanni Rubini, whose performance especially pleased the critics) was killed in a duel in the second act, and that Elena

EXAMPLE 15. Donizetti, *Marino Faliero,* Aria (Israële), Act 3, mm.50–82.

(Giulia Grisi) did not sing an aria until Act 3, both of which meant that the opera granted less space to unbridled lyricism and vocal display than critics might have wished for. One can sense in the reviews a disgruntled awareness that Donizetti was attempting something new and ambitious, mixed with regret that he was not content to replay the best effects from his earlier successes. A few reviews detect echoes of Rossini's *Guillaume Tell* in the new score, for better or for worse. Charles Merruau invoked *Tell* as an "obvious inspiration" for *Marino Faliero,* while the critic for *Le Moniteur universel* wished that it *had* been more of an example for Donizetti, since it showed how political disorder could be set to music in "a harmonious way."[62] *La gazette de France* agreed that the opera's preponderance of *"politique chanté"* was monotonous, and heard in its innovations an homage to Victor Hugo's *Hernani.*[63]

In general, critics were reluctant to engage with the opera's political implications—which was certainly not always the case among Parisian newspapers. A few expressed opinions about Faliero's reasons for joining the conspiracy, coming down more or less equally for and against—some dismissing Faliero's affinity with Bertucci as a "monstrous alliance" undertaken for "frivolous and personal" reasons and others applauding Faliero's valor in risking his own position to "free the populace from the tyranny of the aristocracy and restore their liberty."[64]

The tenor of these reviews suggests that the success of *Marino Faliero,* in Paris and beyond, was hobbled by good intentions and perhaps by a slight misconstrual of local taste on Donizetti's part. Striving to meet the French audience on its own ground by investing a score for the Théâtre-Italien with some of the political seriousness of the works staged at the Opéra, Donizetti stinted on the qualities that audiences most prized and enjoyed: Italian virtuosity and melodic lyricism. But if habitués of the Théâtre-Italien were underwhelmed by *Marino Faliero,* in contrast to the new work by Bellini that had taken the stage earlier that season, the opera may have better pleased the expatriate community. At least one prominent member of that group, Niccolò Tommaseo, wrote of it as "grandiose" music before which "the soul trembled," while he dismissed *I puritani* as a mere *"dramettino."*[65]

When Elena Ferrante wrote (in the passage that provides this chapter's epigraph) that "the neighborhood was connected to the city, the city to Italy, Italy to Europe, Europe to the whole planet," the vision of connectedness across borders was wishful, more hope than fact. Ferrante's "Neapolitan novels" tell the story of a protagonist with deep roots in Naples who intermittently strives to extend her intellectual reach beyond the city of her birth; but the events of the novels often attest to the strain, sacrifice, and outright failure that attend such spatial and cultural translations from neighborhood to city to nation and beyond. It requires a vertiginous leap to draw conclusions from the isolated example of *Marino Faliero* about the translation of artistic works across borders and their efficacy as vehicles of soft diplomacy. But then the opera itself is something of a unique case in its combination of a libretto that boasts explicit populist elements, direct creative involvement by a revolutionary activist, and the special status it is granted at the end of Mazzini's essay on opera. Mazzini's vision for a free and unified Italy depended on connections and common cause with other European nations, knit together into the web of "associationism" and concretized politically in the founding of the "Young Europe" movement in 1834, to work in parallel with the older Young Italy. Yet the opera's reception—the obstacles to its successful translation from the exile community around the rue Quincampoix to the audience of the Théâtre-Italien in the first *arrondissement* to opera houses back in Italy and beyond—perhaps reflects something of the challenge Mazzini and his allies confronted in trying to raise international support for a political reorganization that would return Italian rule to its own people. The eventual success of those efforts relied on international support—most of it at first unofficial, through private channels—gradually building into official support for an autonomous Italian nation from the governments of European nations as well; and it is well known that cultural works and the promotion of positive images of Italy were crucial in winning that international endorsement. In the chapter that follows we shall see that such acts of translation were perhaps easier to effect through light salon music that functioned almost as a musical form of picture postcards than through earnest political dramas.

FIVE

Parlor Games

GRIDANDO LIBERTÀ!

My second story of exiles in Paris begins from a detail, a musical mania that formed around a particular melody by Vincenzo Bellini, and one of its many contemporary adaptations. In the cabaletta from the bass duet in *I puritani*, the two basses step outside of the opera's dreamy and nonteleological plot for an isolated moment of patriotic fervor; for their homeland, they will take up arms and gladly face death:

> *Suoni la tromba, e intrepido*
> *Io pugnerò da forte,*
> *Bello è affrontar la morte*
> *Gridando: "Libertà!"*

(Let the trumpet sound, and fearless I'll fight with all my strength. To face death is beautiful, shouting "liberty!")

Bellini responded to the hot-headed patriotism of Carlo Pepoli's poetry for this number with excitement, writing to his poet that the duet was turning out magnificent and that "the trumpet fanfare will make the liberal hearts that will be in the theater quiver with joy."[1] In that letter he signed off with a (possibly, but not necessarily sincere) *"Viva la libertà!!!"* To other correspondents around this time, though, Bellini wrote that the duet had "a terrifying liberal bent," and correctly predicted that certain key words—especially *"libertà"*—would have to be changed for the opera's export to Italy.[2] He might also have pointed out that the fierce calls for freedom had little or no justification in the plot: in the duet up until this point the two bass characters have been discussing the marriage plans of the heroine, Elvira—and the homeland they are suddenly willing to sacrifice themselves for is England under Cromwell. But he raised none of these objections, and the piece was an immediate, massive success. The day after the première Bellini wrote to his friend Francesco Florimo that

> all the French seem to have become mad, they made such a noise, such cries, that it seemed as if they were astonished to find themselves so transported: but people say that the stretta [i.e., cabaletta] of the duet attacked the nerves of everyone present . . . the entire parterre rose to their feet at the impact of this stretta, screaming, demanding encores, and screaming again.[3]

As much as for the buzzing energy of the voices moving in march patterns, the cabaletta is remarkable for the utter regularity of its phrasing.[4] Every one of the five four-bar phrases begins in exactly the same way: with a leap of a rising third or fourth followed by repeated quarter notes. The effect is of uniformity and single-minded propulsion: a forceful musical analogue for the sentiments expressed in Pepoli's martyr-like poetry.

These are exactly the musical features that were erased when Chopin and Liszt went to work on Bellini's theme as part of the famous collective composition the *Hexameron*. Masterminded by Liszt, who also chose the Bellini theme as a starting point, the *Hexameron* consists of an introduction, six variations, and a finale, with sections contributed by the leading piano virtuosi in Paris: besides Chopin and Liszt, Thalberg, Czerny, Pixis, and Henri Herz all wrote variations. Chopin was assigned the single slow variation, and his approach to Bellini's relentless tune is first to disarm it with cascades of pulseless, "Chopinesque" left-hand triplets, adding a fleeting dissonance between melody and accompaniment in nearly every measure, and then—as soon as he decently can—by transposing the theme to the remote key of G♯ major, with accompaniment reminiscent of the funeral march. The ethereal final section of this short variation was added by Liszt, and the tendency to obscure the martial clarity of Bellini's cabaletta is also characteristic of the other sections that Liszt contributed to the *Hexameron*. Indeed, the only thing all six composers seemed to agree on was the desirability of writing over (in a sense) the square march and clear patriotic outlines of the source melody.

The juxtaposition of these radically different manifestations of Bellini and Pepoli's hymn to liberty attests to the ease with which music—and the messages it carried—circulated between public and private settings in the Paris of the July Monarchy. The original duet was obviously conceived for very public surroundings: it was first heard at the première of *I puritani* at the Théâtre-Italien during the carnival season of 1835, just six weeks before the first performances of *Marino Faliero*. The *Hexameron*, on the other hand, was born into the private (or semiprivate) world of the Parisian salon. Liszt had originally conceived the project as a contribution to a charitable benefit organized by the Princess Cristina Trivulzio di Belgioioso: ultimately, though, the pieces couldn't be assembled in time for the benefit, and the collection was premièred at the Belgioioso salon at a later date. It is tempting to see this distinction between public and private contexts as the reason for the radical difference of affect between the two pieces; but in this chapter I explore something like the opposite idea: that salons were every bit as hospitable as public venues like the Théâtre-Italien to grand patriotic and political statements (in music). Paradoxical as it may seem, it may be that the best way to grapple with opera's complex role in defining and instilling Italian national identity is not through weighty political arguments or grand narratives of activism prompted by music, but through eager amassing of gossip and anecdote and obsessive attention to the many fads and flashes-in-the-pan that chased each other through concert halls and musical journals in the 1830s.

ELVIRA STEPS OFF THE STAGE

Perhaps the most important link between the aristocratic world of the Théâtre-Italien and that of the political exiles was Carlo Pepoli, author of the libretto for *I puritani*. The oldest son and heir of a prominent Bolognese land-owning family, Pepoli fell in with the revolutionary generation of the 1820s and served in the provisional government that briefly held power in the province of Romagna after the 1831 uprising. When the rebellion was quashed, the positions Pepoli had held as head of the Guarda provinciale and prefect for the cities of Pesaro and Urbino earned him imprisonment in the Spielberg, a sentence that was commuted to exile thanks to French intervention.[5] Once he arrived in Paris he renewed his acquaintance with Rossini and took on a few libretto commissions to supplement his main income as a tutor of Italian.[6] Pepoli tends to appear in Bellini biographies as the fallback to whom Bellini turned after his break with Felice Romani, and as a neophyte who required instruction in the very basics of operatic expression.[7] However, an address Pepoli delivered to prize-winning students in Bologna in 1830 reveals not only a surprisingly broad grasp of operatic repertoire but also some forceful ideas about how music could provoke political feeling. Pepoli adopts a modern aesthetic agenda, condemning vocal ornamentation as a dilution of dramatic sense and attacking imitation as cheapening music's inherent, nonverbal language. After touching on exemplary passages from operas by Morlacchi, Vaccai, and Bellini, Pepoli turns to the "Marseillaise," arguing that there music and poetry meld perfectly to arouse feeling and provoke action. In a phrase that strikingly anticipates the language of the martial duet he would write for I puritani a few years later, Pepoli proclaims, "For this song, the people fight, win, triumph: Europe and the world shouted 'Liberty!' [gridavano Libertà]"[8]

Amid the piecework Pepoli picked up during these years was the poetry for a pair of song collections by Rossini and Saverio Mercadante, published respectively in 1835 and 1836.[9] The two collections converse clearly with one another, suggesting that they may have been conceived for the same audience, or that Mercadante's songs sought to capitalize on the success of the recent publication by the elder statesman Rossini. The link between the two collections is revealed first of all by their titles: Rossini's rather generic title, Soirées musicales, becomes in Mercadante's hands the more evocative Soirées italiennes. For Rossini, Pepoli penned an assembly of eight faux-folk poems whose images, verse rhythms, and pastoral allusions create a vision of Italy that is predominantly nostalgic and touristic although at the same time surprisingly eroticized. The collection is rounded out to a dozen songs with four settings of Metastasio texts.[10]

Both collections balance postcard-like images of characteristic scenes and nostalgic dips into the pastoral with an occasional song that offers a more direct expression of love (see table 2 for a comparison of the two collections).[11] While the Metastasio texts included in Rossini's Soirées musicales hark back to pastoral tropes of love and courtship, the poems Pepoli contributes to both collections seem to flow rather from the tradition of Italian travelogues that stretches back to Madame de Staël's Corinne, ou l'Italie (1807) and Goethe's Italian Journey (1816–17). Most of these regional topoi are stereotypical enough to seem part of a broad cultural legacy, sparkling but inert evocations of some of Italy's most recognizable locales: the Alps (in Rossini's "La pastorella dell'Alpi"), Venice (in his barcarolle "La gita in gondola"), and Naples (in the well-known tarantella "La danza").

The scene depicted in "La pastorella dell'Alpi" could almost have been pilfered from Goethe. As he traverses the Brenner Pass into Italy, Goethe is

Rossini, *Les soirées musicales*, texts by Metastasio and Carlo Pepoli (1835)	Mercadante, *Les soirées italiennes*, texts by Pepoli (1836)
1. La promessa (Metastasio) [canzonetta]	1. Il desiato ritorno [barcarolle]
2. Il rimprovero (Metastasio) [canzonetta]	2. La primavera [pastorale]
3. La partenza (Metastasio) [canzonetta]	3. L'asilo al pellegrino [chanson]
4. L'orgia [arietta]	4. Il pastore svizzero [tyrolienne]
5. L'invito [bolero]	5. La serenata del marinaro [serenade]
6. La pastorella dell'Alpi [tirolese]	6. Il zeffiro [polonaise]
7. La gita in gondola [barcarolle]	7. Lamento del moribondo [romance]
8. La danza [tarantella]	8. La zingarella spagnuola [bolero]
9. La regatta veneziana [notturno for two sopranos]	9. La pesca [duet]
10. La pesca (Metastasio) [notturno for two sopranos]	10. Il brindisi [duet]
11. La serenata [notturno for soprano and tenor]	11. La caccia [duet]
12. I marinai [duet for tenor and bass]	12. Ilgalop (text: G. Crescini) [duet]

impressed by the prosperity and apparent contentment of the merchants at an open-air market: "The sun was shining brightly when I arrived in Bolzano. I was glad to see the faces of so many merchants at once. They had an air about them of purpose and well-being. Women sat in the square, displaying their fruit in round, flat-bottomed baskets more than four feet in diameter."[12] The initial image of Pepoli's Alpine text follows Goethe quite closely, personifying the Alps as a pretty woman proffering a cornucopia of fruit: "*Son bella pastorella, che scende ogni mattino, ed offre un cestellino di fresche frutta e fior*" (I am a beautiful shepherdess, who descends each morning to offer a basket of fresh fruit and flowers). But Pepoli's shepherdess, individualized and flirtatious, goes on to talk of inviting the interlocutor into her garden to sample the "rosy apples," giving the song an erotic tinge entirely lacking in Goethe's chronicle (see example 16). The juxtaposition of the shepherdess's crystalline yodeling with the frank invitation of her words makes an ironic interpretation irresistible, and many of the Rossini songs seem to play on the same doubleness and sense of secrecy, or barely concealed meaning.

Mercadante's collection, identically constructed of eight solo songs and four duets, can be heard as either homage or corrective to Rossini. Mercadante matches the characteristic songs in Rossini's collection almost note for note.

EXAMPLE 16. Rossini and Pepoli, "La pastorella dell'Alpi," from *Soirées musicales*, mm. 1–32.

Mercadante's Venetian barcarolle ("Il desiato ritorno") is less dark than Rossini's and lacks the folk-like invocations of the physical labor of rowing (as in Rossini's refrain, *"Voga, voga, marinar"*). Mercadante's tyrolienne ("Il pastore svizzero") not only follows Rossini in including a feint at yodeling but also dares to quote the overture to Rossini's *Guillaume Tell* in its piano prelude. Both composers include a song entitled "La pesca," in which sport fishing is given a sexual spin: for this particular pastoral topos Rossini drew on an existing Metastasio text, which Pepoli then imitated for Mercadante. Whereas the poems Pepoli supplied to Rossini all depict communal activities or generic scenes of courtship, the Mercadante cycle also contains two songs that could be described as lyric rather than picturesque. There is a *canzonetta* sung by a troubadour who wanders in lonely, loveless exile ("L'asilo al pellegrino"), and a fragmented, incoherent lament in the voice of a man who is about to die of unrequited love ("Lamento del moribondo"). It is tempting to see in these two poems and the music they elicit from Mercadante a nascent romantic sensibility that is absent from Rossini's songs; the intrusion of the suffering artist into the calculated musical discourse of the salon. But if so, the intrusion is rather choreographed, as if the isolated but hyperarticulate romantic outcast is just another type, to be depicted alongside the shepherd and the gondolier and the fisherman.

The images of Italy presented in both collections seem distanced and idealized, perhaps packaged for foreign consumption. The French listeners who heard these songs in salons may have experienced them as musical analogues of the Grand Tour; but for Italian audiences their picture-postcard aesthetics must have conveyed a slightly different message. Besides their kinship with travel narratives like de Staël's *Corinne,* the songs participate in a discourse of the picturesque that was becoming popular in the 1830s through periodicals such as the *Cosmorama pittorico,* which reproduced lithographs of characteristic scenes from around Italy and beyond its borders, along with brief descriptive texts. From its base in Milan, the *Cosmorama* provided northern Italian readers with images of their own region alongside views of the south, from the eruption of Vesuvius to peasants dancing a tarantella. Literary critic Nelson Moe has suggested that the circulation of these images of far-flung locales and distinctive cultural practices was key to helping Italians imagine themselves as diverse yet connected, enabling "a new, pictorial way of articulating bourgeois identity vis-à-vis other peoples and parts of the world."[13] By the 1840s the Catholic nationalist thinker Vincenzo Gioberti was exploiting this nascent pictorial sensibility and anthropological curiosity to promote the idea that Italy's ethnographic diversity made it superior to other, more homogeneous

Rossini, "La gita in gondola" (excerpt)	
Voli l'agile barchetta,	Take wings, my boat
voga, voga, o marinar,	o sailor, row, row,
or che Elvira mia diletta	as my dear Elvira
a me in braccio sfida il mar.	braves the sea in my arms.

Mercadante, "La serenata del marinaro"	
L'estrema volta è questa	This is the last time
Che udrai il Marinar	you will hear the sailor
Per notte azzurra e mesta	in the blue, sad night
Cantar e remigar.	singing and rowing.
Se ognor tu sei crudel	If you cruelly reject
Al fido mio pregar,	my devoted pleas
Io piegherò le vele,	I will fold up my sails
M'affonderò nel mar.	and drown myself in the sea.
Se udrai la sera, o Elvira,	If you hear in the evening, oh Elvira,
Un'aura sibilar,	a whispering breeze,
È un'ombra che sospira,	it is a shadow sighing,
È il morto Marinar.	it is the dead sailor.
L'estrema volta è questa	This is the last time
Che udrai il Marinar	you will hear the sailor
Per notte azzurra e mesta	in the blue, sad night
Cantar e remigar.	singing and rowing.

countries. In his influential 1843 book, *Del primato morale e civile degli italiani,* Gioberti posited a "national personality" divided just as "the human body is divided into various organs and members, each of which, besides its participation in the common life, has a mode of existence and life proper to it."[14]

The frequent double entendres and delicate innuendo that permeate Pepoli's poetry for these songs imply an intended audience of sophisticated insiders, listeners primed to laugh at the same jokes, decode the same veiled meanings. This impression that the songs were conceived partly for a tight-knit community of like-minded listeners is reinforced by another detail of their texts, an intrusion that hints at a conscious, playful, and rather cryptic interplay between opera and solo song. Both the *Soirées musicales* and the *Soirées italiennes* contain songs that feature a character named Elvira, echoing the name of the heroine in *I puritani*.[15] This Elvira is not a seventeenth-century Puritan like her operatic counterpart; she is apparently Italian, floating between various aquatic and sylvan locales. Otherwise she is featureless, almost interchangeable with the nymphs and rustic maidens of the surrounding pastoral songs. In Rossini's *Soirées musicales,* a gondolier sings as he rows in a calm, moonlit lagoon, his beloved "Elvira" in his arms (see table 3). Mercadante's song "La serenata del marinaro" retains the maritime setting but reverses the mood, transporting the boatman and his love to Naples (to judge by the rhythms). Instead of a celebration of fulfilled love and rippling motion, Mercadante forges a bitter, suicidal plaint, or rather a coercive threat. *This* sailor thinks longingly or angrily of the watery death he will embrace if Elvira rejects his love, and warns that his ghost will haunt her, its sighs mixed in with the breeze (see example 17).

These glancing mentions, severed from any context, would not seem so striking were Elvira a more common name in this repertoire. The Rossini and Mercadante collections, like other salon songs of the time, frequently have the speaker name the love object who is being addressed or sighed for, but those women usually go by one of the standard names from the pastoral canon— Nice and Bice, Tirsi and Aminta all make appearances, as does an Eloisa. But the name "Elvira" is rarely used in poetry or music: with the exception of Donna Elvira in *Don Giovanni,* the only other Elvira in music seems to have appeared in a set of three Vivaldi cantatas, where she is paired with a lover named Fileno.[16] The song that follows "La serenata del marinaro" in Mercadante's *Soirées italiennes* lays to rest any doubt that the nomenclature might be accidental, by pairing Elvira with a lover named Arturo, just as in the opera. "Il zeffiro" stages a playful love-scene-at-a-distance between the two: Elvira enlists a gentle breeze to travel to Arturo, first to ruffle his hair, then to breathe her name into his ear (see example 18). The Elvira of Bellini's opera could never sing anything so carefree. The song's bright, flirtatious tone bespeaks a far less tentative, less intense persona than that of the operatic Elvira. It is as if Pepoli tossed in these recognizable names without concern for the surrounding context, perhaps hoping that listeners would notice the allusion and enjoy a momentary thrill of recognition.

CHARADES (PERFORMANCE)

Why bury allusions to a popular opera of the moment in a set of solo songs about a completely different subject? One answer might have something to do with Pepoli's desire to drum up publicity or to lay claim to the *Puritani*

EXAMPLE 17. Mercadante, "Serenata del marinaro," from *Soirées italiennes,* mm.18–45.

EXAMPLE 18. Mercadante, "Il zeffiro," from *Soirées italiennes,* mm.17–39.

libretto. But such explanations seem both trivial and out of step with the playfulness and the subtlety of the connections between song and opera. To understand the messages borne by these fleeting appearances of Elvira and Arturo, it might be necessary to enter the world of the salons, to study the dialects—both verbal and musical—in which their habitués communicated. To do this means sinking for a moment into the plush fabric of gossip and anecdote that comprise the only surviving record of salon culture.

Most of the individual songs from the *Soirées musicales* and the *Soirées italiennes* bear dedications, some to influential and titled Parisians, others to singers. Mercadante's collection includes songs inscribed to three of the four members of the *Puritani* quartet, with only Giulia Grisi left out. Another of the *Soirées italiennes* songs is dedicated to Madame Orfila, a singer who hosted a salon attended by Rossini; and yet another to the daughter of Adolphe Thiers, the French politician and journalist who was an intimate of Cristina Belgioioso.[17] It could have been at Madame Orfila's salon that some of these songs had their first hearings, or at the home of the Princess Belgioioso, or of the Comtesse de Merlin.[18] David Tunley's survey of repertoire performed at the salons yields two mentions of "romances by Mercadante," both dating from 1838. In March some romances by the composer were heard at the salon of Madame Rinaldi, and in February "airs by Mercadante and Marleau" were performed at Merlin's salon by singers who included the Comtesse de la Sparre, the Prince Poniatowski, and bass Luigi Lablache.[19] I have found no corresponding mention of songs from Rossini's *Soirées musicales;* but since only a tiny minority of salon gatherings received attention from the musical press, this silence hardly indicates that the Rossini songs were *not* performed in salons.

The Princess Belgioioso was by far the most overtly political of the *salonnières*. Like Carlo Pepoli, she lived in Paris under duress: the only significant female presence in the Giovine Italia circle and perhaps the only woman to be directly involved in the anti-Austrian conspiracies of 1831, Belgioioso had fled Italy just ahead of the authorities, passing through Geneva before settling in Paris. The princess sang and played piano, and on at least one occasion she sang in trio with the Comtesse de la Sparre, a professional singer to whom Mercadante's "Il zeffiro" is dedicated.[20] Belgioioso's salon is remembered as the venue for the famous 1837 benefit for the Italian exiles, which became the setting for the duel between Liszt and Thalberg, as well as the occasion for which the collaboratively composed *Hexameron,* derived from Bellini's "Suoni la tromba," was commissioned. Belgioioso was also a prolific journalist and, later in life, an activist on women's issues.[21] In the "memoirs of exile" she published in 1850, Belgioioso says little about her own salon, but she recalls other such gatherings in near-Utopian terms. Recalling the salon hosted by Madame Recamier, Belgioioso's memory turns to the easy mingling of opposites and to escape from official politics and rigid hierarchy. Her home in the Faubourg Saint-Germain was a space

> between the court and the academy, where great men and women acted like poets, where one chatted as much as one disputed, where if someone dared to coin a new word, those words would enter straightaway into the dictionary of the Académie, where we had such good fun that it was sometimes possible to forget about Versailles—that is to say the place where they hand out sinecures, pensions, honors of all kinds, and even more important, that is the measure for grace, elegance, and beauty.[22]

In emphasizing the irrelevance of Versailles, Belgioioso anticipates what has become the established assessment of the social role of the salon as a place of free social and political concourse, crucially autonomous from the court.[23] Yet for all the emphasis on fun and on oblivion to the workings of official power, Belgioioso also glancingly acknowledges the considerable cultural power wielded within these loosely knit institutions, where casual wordplay could transform the dictionary.

Almost as prolific as Belgioioso, the Comtesse de Merlin also published memoirs of her Cuban youth (in four volumes) and several novels. In *Les lionnes de Paris,* an 1845 *roman à clé* published under a pen name, she paints unflattering portraits of Belgioioso and of salon culture in general. The novel centers on four formidable women who move into Parisian society, take and discard lovers, and (mostly) come to tragic ends. The book's final section focuses on Giuditta, duchess of Ferraro, a thinly disguised Belgioioso, who is described as narcissistic, eager to show off her every achievement, and easily bored, passionate about political causes only as long as they attract attention. Merlin's Giuditta informally separates from her husband (as did Belgioioso) and becomes involved with a founding member of a secret society, clearly modeled on Mazzini's Giovine Italia movement. In keeping with the novel's lugubrious tone, its assessment of salon life is scathing and almost diametrically opposed to Belgioioso's own account:

> Most of the salons where polite society gathers can be distinguished only by the name of the man of the house, and by the degree of luxury and the

number of lamps that adorn the rooms; they are performances in which everyone believes himself an actor, but in which no one amounts to more than a poor bit of the parterre, crowded and confined, jostled and buffeted by the wave; tossed about by the rising tide. We do not look there for men of merit, but for those of position—here powerful men, there the titled, and everywhere dancers. . . . How is it possible to enjoy the charms of wit where conversation, the exchange of ideas, is impossible?[24]

Of course, Merlin writes here in the voice of a fictional narrator who may be taking an extreme position for literary reasons. Yet the evident cynicism of this verdict coincides with historians' conclusion that by the 1830s the salon was a pale shadow of what it had been a half century before, and the influence of *salonnières* correspondingly diminished. After the political fissures and intense factionalism of the revolutionary period and the Restoration, caution and superficial agreement had acquired a new value for the aristocracy and the bourgeoisie. So although the salons continued to be places in which political influence was brokered and bestowed, overt political conversation was frowned on.[25] Merlin was said to forbid it at her own gatherings—because it was so inflammatory and all-consuming but also because her own views were more conservative than those of many of her guests, particularly concerning universal suffrage.[26]

In this new atmosphere of accommodation, music was an important element within a broad constellation of communicative modes. Another of those modes was purposeful *play*. One contemporary account after another attests that the habitués of the salons delighted in the decoding and deciphering of puzzles, allusions, and concealed meanings. One such game, a favorite among the writers who try to evoke the special ethos of the nineteenth-century salon, was an operatic parody created at the Merlin salon in 1840. Entitled *L'Incendio di Babilonia* (The bonfire of Babylon), it featured characters borrowed from *Orlando furioso* and a farcical mad scene, in which both the insanity and its eventual cure were manifested only through changes in the heroine's hairstyle. A scene featuring the villain Ferocino (played by Lablache) stands out for its superb satirical marksmanship:

"Silence!" says Ferocino; "I hear in the forest the gondolier singing the barcarole!"—"In the forest?" says the chevalier-pilgrim of the Légion d'Honneur.—"In the forest!" replies Ferocino. And in fact the barcarole commences; "Zephyr, souffle gentile!' It is something new and strange, this ballad which recalls the barcarole of *Otello*.[27]

However broad its humor, this burlesque was clearly conceived on some level by and for true insiders. To laugh at *L'Incendio di Babilonia,* a spectator would have had to be familiar with the correlation between unbound hair and madness in *Lucia di Lammermoor* and other mad-scene operas, to recall the third act of Rossini's *Otello,* and to agree that barcarolles had become ridiculously common in recent opera.

Another such diversion, this one purely verbal, is narrated by the Comtesse de Bassanville. The setting is again the Merlin salon; the entertainment, a politically charged game of charades:

> I remember ... one evening that took place a short time after one of the summer riots in which Maréchal de Lobau had so handily dispersed the insurgents with the help of fire hoses; people recalled this incident there in a charade that was most amusing.
>
> The word was *Jacqueminot,* and General [Jean-François] Jacqueminot, then a colonel in the National Guard, figured among the players. For the first clue, people mimed a pilgrimage to Santiago di Compostela [*Saint-Jacques* de Compostelle], for the second, a scene with a grain dealer [*minotier*], and for the finale, a riot.[28]

This vignette beautifully sums up how the performative, and topical or political, dimensions of the salon can be melded. In the charade, recent, disturbing political events—the subduing of rebels with fire hoses—are inextricably intertwined with polite conversation and play. It is both fascinating and disquieting that the charade (or the anecdote of the charade) invokes the riot so blithely, oblivious to the rather violent reality behind the homonym of the word "riot." Perhaps Pepoli and Mercadante's casual invocation of the operatic Elvira and Arturo in their songs could be seen as another manifestation of this game-playing spirit, a small riddle that functions socially to create a group of insiders who all share some bit of knowledge, however trivial, and who get pleasure from decoding the concealed message.

ESCHATOLOGIES (PRINT)

The compulsion to connect these songs to a specific salon perhaps flows from the historian's desire to fix those elements of history that are most ephemeral, least documented—and that thus seem most precious and most informative. Within a historiographical atmosphere that privileges documented reception and whatever traces we can find of "ordinary" reactions to music, songs like this become a kind of Holy Grail, because they *must* have been popular, must have been rooted in everyday (albeit aristocratic) discourse. But there is also a musically specific dimension to this quest. The association with a particular salon would ground these rather blank, almost cryptic songs within some precise frame of verbal meaning, as if tying them to an exact performance venue would allow us to get past their proliferation of poetic and musical topoi, and their avoidance of direct expressive utterance. One might even go so far as to say that these aspects of salon song merely magnify the condition of the Italian opera of the time. This music mattered to large numbers of people and perhaps helped listeners articulate a shared sense of taste or communicate common values across geographical barriers. Yet the interpretive vocabulary that exists to talk about individual musical moments gets stuck on cataloguing generic features, or in measurements and assertions of vocal display and auditory pleasure, never quite seeming to touch the real force of the musical experience.

It is thus deeply satisfying to imagine the Rossini and Mercadante songs as part of a conversation among initiates, their allusions and intertextuality quietly building a common vision of Italy among listeners. Yet this vein of interpretation assumes that the songs functioned primarily as performances for specific audiences, that their expressive identities are more firmly attached to live performance than to reproduction and dissemination.[29] Salon culture is clearly part of the story of these songs, but there is also evidence that the vocal music of this period was destined above all for print—for distribution and for consumption at a distance by large numbers of unknown (and fairly unskilled) musicians and listeners, some of them located outside of urban centers. For those listeners and performers who encountered the two *Soirées* collections this way, the songs could not have seemed analogous to charades or to the witty but often highly charged conversations in the salons. A distinct set of reference points and meanings arises when we hear the songs as cogs in a large, mechanized process of cultural dissemination at a distance, rather than as direct communications among a tightly knit group of Italian exiles and Parisian aristocrats.

Musicologist Raoul Meloncelli, who has probably studied the Italian salon repertoire more exhaustively than anyone else, approaches the *"romanza di salotto"* almost exclusively as a phenomenon of publishing.[30] Subject matter

and musical styles were calibrated purely to sell sheet music, and the complex-
ion of any particular song can usually be explained by a desire to capitalize
on the success of an earlier model. Publishers had a strong financial incentive
to retread an already successful poetic or musical template as long as it
continued to appeal to customers. These aesthetic calculations became more
common, and more sophisticated, Meloncelli suggests, toward midcentury,
as composers and publishers began to realize how central the *romanza* would
be to domestic music making. The life experience or aesthetic predilections
of an individual like Carlo Pepoli have no place in this interpretive model,
much less the tastes or pleasures of a Belgioioso or a Merlin.

Table 4 shows a very partial listing of the thematic ideas and titles that
crop up in Italian songs published in the decade after Rossini's and
Mercadante's collections appeared. Neither the inventory of themes nor the
specific examples listed is anywhere near exhaustive; but even this fragmen-
tary overview indicates the reach of the phenomenon.[31] The sheer number of
song collections that play on the idea of a place recently left and fondly
remembered suggests that nostalgia and loss had themselves become a distinct patriotic topos, an idea that is supported by the contemporaneous
efflorescence of piano miniatures by Polish exile composers with titles alluding to homesickness and exile.[32]

Perhaps the most unexpected thematic group to appear in table 4 is the
category of songs spoken in the persona of a man about to die, and suffering
from unrequited love. This cluster of songs is different from the others in that
its currency in the 1830s and 1840s may be traceable to a single, massively
influential poem: Giovanni Luigi Redaelli's "Odi d'un uom che muore."
Redaelli (1785–1815) was based in Cremona, his career nearly coterminous
with Italy's Napoleonic period and with the career of the much better known
Ugo Foscolo. His fame now rests mainly on the fictionalized portrait that
Stendhal created of him in the essay *De l'amour* (1822). Stendhal disguises
Redaelli as the melancholy military man "Salviati," whose journal entries
documenting a doomed and adulterous love affair Stendhal reprints (supposedly) verbatim. In a long footnote to the chapter dedicated to Salviati,
Stendhal prints a composite of three of Redaelli's poems, including the complete deathbed ode.[33] He died of tuberculosis in 1815 at the age of thirty,
reportedly dictating "Odi d'un uom che muore" from his deathbed.

This at least was the account often given in explanatory footnotes
when the poem appeared in nineteenth-century anthologies. In the 1843
anthology *Il parnaso italiano,* the footnote not only sketches the eschato-

TABLE 4 Themes in Song Collections, c. 1835–1845

Nostalgic memory of a place recently left (titles of collections):
  Donizetti, *Nuits d'été à Pausilippe* (1836)
  Donizetti, *Un hiver à Paris* (1838–39; retitled *Rêveries napolitaines,* pub. Naples)
  Donizetti, *Soirées d'automne à l'Infrascata* (1839)
  Donizetti, *Inspirations viennoises* (1842)
  Pacini, *Souvenir de Florence pendant l'hiver à Paris* (also as *Souvenirs... pendant l'hiver de 1835*)
  Dario Fabiani, *Una sera sul Canal Grande* (early 1840s)
  Fabio Campana, *Souvenir de Bains de Lucques, Ricordi di Milano, Souvenirs de Rome,* etc.

Sailor's laments:
  Mercadante, "La serenata del marinaro" (*Soirées italiennes,* 1836)
  Donizetti, "Sovra il remo" (1844, Luigi Mira)
  Pacini, "Bella nel dì novello" (1844)
  Donizetti, "Il barcaiuolo" (*Nuits d'été,* 1836)

Exile/pilgrim songs:
  Mercadante, "Date asilo al pellegrino" (*Soirées italiennes,* 1836)
  Pacini, "Il pellegrino" (1843, anon.)
  Dario Fabiani, "Il pellegrino, il cavaliere, e il trovatore" (A. Maffei)

Dying man (and woman) songs:
  More than thirty settings of Giovanni Redaelli's "Odi d'un uom che muore," between 1820 and 1845, including songs by Donizetti ("Amore e morte," 1839, in *Soirées d'automne*), Marco Aurelio Marliani, and Rossini ("Amore e morte," *Pechés de vieillesse: Album italiano*)
  Mercadante, "Lamento del moribondo" (*Soirées italiennes,* 1836)
  Donizetti, "È morta" (1842, Carlo Guiata)

logical circumstances surrounding the poem's inception but connects it immediately to song: *"Versi dettati dal Redaelli moriente; furono posti in musica da valentissimi maestri"* (Verses dictated by the dying Redaelli; they were set to music by the most eminent composers).[34] By the time it was anthologized, Redaelli's poem had been set by at least twenty different composers, the initial attraction probably spurred by the poem's flexible *settenario* (seven-syllable) meter and the compact emotional intensity of its sixteen lines.

> *Odi d'un uom che muore,*
> *Odi l'estremo suon;*
> *Quest'appassito fiore*
> *Ti lascio Elvira in don.*

Quanto prezioso ei sia
Tu dei saper lo appien;
Nel dì che fosti mia
Te lo involai dal sen.

Simbolo allor d'affetto
Or pegno di dolor
Torna a posarti in petto
Questo appassito fior.

E avrai nel cor scolpito
Se duro il cor non è
Come ti fu rapito
Come ritorna a te

(Hear the words of a dying man, hear the last sounds; this faded flower I leave you, Elvira, as a gift. You must know how precious it is: the day you became mine I stole it from your breast. Then a symbol of our love, it is now a token of sorrow. Place it once more on your breast, this faded flower. And you will have engraved on your heart, if your heart is not too hard, how this flower was taken from you and how it returned to you.)

Redaelli's poem and its early reception encapsulate the twisted relation between romanticism and early-nineteenth-century print culture. Almost everything in the language of the poem suggests unicity, irreproducibility. Not only was "Odi d'un uom che muore" framed as its author's final utterance; it was the only work from Redaelli's extensive oeuvre that was widely reprinted and anthologized. Isolated on the page with its tear-stained history recorded in a footnote, hemmed in by the garrulous output of contemporaries such as Vincenzo Monti, Giuseppe Parini, Silvio Pellico, and Alessandro Manzoni, this little poem gives the impression of secrecy, rarity, and the utter immediacy of the poet's experience translated into verse. Yet this aura of individuality is illusory. Most glaringly, the conventionality of the poem's imagery belies—if not quite undermines—its pose as an ultimate, unbounded outpouring of grief. Like much Italian verse of the period, the poem efficiently packages a number of strong romantic symbols into neat rhetorical units: the plaintive cries of the dying man, the withered flower as symbol of past happiness and subsequent loss, the whole sad tale carved forever into the stony heart of the beloved . . .[35] The aura of specificity is further softened by the fact that this is just one in a series of five poems in which Redaelli keened over his lost love. The same Elvira makes appearances in four other poems, always in connection with the imagined death of Redaelli's poetic avatar. In one sonnet, the poet imagines Elvira hovering over his tomb with her hair unbound (presumably out of grief), strewing flowers on his grave and piously calling out his name; in another poem she takes up the lyre that lies by his tomb and exchanges cries with her expired beloved.[36] The pattern of replicating intensely private feeling in a series of copies achieves a kind of logical culmination in the poem's musical reception, in its enthusiastic embrace by so many now-forgotten composers and its eventual posterity precisely *as* material for song.[37]

The combination of the poem and Redaelli's personal history exerts a powerful allure, and it could be fascinating to examine the many musical responses to "Odi d'un uom che muore." But in the present context, Redaelli and his deathbed poem are significant mainly as precursors: as a possible antecedent for the naming of Bellini's operatic heroine, and as a cornerstone of the genre of poems written in the voice of a dying lover popular in the 1830s and represented in the song "Lamento del moribondo" from Mercadante's *Soirées italiennes*.[38] Pepoli probably knew Redaelli's poetry—from 1843 on, both poets were anthologized in Antoine Ronna's *Parnaso italiano*.[39] Whether or not Redaelli's Elvira has any direct connection to the operatic character is impossible to say with certainty. Pepoli and Bellini wavered more than once about what to call their heroine, switching in sub-sequent libretto drafts from Elvira to the more innocent (and more common) Eloisa and back again.[40] Redaelli's Elvira, although a powerful presence in the poems, has few distinguishing features. She is blond and beautiful, she weeps and strums the lyre, and behaves in all respects like a typical romantic muse. If this Elvira did inflect the characterization of Bellini and Pepoli's heroine, it would have been in the direction of passivity and romantic mysti-cism, for Elvira is dreamier and more volatile than most operatic heroines, famously veering into madness at three separate moments, returning to her senses only to be set off by some new disappointment or fear.

The narrative frame for Mercadante's "Lamento del moribondo" is nearly identical to that of "Odi d'un uom che muore"—a dying man makes a final, grandiloquent proclamation of love to an absent, probably indifferent woman. Even so, Pepoli's poetry strikes a tone at once more dignified and more direct. Where Redaelli begins with the full frontal command *"Odi,"* twice repeated, Pepoli's verses recast the same plea at a remove, in terms of memory: *"Non scordar gli estremi accenti d'un meschin che per te muore"* (Do not forget the dying cries of the unfortunate who died for you). And at the poem's conclusion, where Redaelli coldly fantasized that the story of their failed love might be engraved on Elvira's heart, Pepoli's verse remains utterly in the present moment, quite vividly depicting the speaker's death.

Mercadante's music for the song embodies an expressive contradiction, albeit one familiar to those who appreciate the Italian music of the early nineteenth century. The "Lamento" is built from an elaborate lexicon of conventions for projecting strong emotion, packed with mimetic devices for physical collapse and emotional breakdown. The vocal line for the opening stanza is constructed almost completely from sustained sigh figures and the piano supports the singer with chains of throbbing syncopations (see example 19, mm.17–22). The opening section revels in expanses of empty space, whether in the silences between distinct gestures in the piano prelude or the unisons, in the lean voicings in the accompaniment, or the small gasps between chunks of the vocal melody. In his setting of the poem's last quatrain Mercadante exploits many of the same topoi for grief and physical collapse but adds a tinge of realism at the actual moment of death. As the speaker begins to lose strength (*"Più non veggo . . . io manco"*), the spaces between vocal gestures expand and the voicing thins out yet more, until the voice is left alone on the final repetition of *"t'amo"* (see example 20, mm.63–72). The song's last word, *"Addio,"* is sung on a sudden fortissimo, its bitter finality underlined by a downward fifth leap and a descending chromatic scale, staccato, in the bass (mm.75–76). The effect recalls operatic death scenes, but the final moments of this suffering soul are more extreme—more rhythmically distended and less vocally virtuosic—than in any opera of the period. The overall effect resembles a pleasurable sleight of hand. As listeners we seem to have been privy to a unique moment of self-revelation and extremity. Yet this intensely individual utterance is phrased in a poetic and musical vocabulary that is familiar, generic, and thus easily grasped in all its force. In this sense, Mercadante's "Lamento" instantiates the delicate balance between unicity and dissemination that is fundamental not only to romantic print but also, perhaps, to the special flavor of *Italian* romanticism.

One of the obstacles for historians seeking to link the aesthetic developments of the early nineteenth century to Risorgimento politics has been the strong conservative strand in Italian literature and music. Rather than making sharp, "revolutionary" breaks with existing styles, most Italian writers preferred to nourish their work on a carefully cultivated canon of works from the past that showcased the most admirable elements of the national spirit. (Thus many literary histories of the time proudly dubbed Dante, Ariosto, and Shakespeare as exemplary romantics.) And in opera, the melodic styles and aria forms that audiences had come to expect prevailed over composi-

EXAMPLE 19. Mercadante, "Lamento del moribondo," mm.1–28.

EXAMPLE 20. Mercadante, "Lamento del moribondo," mm. 61–79.

tional experiment, even in works whose subject matter might venture into the territory of gothic thrills.

Despite this, most historical inquiries into the reciprocal links between culture and politics in the Risorgimento have, as we saw in chapter 1, emphasized heroic subjectivities and revolutionary narratives. What is perhaps most interesting about Carlo Pepoli's poetry for the two *Soirées* collections, and about the musical styles in which that poetry was clothed by Rossini and Mercadante, is their almost complete avoidance of the heroic plane. The collections are mosaics of anonymous characteristic scenes, voiced by personae who are anything but heroic, some of whom barely count as speaking subjects at all: the sailor rowing steadfastly, the flirtatious merchant of fruit and flowers, the lovelorn girl appealing to the breeze and the brook to confirm that her love is reciprocated . . . The illustrative canvas is scaled back for the salon or the parlor, certainly, compared to the larger-than-life characters and scenes that often dominated opera. But it is just as significant that these various subgenres—the songs of the eroticized shepherdess, the sailor's suicidal laments, and the dying man songs—militate against any kind of dialogue with everyday reality. Their characters are, almost without exception, abstracted from all family ties or practical backdrops. These songs would be unlikely to inspire identification, emulation, or heroic action in listeners, as Pepoli had imagined could happen when word and music were perfectly fused in the Marseillaise; but they might forge subtler connections between listeners and between the various images they evoke. The thread that connects all of the various picture postcards and melodramatic poses of this song repertoire is a strong undercurrent of regret, loss, and distance. Perhaps one important purpose served by the proliferation of songs on each of these themes is to fabricate through quantity and repetition a sense of recovery and plenitude, to beat back the alternately flat and overwrought images by embracing them, over and over again.

SIX

Progress, Piety, and Plagiarism

VERDI'S *I LOMBARDI* AT LA SCALA

"MEN WHO THOUGHT OF ITALY . . ."

Not only are Italians innately, inescapably operatic; even their revolutions devolve into operatic spectacle. These are the familiar assumptions behind several irony-drenched entries in the diary of the Count Joseph Alexander Hübner, an Austrian diplomat who was sent to Milan as an emissary during the 1848 revolution. The most extended of Hübner's operatic analogies was inspired by a mid-May demonstration before the seat of government in the Piazza San Fedele, during which republicans and the supporters of the Savoy monarchy known as "constitutionals" hurled invective at each other.

> From three in the afternoon until eleven at night one could admire the strength of the lungs and the resonance of the throats of this populace. Each one seemed to have been born for the Opéra. People say tenors are rare. False: the impresario of La Scala could easily have found one in this crowd. . . . The simple fact that such scenes could occur under the eyes of the governors and could be prolonged for eight hours, without being forcibly terminated, proves how precarious is the current state of affairs.[1]

Elsewhere in his journal for that year, Hübner described bourgeoisie on the barricades during the *cinque giornate* (the "five days" of revolution in Milan during the spring of 1848), who kitted themselves out with cockaded *"chapeaux Ernani"* to infuse their otherwise tentative revolutionary acts with a theatrical intensity. Theatrical costuming aside, Hübner chortled, the revolutionaries "seemed a little embarrassed by their guns, which they shifted nervously from one shoulder to the other, a bit shocked by the roles in which they had been cast." Summoned to a meeting with the provisional government the same week, Hübner experienced the décor of their headquarters as reminiscent of "an evening at La Scala, during a performance of [Verdi's] *Ernani* or [Donizetti's] *Dom Sébastien*."[2]

Hübner's persistent return to operatic comparisons in order to puncture the pretensions of the revolutionaries is a negative image of the many anecdotes that celebrate opera as a means of political expression under conditions of censorship and foreign domination. Where Hübner figured the operatic as self-important posturing and empty vocalizing, the overwhelming tendency in accounts from later in the century, and beyond, invests opera with a power to transcend the stage, to articulate sentiments through singing that could not be articulated in words, and to provide ready-made narratives that allowed ordinary Italians to imagine themselves as political actors.[3] But Hübner's remarks are significant also simply because they are among the few instances in which opera, and Verdi, were invoked during the events of 1848. Roger Parker's careful reading of the Milanese press did more than discredit the myth of the spontaneous, unruly encore of "Va pensiero" at the first performance of *Nabucco*. Parker has also shown that the works, and even the name, of Verdi were surprisingly absent from concert programs and newspaper coverage in Milan during the few months in 1848 when the revolutionaries held power and the city was not under Austrian rule.[4] Work by Parker and others since has established that no reviews of Verdi's operas from the 1840s alluded to parallels between the situation of Italians under Austrian rule and the plight of the Hebrews in Babylonian captivity (in *Nabucco*) or the Lombard crusaders "liberating" the Holy Land (the subject of Verdi's next opera, *I Lombardi alla prima crociata*). Nor are there many hints that opera was adopted at any point in the 1840s as an expression of popular sentiment, either spontaneously or in scripted manifestations. The strict censorship enforced in Milan and elsewhere in the Italian peninsula was partly to blame for this; but censorship did not completely prevent critics from alluding to the current political situation, and reviews of the new paintings on exhibit at Milan's annual academy exhibitions do not shy away from hints about the political relevance of the art on display. What is more, reports in the foreign press, where one might expect to find ideas and interpretations that were current in Italy but impossible to publish openly there, do not construe opera in these political and allegorical terms.

In the rush to demythologize, it can sometimes appear that all connections between Verdi and the Risorgimento are being dismissed or that opera played no role in the formation of political opinion at the time. But there is no doubt that by 1859 both Verdi's name and his music were adopted as symbols of the pro-Unification movement.[5] And focusing on the period in the spring and summer of 1848, when the revolutionaries were in control of Milan and censorship was lifted, Philip Gossett has shown that the music publisher Ricordi quickly released dozens of new patriotic and martial choruses, which seemed to draw on the musical and poetic language of Verdi's choruses, suggesting influence or at least common cause.[6]

This centrality of wide dissemination and popular participation to the music's political currency is one thing that sets Verdi's music apart from the music of the preceding decades. With earlier operatic repertoire, political meaning often depended on secrecy and concealment, the assumption being that what was most important about these works and the conversations they inspired was missing from their public faces and had to be read between the lines. The ludic connections between Bellini's *I puritani* and the poetry penned by Carlo Pepoli for the salon songs of Rossini and Mercadante suggested a surreptitious mode of communication among initiates, perhaps analogous to the rituals of the Young Italy movement and other secret societies. In a similar way the Neapolitan vogue for operas about Queen Elizabeth I and Mary Stuart gave prominent play to the fear, gossip, and secrecy that Italian spectators imagined as governing the Tudor court. Even the appeal of Salvatore Viganò's ballets can be traced to their esoteric quality, the imperative they issued for critics and fans to speculate about what their bizarre concatenation of symbols and events might mean. Within this historical mentality, contemporary journalism, too, is sometimes most interesting for what it does not dare to say, or simply leaves unsaid.

The situation around Verdi is different in at least one important way. Hidden meanings continue to play a role, not least informing the methods of modern musicological interpreters. But Verdi's music was immediately released into a wide public arena, extending from the stage out into the street, the rhetoric flamboyant and the sheer volume often very loud. Verdi's declarative, extroverted music arrived on the Milanese stage just as voices in support of "Italy" became blunter and more vigorous, and as the Austrian government began to recognize that it was opportune to permit more open discussion of progress and of the national question in the press.[7] Antonio Ghislanzoni, who would much later write the libretto for Verdi's *Aida*, may have been noticing the very beginning of this shift when he wrote in his sketch of Milanese life in the 1840s:

Men who thought of Italy, who trembled under the yoke of foreign domination, who hated Austria, were few and far between. The majority did not realize that such a thing as Italy existed. Even so, some among them agitated secretly, some wrote, some took on the dangerous task of disseminating the writings of Mazzini. Back then it was risky to talk politics, even with one's closest friends. Those who dared fell under suspicion of espionage. Silvio Pellico's [I miei] Prigioni was considered an ultra-revolutionary book. Some people, trembling, dared to declaim the warlike verses of Berchet, within narrow circles of cognoscenti. Such declarations began around the year 1842.[8]

The way Ghislanzoni pinpoints a precise moment when national sentiment was given voice should both raise suspicions about the accuracy of his account (which was published decades after the events he chronicles) and remind us of the extreme volatility of this milieu. In this world, both private opinion and the possibilities for expressing that opinion changed almost day by day. As political views became more forceful and were articulated more openly, the new sonic force and dramatic intensity of Verdi's early style provided a similar spike in direct expressive power on the opera stage, which—coincidental or not—quickly began to seem causally related to the increased heat of the political sphere.

One thing I hope to do here, by tracking the reception of one of Verdi's operas from the early 1840s, is to understand more about how attitudes to opera evolved from the mood around the première of Nabucco, when critical reactions focused most of all on the new challenges Verdi's style posed to voices, to the all-out lionization of the composer just before and after Unification. If the secrecy and obliqueness that governed the interplay between musical culture and political conversation around 1835 gradually gave way to overt display by the mid-1850s, how was this transition managed and what role did Verdi play? Some answers are suggested by the traffic between private sociability and theatrical display that shaped Verdi's second big success at La Scala, I Lombardi alla prima crociata (1843), and by the opacity of the opera's critical reception.

MILAN AS JERUSALEM?

Where Nabucco is usually seen as an ingenuous creation by an untested composer from the Emilian countryside, I Lombardi is more calculated—designed to replicate Nabucco's success and reflecting the tastes and aesthetic interests of the new acquaintances Verdi acquired when he became the toast of Milan. One door that *Nabucco* opened for Verdi led to the salon of the Countess Clara Maffei, where he came into contact with many of Milan's leading artists and intellectuals. The Maffei salon was to evolve into the leading venue for conversation and cultural activity of a Mazzinian bent, especially after Maffei's divorce and her new liaison with the progressive journalist Carlo Tenca. But in the early 1840s the tenor of the proceedings was apparently more moderate: pro-Italian but not overtly anti-Austrian and not oriented toward revolution.[9]

One of Verdi's debts to the Maffei circle was probably the plot of *I Lombardi*, which was drawn from Tommaso Grossi's 1826 epic poem of the same name. Grossi was such an intimate in the Maffei salon that it was he, in his professional capacity as notary, who drew up the legal papers when Maffei and her husband Andrea divorced in 1846. But Grossi's sprawling retelling of Tasso's *Gerusalemme liberata* had enjoyed one of the largest print runs of any Italian literary work, so Verdi and his librettist Temistocle Solera would hardly have had to be initiates of the Maffei circle to have known of it.[10] The poem's action is spread over several decades and locales, presenting an exceptional challenge for operatic adaptation. The heart of both poem and opera is a love interest between the Christian Giselda, daughter of one of the leaders of the Lombard contingent in the First Crusade, and Saladin (renamed Oronte in the opera), son of the leader of the Muslim forces at Antioch.

With *I Lombardi* Grossi was clearly participating in the new nationalist project of recuperating events from Italian history as models for forming a new nation. Grossi's focus on the participation of nobles from Lombardy in the First Crusade gave his epic an immediate local relevance in the Milanese context, and the central conflict—Christians battling Muslim forces for the control of the Holy Land—could be inflected to project images of Italian virtue and valor, although cheering for the Christian forces was far from the only option for poets and historians who wrote about the Crusades. Another intimate of the Maffei salon, painter Francesco Hayez provided engravings to illustrate the first edition of Grossi's poem, and in the mid-1830s Hayez exhibited three paintings on scenes drawn from Grossi at the salon of the Accademia Brera.[11]

By the time Verdi and Solera's opera took the stage at La Scala in 1843, the Crusades—and Catholicism more generally—were beginning to acquire a new political import thanks to the philosopher Vincenzo Gioberti, whose vision for an Italian nation unified in the embrace of the church and under the leadership of the pope won a substantial following beginning with the publication of his *Del primato morale e civile degli italiani* in 1843.[12] Florentine critic Abramo Basevi remembered the mood of the period, looking back from the jaded vantage point of 1859:

> At the time there was a vogue for religion, which completely imbued the philosophy of the day. Theology had invaded every area of knowledge, and, championed as a basis of civilization, Christianity was lent glowing splendor in the writings of certain brilliant authors. It was then that Gioberti wrote those eloquent pages that professed the civilizing power of the Catholic ideal united to Italian spirit, and quickly ignited in our peninsula the great fire that only a few years later buried under its embers all who had stoked it.
>
> In the music of *I Lombardi* Verdi reveals himself to have been inspired by the same enthusiasm for Christianity that Gioberti exhibited in his *Primato morale e civile degli italiani*. . . . No other opera so well embodies the "sacred-modern" character.[13]

Basevi must be accounting here more for what *I Lombardi* came to mean to audiences rather than the intellectual currents that made it what it is. Direct influence of Gioberti's book on *I Lombardi* is nearly impossible since the *Primato* was published only after the opera's première and was not excerpted or discussed in advance in the press. Given the resolutely secular tenor of the Maffei salon, a looser "Zeitgeist"-type connection between the two works, "inspired by the same enthusiasm for Christianity" that impelled Gioberti, seems almost as unlikely. But especially after the election in 1846 of the liberal pope, Pio IX, who was briefly perceived by republicans as the best hope for changing Italy's fate, the war cries of the Lombard crusaders and the celestial sonorities of the scene in which Giselda herself baptizes the fatally wounded Oronte could quite plausibly have stirred the hopes of those who saw a path to an autonomous Italy blazed by the Vatican.

Documentation of such reactions is nonexistent, however, mainly because press notices of operatic revivals normally took the form of terse paragraphs that reported on the adequacy and disgraces of the singers stepping into the familiar principal roles. Reviews of the February 1843 première were much longer but only glancingly engaged with any political resonances the opera might bear. Indeed, the contrast with journalistic notices for Hayez's paintings of scenes from the Crusades is somewhat perplexing. Although the exhibitions of new painting at the Brera were reviewed in essentially the same censored press that was so silent about the topical resonances of Verdi's operas, Hayez's canvasses devoted to images of the Crusades elicited a much more engaged, indeed almost martial, response from critics. Perhaps the most flamboyant among several reviews that allude to the political resonances of the canvasses is an excitable commentary on the painting "Pope Urban Launches the First Crusade in the Piazza at Clermont," exhibited at the Brera salon of 1835.[14] The anonymous critic for the *Annotatore piemontese* places the painting against the backdrop of the seething tensions and inequalities of feudal Europe, all of which resolved into a joyous unity when the pope launched the Crusade:

> If feudalism in Europe sufficed to defend societies against foreign powers, it was not capable of securing domestic peace.... The population enslaved. The nobles unrestrained. Eternal wars. Arts and sciences censored. Literature ignored....
>
> The Cross is the symbol of European brotherhood; Pope Urban displays it in person to the populace.
>
> Oh, epoch of hopes and expectations! All fires were extinguished except rage against the enemies of Christ. All dissent among foot soldiers was calmed by this holy cause, among those who were united by this universal love.
>
> The surging crowd is animated by unanimity. What spaces! what waves! each action, each movement is the expression of an identical conviction, the expansion of the same enthusiasm.
>
> Listen to the groupings closest to the foreground. Oh, the powerful energy of the patriotic word that calls sons to the sacred oath of the religion to which they were born.[15]

In the article's final paragraphs, the writer zeroes in on the composition of the painting in detail, waxing enthusiastic about the way Hayez groups the characters to convey distinct personalities who are at the same time melded into a united crowd.[16] Read in juxtaposition with the bland, circumlocutionary writing on opera of the same period, this essay is remarkable for its willingness to connect the artwork to historical forces, to power, and to collective feeling.

The reviews that greeted the première of Verdi's opera at La Scala in February 1843, in contrast, barely mention Grossi's epic much less the historical and political realities of the Crusades. Most articles make no more than a nod to Grossi, acknowledging that the opera's source is so well known that there is no need for the critic to explain or discuss the plot. The reviews focus instead on pinpointing what is special about Verdi's style in light of the recent (and ongoing) performances of *Nabucco*. With two successful operas at hand to compare, the critics are beginning to assess what the Verdi phenomenon is all about. They all agree that these operas give a much greater role to the chorus than ever before—and they acknowledge the special appeal of the Act 4 chorus "O signore dal tetto natìo." The word *"filosofico"* and its synonyms echo through the reviews, as critics strive to identify what makes Verdi stand out from the operatic surroundings. At the same time, the reviews resound with a slightly puritanical contempt for the old Rossinian *"leggerezza"* that is easy to read in national terms: Verdi is seen as a restrained, syllabic, dramatic composer, who differentiates characters with distinctive motives, and as weightier and more balanced than his predecessors.[17] It is almost as if the challenges of Verdi's style (which after all was not *so* different from that of the operas of the past five or ten years) coincided with the emergence of a professional language of criticism in Italy, or as if critics took the Verdi premières as an excuse to demonstrate their technical expertise.

The stark differences between the tone of opera criticism and these responses to Hayez may have something to do with changes in censorship restrictions in the eight years between the Hayez exhibition and the première of *I Lombardi*. Writing in 1846 under the double cover of anonymity and publication abroad, the patriot Luigi Torelli had characterized Lombard censorship as truly draconian:

> Any writing, therefore, that even remotely tries to depict the unhappy state of a certain class of person, or town, or region, is prohibited or mutilated, because there must be no suffering under the Austrian government, at any cost. Any writing that recalls, in colors at all vivid, the actions of a people who liberate their country from a foreign yoke, is prohibited and mutilated, because it could inflame the souls by example and disturb the peace of the most contented people on the face of the earth. Any writing that, even at arm's length, points towards the absurdity or flaws in a law, or any other abuse by the magistrates, is prohibited or mutilated, because one must not in any way suggest that the government can create a bad law or an imperfect one, or appoint an inept or dishonest functionary.[18]

But it seems more likely that critics' willingness to connect Hayez to political ideas such as the individual and the collective stems from differences in the status of painting and opera—perhaps with the event-based and simultaneous nature of operatic experience as compared to the more leisurely and contemplative act of viewing a painting. Operas could, if successful, be depended upon to travel, to be taken up in new cities and towns soon after their premières, while paintings were more spatially fixed, although distributed through the medium of engraving. Opera also played to much larger and more socially mixed audiences than did art exhibitions, so that even published reviews of the artistic salons would partake more of the freer language of the salon than of frankly public space. Perhaps even more significant are the two art forms' distinct modes of consumption: crucially, paintings are rarely viewed by large groups of spectators all at once, whereas the simultaneity of the operatic experience means that audiences can not only gauge each other's reactions but also react with immediacy, a process that can spark groundswells of popular approval or disapprobation.

If journalists reporting on opera were constrained by the expectation of stricter censorship *and* by the challenge of translating abstract musical processes into words, then it becomes tempting to speculate about what they might "really" have wanted to say in their accounts of *Nabucco* or *I Lombardi,* and a small step from there to assuming that they would have noticed and cared about the same things today's listeners hear in the operas. In the chapter's final sections I shall return to the reception of *I Lombardi* to suggest some ways of reading through the reticence imposed by censorship to get a credible glimpse of the opera's contemporary relevance. But first I want to look at how Verdi's opera configures its heroes and villains against the background of the First Crusade, and more generally at the affordances Verdi and Solera's text offered to spectators and critics thinking about the links between power and religion, about what it meant to belong to a community, and about the role of belief in inspiring action. As we shall see, a swerve of perspective midway through the opera significantly blurs its moral and political stance, so that *I Lombardi* seems at times to embrace the late-model French-revolutionary values of equality and fraternity, and at others to incline toward the proselytizing tone of the Catholic-liberal agenda.

INEXORABLE ORIENTALISM

No less than the stories of Marino Faliero or Queen Elizabeth I, the Crusades were an object of fascination and of historiographical reevaluation for nineteenth-century writers—and as with those other fashionable historicist topics, the stakes of narrating or representing them were complex.[19] Most theatrical works that treated the Crusades would have been indirectly informed by Joseph Michaud's widely read *Histoire des croisades,* first published in France between 1817 and 1822.[20] Reversing the Enlightenment critique of the Crusades as superstitious and savage, Michaud espoused an ideological view based on complete identification with the crusaders, whom he depicted as engaged in a struggle to preserve Western civilization against the forces of violence and disorder.[21] That posture of identification was shared by Mazzini, who in his *Duties of Man* ventriloquized the cry of the crusaders as a proclamation he hoped to hear for a new uprising: "The cry which has resounded in all great and noble great Revolutions, the '*God wills it! God wills it!*' of the Crusades, alone will have the power to rouse the inert to action, to give courage to the timid, the enthusiasm of sacrifice to the calculating, and Faith to those who distrust and reject all mere human ideas."[22]

That *I Lombardi* and several earlier Crusades-themed operas took a less Manichean view of the conflict can probably be credited to their common source in an immensely popular novel that predated the publication of Michaud's history, Sophie Cottin's *Mathilde et Malek-Adel* (1805). The novel's impact in Italy can be glimpsed through a cluster of libretti that took *Mathilde et Malek-Adel* as their source.[23] These operatic adaptations suggest an orientation toward religious tolerance and reconciliation, quite different from the single-minded "rage against the enemies of Christ" and disdain for Muslim culture that the Piedmontese critic perceived in Hayez's painting in 1835. Where the anonymous art critic seems to have been reading Michaud and absorbing his oppositional view, Italian librettists at the same moment were apparently more captivated by the empathetic perspective of Cottin's novel.

All four operas cast the Muslim leader Malek-Adel as the romantic hero and crusader Guido di Lusignano as villain. In Giovanni Pacini's *I crociati a Tolemaide* (Turin, 1830), Malek-Adel has many of the attributes of Rossinian heroes and heroines; the role is assigned to a trousered contralto who is introduced singing from a boat, apostrophizing nature, in an echo of the opening scene of *La donna del lago*. Matilde and Malek-Adel each embrace the other's faith, and when they marry in the opera's second act it is without any public ceremony or participation by their communities; but the union is blessed by a bishop who happens to be nearby. Pacini also prefigures Verdi and Solera by showing the heroine at her first entrance weeping over her impossible love for a pagan, with whom she has fallen in love while a prisoner.

Carlo Pepoli's libretto for the Théâtre-Italien recasts Cottin's plot and characters in a mold that seems borrowed from Pepoli's previous great success at the Italien, *I puritani*. In his 1837 *Malek-Adel* (with music by Michael Costa), the central clash of cultures and faiths is embellished with generous lashings of gothic color. Scenes are played out against backdrops of ruined buildings and misty landscapes; Lusignano and Richard the Lionhearted sing a cabaletta that is also an oath of brotherhood; and the chorus sings often from offstage. In the last act Matilde becomes a nun at Mount Carmel and, in a vision, hallucinates that she is being pursued by a bloody ghost. Malek-Adel follows her to the doors of the convent, where he is inspired to convert to Christianity by the sound of the nuns' voices emanating from inside the church. Pepoli's *Malek-Adel* resembles *I puritani* also in blurring the distinctions between sympathetic and villainous characters, so that it is hard to glean a clear message about Christianity or crusades. Yet there is no ambiguity about the central axis of good and evil, and the opera's final moments are given over to a saintly death scene for Malek-Adel, who dies in Matilde's arms on the steps of the church after being wounded in battle by Lusignano.

Compared to these antecedents, Solera's libretto downplays the antagonism between the leaders of the opposing forces—and also minimizes private sentiment in favor of pageantry and choral tableaux. Solera dispenses with the conventional love triangle, which would have placed a rival for the soprano's affection among the leaders of the Crusade, and displaced that male conflict instead on to the brothers Arvino and Pagano. Long before the action begins, the two were rivals for the love of the same woman, who married Arvino and gave birth to a daughter, Giselda. The rivalry is reignited when Pagano returns from exile and learns that Arvino has been named leader of the Lombard forces in the First Crusade. Seething with jealousy, Pagano tries to murder his brother, but the blow misses its mark. To give thanks for her father Arvino's survival, Giselda undertakes a pilgrimage to the Holy Land. She is promptly captured by infidels, and while she is held as a prisoner at Antioch she falls in love with Oronte, son of the Muslim leader Acciano.

Giselda is depicted throughout as committed to a middle path that privileges humanity over rigid belief. In a duet that replays a stock scene from the Malek-Adel operas of the 1830s, she dismisses any allegiance to land, soil, or family in favor of pure communion with her beloved: *"Tu sei patria, vita e ciel per me"* (You are homeland, life, and heaven for me). In the final scene of the second act, after receiving the (false) news that her betrothed has been killed by the crusaders, she indicts her father and the army he leads for their brutal treatment of the Muslim inhabitants of the Holy Land. Her tirade takes the form of a cabaletta, which is interrupted by a vision of the horrors of the battlefield. The words she sings hinge on a reversal of the Crusades' defining cry: *"Dio nol vuole,"* she insists, in opposition to the ringing proclamation, *"Dio lo vuole,"* that historically impelled the Crusades.

No! giusta causa—non è d'Iddio
(quasi colpita di demenza)
La terra spargere—di sangue umano;
È turpe insania—non senso pio,
Che all'oro destasi—del musulmano!
Queste del cielo—non fûr parole:
No, Dio nol vuole—No, Dio nol vuole!

(No! it is not God's just cause [*as if struck by madness*] to bathe the earth in human blood; it is wicked insanity, not a pious feeling, aroused by the gold of the Muslim! These were not Heaven's words: *No, God does not will it, no, God does not will it!*)

The rejection of the crusaders' cry returns in the cabaletta's culminating phrase, positioned to release the accumulated tension of the vision's diminished sonorities and creeping chromatic lines into a broad, syncopated G-major phrase that assertively spans the soprano's range (see example 21).

Giselda is alone among the opera's characters in consciously rejecting violence and factional division. But the scenes in Act 2 in which the opposing groups are introduced endow the two factions with unexpected symmetry and equivalence. Both choruses are built around a sequence of tension and release. Chromaticism, extreme volume, and repeated accents give way to accessible march melodies with *banda* accompaniment, and the arrival of the march topos tempers the initial tone of savage belligerence to perform a ritual transformation of bloodthirsty warriors into noble citizenry.

At first the chorus of Muslim ambassadors calls down the punishment of Allah on the rampaging crusaders; but that music quickly gives way to an oath of brotherhood rendered as a lush march in the relative major. Hearing their leader, Acciano, describe the atrocities he has seen the Christians perpetrating, the chorus of Muslim ambassadors responds at first with fury, calling down the punishment of Mohammed and Allah on the rampaging crusaders. The musical style throughout this opening section is dotted with classic orientalist signifiers: strong beats are reinforced with grace notes that imitate drum rolls; semitones and flattened seconds are prominent melodically; twice the chorus converges on a diminished sonority in *fortissimo,* initiating a chilling echo effect (for one representative passage, see example 22). But after a few of these shouts of rage, the Muslims swear to forget their differences and act "as one single man," and their style for a moment becomes indistinguishable from other groups bound by an ethnic identity or by affinity: the Muslims could almost be confused with the

EXAMPLE 21. Verdi, *I Lombardi,* Act 2, Rondò-finale (Giselda).

EXAMPLE 22. Verdi, *I Lombardi*, Act 2, Coro di Ambiascatori, mm.17–21.

knights of death in *La battaglia di Legnano* resolving to block the advance of
Barbarossa.

> *Giuriam! Noi tutti sorgere*
> *Com un sol'uom vedrai,*
> *Scordar le gare, e accenderne*
> *Un'ira sola omai.*

(Let us swear! We will rise like a single man, you will see one man; we will
forget our differences and rise with a single fury.)

The harsh unisons and chromatic colorations of the opening section are
replaced with rich but decidedly Western-sounding harmonies, and *banda*
accompaniment lends the voices a mood of immediacy and resolve (see example 23). This elevated tone is short-lived: after just eight measures, the chorus
is again cursing the invader, its vocal lines again colored with semitones and
syncopation.

The chorus for the crusaders later in the act adheres to the same double
logic, beginning with a searing prophecy of the punishment that will befall
Allah and the infidels ("Stolto Allhà"). The first quatrain of poetry is set in
an angry, screeching idiom whose chromatic logic could be parsed as "orientalist" as easily as that of the Muslim chorus (see example 24). But with the
onset of the second quatrain (example 25), the rant gives way to a march sung
in unison, in the parallel major. The shift of styles is motivated by the mention of the radiant cross in line 5, and the chorus closes with a return to its

EXAMPLE 24. Verdi, *I Lombardi,* Act 2, Duettino ed Inno dei Crociati, mm.54–58.

fierce opening strain and a new segment of *banda* music (without voices) that accompanies the crusaders' movements across the landscape.

The even-handed depiction of the two choruses and the force of Giselda's plea for tolerance are weakened, if not completely negated, by the events of the opera's fourth and final act. The reversal of perspective is almost acute enough to merit discussion of *I Lombardi* in terms of the kind of "Bruch" that plagues interpretation of *Die Zauberflöte.* In the last act, the volatile Giselda experiences a second vision, this time of Oronte, who returns from the dead to assure her that he is in the (Christian) Heaven and—in a move that suggests he has embraced the crusaders' cause—to promise that the pool of Siloe outside the walls of Jerusalem will flow again with water to quench the thirst of her people. After a moment of uncertainty Giselda concludes that the apparition is real (*"Non fu sogno!"* / It was not a dream), and she imagines urging her people to rush to the city walls to drink from the source.

After the crusaders, still thirsting in the desert, wallow in memories of their verdant Lombard homeland in the famous chorus "O Signore dal tetto natìo," Giselda rushes in, shouting *"al Siloe!"* Arvino urges his

EXAMPLE 25. Verdi, *I Lombardi,* Act 2, Duettino ed Inno dei Crociati, mm.67–74.

people to drink, then scale the walls of the city, a suggestion they eagerly take up in the chorus "Guerra! guerra! impugni la spada" sung to the same music as the Act 2 crusaders' chorus, "Stolto Allhà." As in Act 2, the fevered opening strain of the chorus yields to the unison march theme, then to the recurring *banda* theme that represents the crusaders on the march. In this reprise, however, the stage band music expands into a long orchestral interlude in which the crusaders' theme is pitted against the march theme from the Act 2 Muslim chorus (their "oath of unity"), played in snatches by orchestra alone. The alternation of themes depicts the battle for Jerusalem; the crusaders win, and their melody concludes the scene. In the final moments of the opera, a scrim rises, and as the crusaders sing a hymn of thanks and praise, the city of Jerusalem is revealed: "On the walls, on the towers, fly the crusaders' banners, illuminated by the first rays of the sun from the east."

Early reviews of *I Lombardi* seem oblivious to the last act's sudden shift from criticism of the crusaders to full embrace of their cause. Nor do critics comment on the opera's treatment of the historical events it depicts, or even on broader topics such as religious fervor or the power of collective action. In reviews and in more feuilletonistic contexts, the discourse is concerned with accounting for the opera's musical style and what is new about it.

In keeping with the consistent emphasis on stylistic innovation and purposeful drama in the reviews, one note of reserve that crops up more than once concerns Verdi's tendency to interrupt simple melodies with fussy orchestral filigree. Perhaps betraying a slight regret for the flow of unfettered melody lost with the advent of the purposeful Verdi, journalist Geremia Vitali let himself express a twinge of disapproval that the composer interrupted the vocal phrases of the chorus "O Signore dal tetto natìo with "chirping flutes": "It is one of the most beautiful sections of an opera that would be above criticism, if it were not that the continual chirping by the flutes that rises to accompany the voice when the 'fresch'aure volante' are mentioned lends, some think, too cheerful a color to a sorrowful invocation of people who remember and sigh for their native skies."[24]

When read together with a handful of other complaints about orchestral intrusions into vocal melody, Vitali's gripe hints at more than just distaste for old-fashioned imitation of birds, breezes, and brooks. Basevi, the writer who pioneered nationalist-theological interpretations of *I Lombardi,* complained about a similar effect in the heroine's aria-prayer to the Virgin Mary, the "Salve Maria." The problem, for Basevi, lay in the "gothic" ornamental flourishes for flute and clarinet interposed between the sung phrases, ornaments that interrupt the singer "as if they want to give her time to blow her nose or to take a pinch of snuff."[25] These remarks hint at nostalgia for a simpler, more bel canto relationship between voice and orchestra; but also perhaps at a lukewarm response to the angelic flourishes (harp, flutes, high violins) that are so central to the opera's style. The focus on Verdi's ability to streamline melody, strip away outdated ornamentation, and infuse his music with moral purpose suggests that critics heard in *Nabucco* and *I Lombardi* more than just a pleasing new musical style: here and there they credit Verdi with discovering a new *function* for musical drama, and they seem to embrace his musical innovations as a form of progress that is a good in itself.

This association between Verdi and progress emerges clearly in an article that appeared in the "Eco di Milano" section of the *Rivista europea* in March 1843, just a few pages before that journal's review of the première of *I Lombardi*. Writing partly for *"forestieri"* who might want to visit Milan and would appreciate pointers about what to see and do, the scientifically inclined philosopher G. B. Baruffi remarks that he has recently noticed many visitors to the city using the new rail line connecting Milan with Brescia and Padova to come and see the avenues of Milan and to "bathe their ears in the novel sounds of Verdi's *Nabucco*," which they have managed to enjoy despite its reuse of passages from Rossini's *Mosè in Egitto*.[26] Baruffi continues:

> Frequent moral contact renders a population more cultivated, more civil, and more social, just as an abrasive substance cleanses the body. And we can thus see that today nations that possess the largest and more convenient means of transportation and communication are also the most civilized, just as we find the best cucumbers in locations where clear and fresh water flows fastest and most copiously.[27]

The loose chain of associations spun out in Baruffi's article—between the musical novelty of *I Lombardi*, new transportation routes, agriculture, and moral cultivation of the citizenry—may be more purposeful than it appears at first glance. The construction of new rail lines had become controversial under the Austrians, who discouraged the linkage of cities within northern Italy, partly because stronger lines of transport and communication might weaken imperial rule and partly in order to promote the Adriatic port of Trieste, with its proximity to Vienna, over Genoa, which had historically been a key port for northern Italy but which was more closely linked to France. Even by 1846, Camillo Cavour's article about the desirability of constructing a pan-Italian railroad had to be published in Paris rather than in the peninsula.[28]

It was perhaps not quite precisely in 1842, as Ghislanzoni had claimed in his whimsical *Storia di Milano*, but around that time—in gradual stages just before and just after the première of *I Lombardi*—that journalistic and public discourse began to open up, imperceptibly and without any official concessions from the censors. The process began with press reports on industrial improvements, on the annual meetings of scholars from all over Italy, and with the increasing publication and circulation of journals whose main brief was to print statistical tables that measured Italian achievements in comparison with those of other nations, making readers aware of the back-wardness of indigenous technology and production.[29] As John Davis explains it, the Austrians gradually began to see that it would further their aims of governance better to foster progress in the Lombardy-Veneto rather than to maintain the region in an infantilized state of economic dependence. The journalistic assessments of Verdi's style as an advance of dramatic honesty and musical energy perhaps form another strand of a subtle endorsement of progress in all its forms as a national goal.

THE MAKING OF A MYTH

So, did critics impatient with musical filigree and pleased with Verdi's tight, purposeful approach to drama have a fundamental goal in common with the scientists, statisticians, and journalists who worked to promote industrial and agricultural progress in midcentury Italy? Admittedly, this is hardly an obvious or intuitive reading of the reviews of *I Lombardi,* nor a usual way of connecting opera to Risorgimento discourse. To read the criticism this way is to press through a veil of (assumed) self-censorship, putting pressure on recurring or surprising elements in the evaluation of the opera and deciphering them as hints of an underlying agenda about dramatic and musical reform.

Among the reviews of the opera's première, there is just one that does not partake of this obscurantist language. Carlo Tenca's review in *La moda* stands out for its similarity to the ways Verdi is often written about today and has been since late in the nineteenth century. Tenca, a journalist who was romantically linked with Clara Maffei and was an influential voice in her salon, shares the general perception of the critics about the opera's dramatic innovations. But, uniquely, he couches these observations in language that spells out the consequences such drama could have for national consciousness and for action:

> The individualism of affect disappears in the face of this so fervid imagination: and it has sentiments much more vast, more collective, which will agitate the masses, who will embrace whatever contains the most sublime image of nation or of humanity. And it is precisely in the expression of a grand and complex thought that the creative power of Verdi is revealed; it resides in the lament of an entire people who tremble as slaves on the banks of the Euphrates, and the religious aspirations of two nations, who become brothers, bonded by a single prayer; or it is the cry of war that sends the crusaders off to

the conquest of Palestine, it is in the pained moan of those troops, afflicted by thirst in the desert. Even these individual emotions, without which dramatic action cannot exist, need to be reinvigorated for Verdi by a higher or more generous idea; and even love itself must connect to something more exalted that surpasses vulgar complacency, as occurs in *Nabucco* and in *I Lombardi,* where it is elevated by religious exaltation.[30]

Tenca anticipates terms that become common fifteen years later when he assumes an immediate topical relevance for the "lament of an entire people" and the "the pained moan of those troops, afflicted by thirst in the desert." Tenca agrees with his colleagues that Verdi has somewhat downplayed vocal beauty and memorable melodies, and he goes further to suggest that the composer has elevated harmony above melody as a musical value. Tenca's equations between melody as representation of the individual, and harmony as an expression of the collective, suggest that he was an early reader of Mazzini's "Filosofia della musica," which set up a similar opposition, similarly privileging music that developed harmony more fully.[31] Finally, he observes the same sped-up dramatic pacing that other critics considered to be one of the key innovations of Verdi's style, but is more ambivalent about it, noting that the opera "keeps the mind of the listeners in a state of constant tension that is difficult to sustain for the entire length of the opera."

Where Tenca gives a passing mention to *"nazionalità"* (in relation to the masses, "who will embrace the most sublime elements *of nation, or of humanity*"), connections between Verdi and the more charged term *"patria"* were slower to be articulated. The earliest article I have encountered that mentions Verdi and *"la patria"* in the same breath dates from 1846, and its claims are quite oblique. In that year Benedetto Bermani published a pamphlet on Verdi's career to date, in which he anointed Verdi as the "operatic voice our epoch has longed for," an interpreter who combines the light and the serious to strike a balance between the four constitutive elements of serious opera: nation, love, religion, and suffering.[32] Echoing Mazzini's purpose-driven art criticism, Bermani heralds Verdi's role in transforming opera from "pleasant illusion" to an art worthy of sustained attention and analysis. "The errant, libertine, careless artistic spirit no longer holds any seductive appeal for us," writes Bermani; artists now see the imperative to create works that stand up to sustained critical analysis, and recognize that music must "step down from her isolated throne, to fraternize with the sister arts" to create something more rational and more satisfying to the laws of taste.[33]

By 1855 the confrontations between warring peoples and the wistful evocations of distant homelands in Verdi's early operas had been subsumed into an
explicitly national discourse. Writing in the *Rivista contemporanea,* published
in the freer air of Piedmont, the polymath Marco Marcelliano Marcello wrote
in surprisingly explicit terms about the sub-rosa meanings he perceived
behind Verdi's early operas, which he called latent expressions of "the hatred
of foreign domination, the love of liberty, the ache of [Italy's] impotence,
regret for the memory of her great past."[34] With this essay Verdi enters the
pantheon, or the "Risorgimental canon," to use Alberto Banti's term.
Marcello's article rubs shoulders in the *Rivista contemporanea* with contributions on such staples as the poetry of Dante and the philosophy of Antonio
Rosmini (both by Niccolo Tommaseo) and political thought in France (by
Terenzio Mamiani), and his discussion of Verdi strikes all the high notes of
what would become the myth of Verdi as "bard of the Risorgimento."

He hears Verdi's choruses as the true expression of universal desires and
finds their unisons "perfectly suited to depict the unanimity of the plans that
were incubating in so many souls."[35] He gestures toward the topical relevance
of the depictions of tyrannical oppression and longing for the homeland in
Nabucco, I Lombardi alla prima crociata, and *Ernani* and even invokes the
trope of the masses singing opera in the streets: "I remember with what mar-
velous avidity the populace of our Italian cities was seized by these broad and
clear melodies, and with what agreement they walked singing, along the
squalid streets, confronting the grave reality of the present with aspirations
for the future."[36] In a way, the existence of texts like this only compounds the
difficulty of understanding what people may have heard in Verdi. The enthusiasm and clarity of Marcello's language makes it impossible to dismiss the
idea of the political Verdi. But it is equally impossible to take such views as
indicative of sentiments a decade earlier.

PROGRESS AND . . . PLAGIARISM

The passing allusion to similarities between *Nabucco* and the twenty-year-old
Rossini warhorse *Mosè in Egitto* in Baruffi's *Rivista europea* article may be
more than casual.[37] For years music critics had been obsessing over novelty
and recycling, using resemblances to existing works as an excuse to dismiss
new operas, even though the debts often existed only in the imaginations of
the critics. Nor was *I Lombardi* immune to this strain of criticism. About a

month after the opera's première, an article appeared in the *Gazzetta privilegiata di Milano* that accused Solera of having plagiarized several passages of the *Lombardi* libretto from existing libretti by Cammarano, Felice Romani, and a certain Giovanni Pullè. The matter was debated over a series of six articles in various periodicals, coming to a close only when Solera himself published a response in which he essentially admitted the plagiarism and trumpeted that "the author [Pullè] should consider himself honored to be found worthy of having his ugly verses placed in such a beautiful libretto."[38] In his own continued defense, Solera pointed out that in a libretto consisting of over eight hundred lines he had "carelessly" taken only about thirty from existing libretti. Employing a logic that would damn almost all early-nineteenth-century libretti, Solera further argued that Pullè himself should be ashamed, since the entire concept of his *Ernani* libretto, from which Solera had borrowed, was lifted wholesale from Hugo's play, whereas Solera himself had created a drama of considerably greater novelty in *I Lombardi*.[39]

When one examines the passages Solera is supposed to have stolen, the matter becomes even more perplexing, since the poetic language that recurs is usually so standard and conventional that it could fit comfortably into almost any libretto of the period. Among the more distinctive of the seven or eight "plagiarized" passages referred to in these articles is a passage from the Act 3 duet for Giselda and Oronte, that scene in which the lovers decide to run off together, leaving behind both homeland and family. In the duet's lyrical slow movement, Oronte embraces the fate he imagines awaits him if he flees with Giselda:

> *Per dirupi e per foreste*
> *Come belva errante io movo:*
> *Giuoco ai venti e alle tempeste*
> *Spesso albergo ho an antro, un covo!*

(Through thickets and forests / I move like a wandering beast: / tossed by the winds and storms / I often have but a cave or burrow for shelter!)

Oronte's vocabulary here is strikingly reminiscent of opera's many outcasts and exiles: Arturo of *I puritani,* who wanders through the English countryside after being branded a royalist sympathizer by Cromwell's forces; or indeed the bandit Ernani from Verdi's opera of the following year, who incessantly figures himself as alone and unwanted.

The parallel between very different dramatic situations is interesting in that the medieval Muslim Oronte's plaint could just as easily emanate from the lips of a Carbonaro revolutionary of the generation of exiles of 1831. Solera's text is reliant enough on the stock libretto lexicon to stretch the meaning of the term "plagiarism." Those very generic qualities came into focus for Geremia Vitali, who entered into the plagiarism debate mostly as an excuse to point out what he considered grievous shortcomings of both dramatic consistency and poetic invention in Solera's libretto. Responding to Solera's first letter of self-defense, Vitali sneers that "anyone who wants to read through this libretto as a whole will find at least thirty lines that use the word 'heart,' about as many that use the word 'God,' and I don't know how many that use the word 'love' or the word 'Lord.'"[40] But for Vitali the issue is fundamentally one of dramatic construction, which quickly devolves into a question of national identity or local pride. Early in the article he defines his task as to evaluate whether this opera entitled *I Lombardi alla prima crociata* really deserves to be staged by Lombards, in Lombardy, and whether it brings any glory to them or their progenitors. After a methodical consideration of each character's words and actions, Vitali's answer is a resounding no. The only admirable character, the only one whose actions are consistent, is "the Turk" Oronte, and he thus must be considered the opera's protagonist. "Can you explain to me," Vitali expostulates, "how an opera can be called *I Lombardi alla prima crociata* in which the most virtuous character is a Turk? and in which we see so many evil-doers and hear them praying at least ten times?"

One lesson to be drawn from this passage, then, might be as a caution against heralding *I Lombardi* as historical drama, when swathes of its libretto can be revealed as interchangeable with *Hernani* or *Pia de' Tolomei* or *Parisina*. Yet this little scandal is also another indication of the value attached to progress—to demonstrable novelty and its attendant value for spectators. For critics writing in the 1830s and 1840s, the only *good* borrowing was one that resurrected the pure old Neapolitan school of melody associated with Paisiello and Cimarosa (stylistic debts that critics were equally capable of conjuring up purely in imagination). It seems a pleasing poetic justice that not long after this, Solera relocated to Spain, and when he returned to Italy in 1871 set up in Florence as a merchant of antiquities, selling vestiges of the pasts (of all nations) to newly unified Italians.

One conclusion we can draw from this snapshot of Verdi's early critical reception is that the absence of references to nation or contemporary politics in the reviews of *Nabucco* cannot be taken as a complete or straightforward record of reactions to the opera, any more than can the excitable patriotic glosses that emerged shortly before Unification and gradually became a default language for discussing Verdi. The circumspection of the critical language, which seems in inverse proportion to the brashness and legibility of Verdi's early style, perhaps has to do with the particularity of opera as a medium, and of the opera house as a venue. The ease with which critics interpreted the paintings of Hayez as statements about nation, in contrast with the tortured language of Verdi's early critics, hints at a desire to dial down the volume of operatic expression, or to counterbalance its blatancy of address. At the same time, the blank, impenetrable surfaces of Verdi criticism may be a sign of listeners' uncertainty about what the nature of the operatic artwork actually was and where its meaning might reside—an unease that was gradually resolved as the job of critic became professionalized and strong interpretive models proliferated.

The reach of censorship and self-censorship, as well as the conventions of musical criticism, make it necessary to read below the surface of reviews—to attend to strange details and probe for subtexts, as in the analogy between streamlined drama and progress. A figure like Carlo Tenca occupies a crucial position in the evolution from indirect, repressed criticism to unfettered patriotic appropriation, and his example can tell us a good deal about the formation of cultural opinion around opera during the period. An outlier in terms of his critical vocabulary but very much an insider in the progressive circles within which Verdi also moved, Tenca likely helped to establish the lexicon for later writing about Verdi and about opera.

The point is not that writers like Tenca, Bermani, and Marcello elevated Verdi to a position of political relevance. Opera had long been a privileged venue for conversation, congregation, and convening of like-minded communities of listeners. What seems to have happened in the 1840s is that it began to matter more what the operas were, and how they were constructed musically and dramatically. In other words, opera's social importance was no longer so thoroughly lodged in the possibilities of the *opera house* as venue, divorced from repertoire or style. Now specific sounds, musical processes, and dramatic devices became more influential, beginning with the centrality of the chorus and the perception of sped-up, ultrafocused drama in Verdi's early works. It would be another fifteen years before journalists developed suitable metaphors and catch-phrases to translate the complexities of Verdi's style into terms that would travel and reproduce themselves across time and space. As always, that process meant highlighting some facets of the operas and ignoring others, and a look back at the first phases of their reception reminds us of the halting steps, the exaggerations, and dead ends that go into the shaping of a cultural archetype.

Such a process would account for the powerful sense of release, satisfaction almost, that one senses when Marco Marcelliano Marcello was finally able to wax lyrical, in 1855, about hordes of protesters singing Verdi choruses in the streets. It is almost as if Verdi's operas *became* political in stages, as the surrounding discourse evolved.

Conclusion

I LOMBARDI MIGHT SEEM A STRANGE PLACE to conclude a study of opera and political opinion in nineteenth-century Italy; but all the factors that make it a perverse endpoint are also strong reasons for ending here. To pursue Verdi's career further into the 1840s would mean wrestling with the seductive narratives that have grown up around these works, from *Nabucco* on. Those stories lean heavily on plot and setting, arranged around clusters of operas that feature feisty local groups resisting conquest by invaders (*Attila, Alzira, La battaglia di Legnano*), or forceful female warriors (*Giovanna d'Arco, Attila*), or brooding Byronic outsider-heroes who command ragtag bands of rebels and outsiders (*Ernani, Il corsaro, I masnadieri*), or eloquently lamenting exiles, alone or in groups (*I due Foscari, Macbeth*). As a work that does not fit easily into these frameworks and is unencumbered by the weight of myth and emotion attached to "Va pensiero," *I Lombardi* may be just the right place to lay this inquiry to rest.

Continuing further into the 1840s would also mean thinking seriously about the adaptations of Verdi's music for political demonstrations and ceremonies, occasions that became more and more common in 1846 and 1847. And it would mean finding out more about what the name "Verdi" and the sounds and ideas associated with it came to mean in various locales in 1848, during the revolutions and in the grim and reticent atmosphere that held sway for several months after the revolutions were suppressed. Before 1848, appearances of Verdi's music (or opera in general) in political contexts centered almost exclusively on one choral number, and one political message. The chorus "O sommo Carlo" from *Ernani* was performed on at least a dozen occasions to honor Pope Pio IX, with the name "Pio" substituted where the characters in the opera laud the newly elected Holy Roman Emperor,

"Carlo."[1] These manifestations began after Pio IX declared an amnesty for Italians who had been exiled for political activity, an action that sharply increased his popularity among republicans.[2]

It would almost certainly be possible to unearth more accounts of occasions on which the *Ernani* chorus or other Verdian melodies were employed in honor of Pio IX, and perhaps also linked to other causes and celebrations. In a fairly cursory browse through the digitized issues of newspapers from the 1840s, I recently came upon two additional performances, and their circumstances are intriguing enough to suggest that more research into what else went on at these events, who sang, and how they were organized logistically would be rewarding. What can we make of the fact that "O sommo Pio" was performed at an 1846 festival in the Piedmontese town of Lomellina otherwise devoted to showcasing advances in agronomy? Or of the chorus's interpolation between the acts of *I Lombardi,* in which the banners of the crusaders were replaced with banners bearing the insignia of the pope?[3]

When simply listing off performances of the chorus it is easy to forget that the music as it appears in the opera is far from simple or easy to sing off the cuff. In its original context, the texture shifts frequently—from a lyrical opening statement for baritone alone (the easiest section to imagine taking on a life of its own as an anthem) to ponderous declamation to a slightly shrill choral apotheosis. It seems most likely that the version of the chorus performed at these political manifestations was trimmed down to just first solo section, was arranged for group singing. There does not seem to be any surviving sheet music or lyric sheets for these performances of "O sommo Carlo" as occasional music; but it is difficult to imagine that the music was not rearranged to render it more homogeneous, more affectively unified, and easier to sing. It would also be fascinating to know whether anyone hearing the chorus adapted this way ever remarked on the irony of repurposing a chorus originally sung to thank an emperor for his clemency to a group of revolutionaries who conspired against him as a hymn honoring a pope friendly to a new vision of Italy (if not to outright revolution).

The wealth of material printed and the ease of consulting it in the age of Google means that it has become much easier to add to the register of political uses to which Verdi's music, and operatic music in general, was put in 1848 and after, although we are perhaps not much closer to penetrating the real significance of these appropriations and allusions. A popular recurring feature in the uncensored revolutionary feuilletons of 1848 were humorous pieces that narrated recent military and political events via bits of plots and characters from popular operas. In September 1848, for example, the

Florentine paper *Il popolano* republished an item from a Venetian satirical paper announcing an (obviously trumped up) "Artistic/Instrumental Accademia (or concert)," its structure a cross between the design of a ceremonial cantata and the miscellaneous programming of contemporary instrumental/vocal concerts.[4] The drama's settings progress through sites crucial to the defense of Venice from Austria—Isonzo, the Campi di Goito (the location of an unsuccessful battle, near Mantua), and eventually Milan and Naples to whom the Venetians turned unsuccessfully for external support. The main characters are Generals Nugent (leader of the Austrian forces outside Venice) and Durando (leading the Italian rebels). The anonymous author expertly weaves together brief passages from *Ernani, Beatrice di Tenda,* and Luigi Ricci's comic opera *Chi dura vince.* At the climactic moment, the Venetian revolutionary leader Daniele Manin inhabits the role of one of the medieval founders of Venice, quoting a stanza sung by the soldier Foresto in Verdi's 1846 opera *Attila;* but as Foresto/Manin rounds off his lyrical hymn to the *"patria,"* he is interrupted by the entrance of the popular Austrian ballerina Fanny Elssler, who rounds out the evening by dancing her famous polka with the Duke of Reichstadt, a high-ranking Habsburg noble.

Farcical allusions to opera like this were balanced by more serious, even tragic appropriations, such as the contrafact of Gilda's narration from Act 2 of *Rigoletto* ("Tutte le feste al tempio") as a lament for the Bolognese martyr Ugo Bassi, a Catholic priest and patriot who urged his congregants to take up arms against foreign rule and was executed by the Austrian government in 1849.[5] We can only speculate about why *this* melody from Verdi was adapted as Ugo Bassi's dying lament (and it seems to be one of only a few instances in which Verdi's tunes were retooled for popular, patriotic ends). Equally, there seems to be no way of knowing how quickly Gilda's utterance was taken up as a patriotic lament; but the melancholic and nonconfrontational style hint at an origin in the earlier phases of the Italian struggle for autonomy and unification, soon after *Rigoletto*'s 1851 première.

Such invocations of scenes and figures from opera and ballet tell us more than simply that readers knew these scenes inside out, or that the opera provided a primary trove of cultural references. They also reinforce what much of the journalistic criticism discussed in these pages also indicated, and what we know from social histories of operagoing: that opera was consumed as a series of discrete moments of intensity and signification. Even evening-long performances of complete operas mattered to listeners and critics mainly as a series of pithy lines, catchy tunes, and indelible performances of single arias or ensembles. The censors too reacted this way to the works and performances they reviewed. Although censorship standards were wildly inconsistent from one city to another, and even from day to day, certain powerful words and phrases (especially invocations of *"libertà"* and *"patria"*) were reliably struck from libretti.

And yet I would not want to confuse this habit of detaching bits of words and music from their narrative context with a situation in which any passage of music could signify anything, or any political or emotional idea could be attached to no-matter-what sung phrase. The specter that I'm trying to beat back here is that of the communist "Internationale," as discussed by Eric Drott.[6] Drott shows that the opposing groups in the 1968 protests in Paris adopted musical slogans and anthems almost interchangeably, responding to the affordances offered by each song and to their recent and remote histories of associations with other political movements. The operatic events and the discourses surveyed in this book do not indicate that any meaning at all could be attached to any operatic excerpt. Indeed, the vigorous attempts of critics and philosophers early in the century to enforce what they thought were the proper relations between word and melody, and their censure of Rossini's breaches of those relations, indicate a certainty that words and music do not fit together any which way.

The foregoing chapters have touched on a number of different roles that opera played in the verbal discourse and in everyday experience (to the extent that these are separable for the historian) in early-nineteenth-century Italy. If there is a constant across these disparate ways of apprehending how opera matters to political realities, it lies in the ways listeners respond to pacing and to isolated effects of sound. In Mazzini's account of Donizetti's *Marino Faliero,* for example, it was the sustained dramatic momentum of the extended *parlante* section and the jabbing violin melody, like a knife penetrating the doge's breast, in the scene between Bertucci and Faliero that so vividly evoked the conditions that might motivate someone to join a revolutionary conspiracy. Critics who saw Donizetti's *Elisabetta* or *Maria Stuarda* also connected pacing and gesture to questions of authority and legislation when they quibbled about whether this or that prima donna was commanding enough to portray a queen. Even the dismissal of Rossini and the lionization of Salvatore Viganò by writers in the romantic debates of 1816 were based in a preference for music that moved forward more quickly, that was choreographically keyed to the stances and gestures of characters rather than dwelling on the more static representation of a seashore or a prison setting. And

Verdi's achievement in *I Lombardi* was heard in terms of technological advances, the new orchestral effects and new challenges his music issued to the voices positively received as manifestations of the progress of which Italy so urgently felt the need by the 1840s. These pluralistic yet still somehow coherent impressions of how opera communicated to Italian audiences before Unification invite us to attend to opera in new ways ourselves, to tune back into those scattered sonic effects and small-scale modes of organizing dramatic time that were so audible to listeners like Stendhal and Abramo Basevi but have since often seemed too obvious and too insignificant to notice. The sum of these critical impressions also, I think, finally and decisively dispatches the presence evoked in this book's title. Not only are Italians by 1848 no longer "waiting for Verdi" to give them voice or to invest opera with true political relevance; they were never waiting at all.

NOTES

CHAPTER 1. RISORGIMENTO FANTASIES

1. Alfonso Bertoldi, ed., *Epistolario di Vincenzo Monti,* vol. 4 (Florence: Le Monnier, 1929), no. 1189 (8 May 1816), 297; quoted in Alberto Zedda, ed., *La gazza ladra* (Pesaro: Fondazione Rossini, 1979), xxii. In another letter, on 28 May, Monti eviscerates the competing libretti one by one, listing their shortcomings in an amusing vein. Among Monti's complaints are lapses of grammar, poetic structure, structure of the action, sparsity of scenic effect, and the possibility that one of the works would require more good singers in main roles than La Scala could supply. The titles of the competing works remind us that classical subject matter was still overwhelmingly dominant: *Calliroe, Le Amazzoni, Polifemo, Piramo e Tisbe, I supposti pastori, Antioco,* and *Il salto di Leucade.* Not enough information survives about La Scala's libretto competition to date it precisely, but it is possible that the entire event was conceived and publicized after January 1816. We know only that Monti was reading submissions in May of that year, when he lamented the generally low quality of Italian poetry in a letter to his fellow judge Angelo Petracchi.

2. *Corriere delle dame,* 14 June 1817, 186.

3. Anne Louise Germaine de Staël, "Sulla maniera e l'utilità delle traduzione," *Biblioteca italiana* (January 1816), trans. Pietro Giordani; reprinted in Carlo Calcaterra and Mario Scotti, eds., *I manifesti romantici del 1816, e gli scritti principali del "Conciliatore" sul Romanticismo,* 2nd ed. (Turin: Unione Tipografico Editrice Torinese, 1979), 83–92. The *Biblioteca italiana* was the official journal of the new Austrian regime in the Kingdom of Lombardy-Veneto (encompassing Milan and Venice) from 1815, but its first editor, Giuseppe Acerbi, engaged as contributors a number of noted patriots, including Vincenzo Monti, Pietro Borsieri, Ludovico di Breme, and Silvio Pellico. The *Corriere delle dame* was also pro-Austrian. On the *Biblioteca italiana,* see Calcaterra and Scotti, *I manifesti romantici,* 154 n1; and Martin Thom, *Republics, Nations, and Tribes* (London: Verso, 1995), 271–72; on the *Corriere delle dame,* see Calcaterra and Scotti, *I manifesti romantici,* 177 n2.

4. Staël, "Sulla maniera e l'utilità delle traduzione"; excerpt reprinted in Michele dell'Acquila, ed., *Primo romamticismo italiano: Testi di poetica e critica* (Bari, 1976), 139. Staël goes on to suggest that the Italian mind would profit from musical settings of good dramatists like Casti or Metastasio.

5. Leopardi, *Discorso sopra lo stato presente dei costumi degl'italiani,* ed. Augusto Placanica (Venice: Marsilio, 1989), 131–32; written in 1824 but first published in *Scritti vari inediti dalle Carte napoletane,* ed. Giovanni Mestica (Florence: Le Monnier, 1906). By far the most common "spectacles" in 1824 would have been performances of operas by Rossini and his contemporaries. In addition to spoken theater, which was far less popular than opera, other kinds of "spectacles" would have included displays of poetic improvisation, a variety of equestrian entertainments, and various other types of open-air performance that straddled the boundary between theater and circus. On Leopardi's firsthand experience of opera, mostly in Rome in 1822–23, see Bruno Cagnoli, "Leopardi e la musica," *Atti della Accademia Roveretana degli Agiati* 253, 8/3a (2003): 33–56.

6. Guthrie, *New Geographical, Historical, and Commercial Grammar, and Present State of the Several Kingdoms of the World,* 3rd ed. (London: J. Knox, 1771), 483; translated into Italian by Carlo Barbiellini as *Nuova geografia universal, antica, e moderna* (Milan: Carlo Ant. Barbiellini, 1802). Arteaga also devotes a lengthy footnote to the musical character of the Italian language in his *Le rivoluzioni del teatro musicale italiano* [1773], vol. 1, 2nd ed. (Venice: Carlo Palese, 1785), 88–90n. Arteaga's claims were taken up directly in Girolamo Tiraboschi's *Storia della letteratura italiana,* and elsewhere.

7. Carpani, "Lettera sul *Tancredi,*" *Biblioteca italiana* 10 (April 1818): 10.

8. Stendhal, *Rome, Naples et Florence* (Paris: Le Divan, 1937), entries of 11 and 12 November, 75 and 79–84. Stendhal's account of visiting La Scala is discussed also by Luigi Mareseglia in his *Drammaturgia e romanzo. Primo Ottocento: I generi letterari nel "Conciliatore"* (Bari: Palomar, 2004), 11. On the Caffè dell'Academia, see Sandro Piantanida, *I caffè di Milano* (Milan: U. Mursia, 1969), 54–56.

9. The tendency to match up composers and their works with "ready-made historical frames supplied by the locations in which art was produced or by big-picture histories," which were sometimes "flattened out," is discussed in Nicholas Mathew and Mary Ann Smart, "Elephants in the Music Room: The Future of Quirk Historicism," *Representations* 132 (2016): 61–78, here 61.

10. See Roger Parker, Introduction to the critical edition of *Nabucco,* in *The Works of Giuseppe Verdi,* series 1, vol. 3 (Chicago: University of Chicago Press, 1988), xviii; and Parker's discussion of the issue in his *Leonora's Last Act: Essays in Verdian Discourse* (Princeton: Princeton University Press, 1997), 57; and his *Arpa d'or dei fatidici vati: The Verdian Patriotic Chorus in the 1840s* (Parma: Istituto nazionale di studi verdiani, 1997).

11. David Kimbell, *Verdi in the Age of Italian Romanticism* (Cambridge: Cambridge University Press, 1981), 445.

12. Gossett continues, "By 1844 [the year *Ernani* was composed], Verdi had no need to render problematic his choruses: the public readily understood their politi-

cal subtext"; Philip Gossett, "Becoming a Citizen: The Chorus in Risorgimento Opera," *Cambridge Opera Journal* 2/1 (1990): 41–64, here 57. The term "hermeneutic window" is Lawrence Kramer's, from his *Music as Cultural Practice: 1800–1900* (Berkeley: University of California Press, 1993).

13. "Review of Lucy Riall, *Garibaldi: The Invention of a Hero*," *New Republic*, 16 August 2007.

14. On operatic forms as containers for the expression of political feeling, see Simonetta Chiappini, *O patria mia: Passione e identità nazionale nel melodramma italiano dell'Ottocento* (Florence: Le Lettere, 2011); and Chiappini, "From the People to the Masses: Political Developments in Italian Opera from Rossini to Mascagni," in Silvana Patriarca and Lucy Riall, eds., *The Risorgimento Revisited* (London: Palgrave Macmillan, 2012), 56–76. Even Richard Taruskin, more often skeptical in such matters, embraced an allegorical and populist model of opera as political art when he revived Morse Peckham's 1985 theory that the function of Risorgimento literature and opera was to raise Italians' "level of aggression," to make them capable of overthrowing the Austrians. Taruskin calls the opera of the Risorgimento period "perhaps the first self-conscious political vanguard—an avant-garde in the literal, quasi-military sense—to be actively promoted, even led, by artists," and suggests that "all national art became double-coded: an implicit model, even a manual of action that exemplified what could not be openly advocated by direct public exhortation"; *Oxford History of Western Music* (New York: Oxford University Press, 2005), vol. 3, 570.

15. In his *Political Beethoven* (Cambridge: Cambridge University Press, 2012), Nicholas Mathew adopts a refreshingly concrete definition of the political as music created for and performed in public settings, but also explores the striking parallels between Beethoven's occasional music and the "absolute" music of the heroic period.

16. Sonia Slatin, "Opera and Revolution: *La muette de Portici* and the Belgian Revolution of 1830 Revisited," *Journal of Musicological Research* 3 (1979): 45–62.

17. Eric Drott's *Music and the Elusive Revolution: Cultural Politics and Political Culture in France, 1968–1981* (Berkeley: University of California Press, 2011) focuses on the affordances provided by different musical genres and performances in overtly political contexts. Drott convincingly shows that the same tune can be brandished by different communities, that a song like the "Marseillaise" may promote fellow feeling or stimulate a desire to act, but that it can do so equally for forces from opposing sides of a conflict. Both Drott and Nicholas Mathew also tartly distance themselves from those who collapse the examination of music's political efficacy with advocacy. Drott (5) notes a tendency to celebrate one particular musical subculture for its symbolic resistance to an imagined or constructed mainstream, while Mathew calls out Beethoven scholars of the past for their unexamined assumption that "resistance is the only authentic aesthetic and political stance," which has led many to dismiss compositions by Beethoven and others that serve the regime in power as "inartistic" (*Political Beethoven*, 6). For a study of power and politics that dares to draft musical details and musical conventions as evidence, see Olivia Bloechl, *Opera and the Political Imaginary in Old Regime France* (Chicago: University of Chicago

Press, 2018). While drafting this chapter, I also had the good fortune to read several chapters of Estelle Joubert's *German Opera and the Politics of Sensation, 1750–1815* (Cambridge University Press, 2019), which posits a constellation of critical discourse about opera, aesthetic thought, and political power that both coincides with and has influenced my own approach.

18. As Emanuele Senici has pointed out, we need also to consider the possibility that artworks can function politically even when they depict or imagine worlds that are deliberately beyond, or out of step with, the everyday routines and realities that surround their spectators; "'An Atrocious Indifference': Rossini's Operas and the Politics of Musical Representation in Early-Nineteenth-Century Italy," *Journal of Modern Italian Studies* 17/4 (2012): 414–26.

19. The notion of the Risorgimento as the product of a "spiritual élite" or "directive class" (rather than an economic class) originates with Benedetto Croce's work on the period, especially his *Storia del regno di Napoli* (Bari, 1925). For recent discussions of the various factions in play during the Risorgimento and the shifting power relations among them, see Lucy Riall, *The Italian Risorgimento: State, Society, and National Unification* (London: Routledge, 1994); Denis Mack Smith, *Modern Italy: A Political History* (Ann Arbor: University of Michigan Press, 1959); and his *Mazzini* (New Haven: Yale University Press, 1994); Adrian Lyttelton, "The Middle Classes in Liberal Italy," in John A. Davis and Paul Ginsborg, eds., *Society and Politics in the Risorgimento: Essays in Honour of Denis Mack Smith* (Cambridge: Cambridge University Press, 1991), 217–50; and Lyttelton, "The National Question in Italy," in Mikulas Teich and Roy Porter, eds., *The National Question in Europe in Historical Context* (Cambridge: Cambridge University Press, 1993), 63–105.

20. This new, more positive assessment—replacing the negative view formulated most influentially by Antonio Gramsci—is put forth by Alberto Mario Banti and Paul Ginsborg, eds., *Storia d'Italia*, Annali 22: "Il Risorgimento" (Turin: Einaudi, 2007), especially in the editors' introduction, "Per una nuova storia del Risorgimento," xxviii–xxxiv. For thoughtful overviews, see Maurizio Isabella, "Rethinking Italy's Nation-Building 150 Years Afterwards: The New Risorgimento Historiography," *Past and Present* 217 (2012): 247–68; Paul Ginsborg, *Salviamo l'Italia* (Turin: Einaudi, 2010); and John A. Davis, "Rethinking the Risorgimento?," in Norma Bouchard, ed., *Risorgimento in Modern Italian Culture: Revisiting the Nineteenth-Century Past in History, Narrative and Cinema* (Cranbury, NJ: Rosemont, 2005), 27–55. Silvana Patriarca has suggested that "the Risorgimento" would better be broken down into several constituent movements and patterns of thought; see her "Indolence and Regeneration: Tropes and Tensions of Risorgimento Patriotism," *American Historical Review* 110 (2005): 380–408.

21. In 1882 Antonio Ghislanzoni looked back thus on the 1840s in Milan: "Men who thought of Italy, who trembled under the yoke of foreign domination, who hated Austria, were few and far between. The majority did not realize that such a thing as Italy existed. Even so, some among them agitated secretly, some wrote, some took on the dangerous task of disseminating the writings of Mazzini. Back then it was risky to talk politics, even with one's closest friends"; Ghislanzoni, "Storia di

Milano di 1836 al 1848," in his *In chiave del baritono* (Milan: Brigola, 1882), 159–60. For a longer discussion of this passage and the attitudes it describes, see chapter 6.

22. Alberto Banti, *La nazione del Risorgimento: Parentela, santità e onore alle origini dell'Italia unità* (Turin: Einaudi, 2000); and Paul Ginsborg, "Romanticismo e risorgimento: L'Io, l'amore, e la nazione," in Banti and Ginsborg, "Il Risorgimento," 20, 5–67, especially 38–48.

23. Carlotta Sorba, *Il melodramma della nazione: Politica e sentimenti nell'età del Risorgimento* (Rome: Laterza, 2015); and her "Ernani Hats: Italian Opera as a Repertoire of Political Symbols during the Risorgimento," in Jane Fulcher, ed., *Oxford Handbook of the New Cultural History of Music* (Oxford: Oxford University Press, 2011), 428–51.

24. On the mythification of Verdi as national bard around the time of Unification, see Francesca Vella, "Verdi and Politics (c.1859–1861)," *Studi Verdiani* 14 (2014): 79–120; Michael Sawall, "'Viva V.E.R.D.I.': Origine e ricezione di un simbolo nazionale nell'anno 1859," in Fabrizio Della Seta, Roberta Montemorra Marvin, and Marco Marica, eds., *Verdi 2001: Atti del convegno internazionale, Parma, New York, New Haven, 24 gennaio–1 febbraio 2001* (Florence: Olschki, 2003), 123–31; and Birgit Pauls, *Giuseppe Verdi und das Risorgimento: Ein politischer Mythos im Prozess der Nationenbildung* (Berlin: Akademie Verlag, 1996). Laura Basini has written about the cultivation of this image across the fin-de-siècle and early twentieth century in her "Cults of Sacred Memory: Parma and the Verdi Centennial Celebrations of 1913," *Cambridge Opera Journal* 13/2 (2001): 141–61; and her "Verdi and Revivalism in Post-Unification Italy," *19th-Century Music* (2004): 133–59.

25. See Mary Ann Smart, "Magical Thinking: Reason and Emotion in Some Recent Literature on Verdi and Politics," *Journal of Modern Italian Studies* 17/4 (2012): 437–47.

26. Letter from Gaetano Donizetti to his father, Andrea, 15 February 1831; in Guido Zavadini, *Donizetti: Vita—Musiche—Epistolario* (Bergamo: Istituto italiano d'arte grafiche, 1948), Z. 64, 281.

27. The passage reads in full:

> Honor to these heroes! Honor to all Italy, which is now truly great! The hour of her liberation has arrived; be sure of that. The people want it: and when the people want it, there is no absolute power that can resist. . . . You talk to me about music! What has got into you? Do you think that I want to bother myself now with notes, with sounds? There cannot be any music welcome to Italian ears in 1848 except the music of the cannon! I would not write a note for all the money in the world: I would feel immense guilt at using up music-paper, which is so good for making shells.

Letter of 21 April 1848; in Franco Abbiati, *Giuseppe Verdi*, 4 vols. (Milan, 1958), 1: 745.

28. In a letter to Mameli, Mazzini wrote of his hope that the "Inno popolare" (also known by its incipit, "Suona la tromba") would become "'la Marseillaise' of Italy, a hymn that—to use Verdi's phrase—will make the people forget both the poet and the composer"; letter of 6 June 1848, published in Abbiati, *Giuseppe Verdi*,

1: 758. A few copies of the "Inno" were printed late in 1848, but the hymn was not published officially until 1865. See Roberta Montemorra Marvin, ed., "Introduction," in *The Works of Giuseppe Verdi*, series 4, vol. 1: *Hymns/Inni* (Chicago: University of Chicago Press, 2007), xi–xii. Mameli also penned the words for the Italian national anthem, "Fratelli d'Italia."

29. Beginning in 1859, Verdi served as deputy to the Assembly of Parma Provinces and at the invitation of Cavour as a deputy to the first Italian parliament in 1861. He declined to stand for a second term in parliament but was named Senator of the Kingdom for Life in 1875; Mary-Jane Philips-Matz, *Verdi: A Biography* (Oxford: Oxford University Press, 1993), 428–39 and 610–11.

30. Paul Robinson takes such an approach to Rossini's treatment of Beaumarchais; see his *Opera and Ideas: From Mozart to Strauss* (Ithaca: Cornell University Press, 1985), especially 16–17. Slavoj Žižek echoes Robinson's approach in his passing dismissal of Rossini's *Barbiere*:

> Rossini took a theatrical piece which was one of the symbols of the French bourgeois revolutionary spirit, and totally de-politicized it, changing it into pure opera buffa. No wonder the golden years of Rossini were 1815 to 1830—the years of reaction, the years in which the European powers tackled the impossible task of the *Ungeschehenmachen*, the undoing, the making-it-not-happen of the previous revolutionary decades. Rossini did not actively hate and fight the new world—he simply composed as if the years 1789–1815 didn't exist.

Žižek, "The Undoing of an Event," in Heiko Feldner, Fabio Vighi, and Slavoj Žižek, eds., *States of Crisis and Post-capitalist Scenarios* (Farnham: Ashgate, 2014), 107–26, here 107.

31. Philip Gossett has argued otherwise; see especially his "'Edizioni distrutte' and the Significance of Operatic Choruses during the Risorgimento," in Victoria Johnson, Jane F. Fulcher, and Thomas Ertman, eds., *Opera and Society in Italy and France from Monteverdi to Bourdieu* (Cambridge: Cambridge University Press, 2007): 181–242.

32. Bruno Latour, "Why Has Critique Run out of Steam?: From Matters of Fact to Matters of Concern," *Critical Inquiry* 30/2 (2004): 225–48. On the distinction between the robust networks of actor-network theory and thinner networks that function more like railways or gas pipelines, see Benjamin Piekut, "Actor-Networks in Music History: Clarifications and Critiques," *Twentieth-Century Music* 11/2 (2014): 191–215. The scholar who has come closest to tracing social networks and engagement around nineteenth-century Italian opera in a way that Latour might recognize (although without ever invoking Latour) is Anselm Gerhard; see his "'Cortigiani, vil razza bramata!' Reti aristocratiche e fervori risorgimentale nella biografia del giovane Verdi," *Acta musicologica* 84/1 (2012): 37–63, and 84/2: 199–223.

33. Rita Felski notes that reading texts in relation to historical context is to line them up again as "a list of attributes—economic structure, political ideology, cultural mentality—in order to finesse the details of how these attributes are echoed,

modified, or undermined by a specific work of art." She calls this "a remarkably static model of meaning," in which "the macrolevel of sociohistorical context holds the cards, calls the tune, and specifies the rules of the game"; Felski, "Context Stinks," *New Literary History* 42/4 (2011): 573–91, 577–78; see also her *The Limits of Critique* (Chicago: University of Chicago Press, 2015).

34. Jeremy Commons, *"Maria Stuarda* and the Neapolitan Censorship," *Donizetti Society Journal* 3 (1977): 151–67; Andreas Giger, "Social Control and the Censorship of Verdi's Operas in Rome, 1844–59," *Cambridge Opera Journal* 1/3 (1999): 233–66.

35. Franco Moretti, "Conjectures on World Literature," *New Left Review* 1 (2000): 54–68; reprinted in *Distant Reading* (London: Verso, 2013); Stephen Best and Sharon Marcus, "Surface Reading: An Introduction," *Representations* 108 (2009): 1–21; Heather Love, "Close Reading and Thin Description," *Public Culture* 35/3 (2015): 410–43. See also Marjorie Levinson, "What Is the New Formalism?," *PMLA* 122/2 (2007): 558–69; and Elaine Freedgood and Cannon Schmitt, "Denotatively, Technically, Literally," *Representations* 125 (2014): 1–14.

36. Wye J. Allanbrook, "Theorizing the Comic Surface," in Andreas Giger and Thomas J. Mathiessen, eds., *Music in the Mirror: Reflections on the History of Music Theory and Literature for the Twenty-First Century* (Lincoln: University of Nebraska Press, 2002), 195–216.

37. For influential readings based on the topoi of nineteenth-century opera, without direct reference to Allanbrook, see Melina Esse, "Rossini's Noisy Bodies," *Cambridge Opera Journal* 21/1 (2009): 27–64; and her "Speaking and Sighing: Bellini's Poetics of Restraint," *Current Musicology* 87 (2009): 7–45.

38. Benjamin Walton has written sensitively about Stendhal's idiosyncratic taste and his critical language; see his *Rossini in Restoration Paris: The Sound of Modern Life* (Cambridge: Cambridge University Press, 2007). Emanuele Senici has read the criticism of the time to show that the musical techniques of Rossini's operas (repetition, ornament, indifference to text and dramatic affect, noisiness) may have satisfied specific social needs for segments of the population of post-Napoleonic Italy without directly engaging with the political situation nor offering infusions of national pride or morale-building; see Senici, "Delirious Hopes: Napoleonic Milan and the Rise of Modern Italian Operatic Criticism," *Cambridge Opera Journal* 27/2 (2015): 97–127; "Rossinian Repetitions," in Nicholas Mathew and Benjamin Walton, eds., *The Invention of Beethoven and Rossini: Historiography, Analysis, Criticism* (Cambridge: Cambridge University Press, 2013), 236–62; and his "Introduction: Rossini's Operatic Operas," in Senici, ed., *Cambridge Companion to Rossini* (Cambridge: Cambridge University Press, 2004), 1–8.

39. This was recognized long ago by Gary Tomlinson, who however viewed romanticism mostly as a concatenation of formal features and did not explore its impact on political thought; "Italian Romanticism and Italian Opera: An Essay in Their Affinities," *19th-Century Music* 10/1 (1986): 43–60, here 46–47.

40. Carl Schmitt, *Political Romanticism* [1925], trans. Guy Oakes (Cambridge: MIT Press, 1986). Paul Ginsborg, "European Romanticism and the Risorgimento,"

and Adrian Lyttelton, "The Hero and the People," both in Patriarca and Riall, *Risorgimento Revisited,* 18–36 and 37–55. On Schmitt, see also Victoria Kahn, "Hamlet or Hecuba: Carl Schmitt's Decision," *Representations* 83 (2003): 67–73. For a recent entry in the long-running debate about whether Italy even experienced a romantic movement, see Joseph Luzzi, "Did Italian Romanticism Exist?," *Comparative Literature* 56/2 (2004): 168–91.

41. www.youtube.com/watch?v = EjLQgQEXrcE; accessed 18 October 2016.

42. The two papers discussed here are Marina Romani, "Verdi's Forgetful Consumers: Lega Nord's 'Va pensiero'," and Marcelo Campos Hazan, "*Nabucco*'s Band." The band arrangement of "Va pensiero" is an item from a catalogue of Prussian marches (*Armeemarche-sammlung*) entitled "Geschwindmarsch," arranged by Carl Mangener, based in turn on Tutsch's arrangement.

CHAPTER 2. ACCIDENTAL AFFINITIES: GIOACHINO ROSSINI AND SALVATORE VIGANÒ

1. De Staël, "Sulla maniera e l'utilità delle traduzione"; excerpt reprinted in Michele dell'Acquila, ed., *Primo romanticismo italiano: Testi di poetica e critica* (Bari, 1976), 139.

2. Schmitt, *Political Romanticism.* For critiques of Schmitt's theory, see Victoria Kahn, "Hamlet or Hecuba: Carl Schmitt's Decision," *Representations* 83/1 (2003): 67–96; Ginsborg, "European Romanticism and the Italian Risorgimento," 18–36.

3. Adrian Lyttelton, "The Hero and the People," 37–55, in Patriarca and Riall, *Risorgimento Revisited,* here 37.

4. This description of Viganò's *Psammi* is adapted from a review in the *Corriere delle dame,* 16 August 1817.

5. On the Beethoven collaboration, see Constantin Floros, *Beethovens Eroica und Prometheus-Musik: Sujet-Studien* (Wilhelmshaven: Heinrichshofen, 1978).

6. Ermes Visconti, "Idee elementarii sulla poesia Romantica," Art. 6: "Sul classicismo nella pittura e scultura, e nei balli pantomimici," first published in *Il conciliatore,* nos. 23 through 28 (19 November to 6 December 1818); reprinted in Carlo Calcaterra, ed., *I manifesti Romantici del 1816, e gli scritti principali del "Conciliatore" sul Romanticismo* (Turin: Unione Tipografico Editrice Torinese, 1951), 349–91. The entire run of *Il conciliatore* (September 1818 to October 1819) has been reprinted as Vittore Branca, ed., *Il conciliatore: Foglio scientifico-letterario,* 2 vols. (Florence: Le Monnier, 1948–54).

7. Visconti, "Idee elementarii," in Calcaterra, *I manifesti Romantici,* 385n; emphasis mine. Needless to say, the essay does not include a corresponding section on the aesthetic attributes of opera.

8. Visconti, "Idee elementarii," 59.

9. "Dialogo sulle unità drammatiche di luogo e di tempo," *Il conciliatore,* nos. 42–43 (24 and 28 January 1819); reprinted in Calcaterra, *I manifesti Romantici,* 392–409; and also www.classicitaliani.it/ottocent/visconti_unità_drammatiche.

htm; accessed 11 December 2014. The names of all four interlocutors in this fictional dialogue correspond with real people; but the words they utter are all Visconti's. Alberto Rizzuti makes the point that Paisiello is chosen to represent an older generation, and aptly terms the roles played by Paisiello and Viganò as *"pertichini"*; Rizzuti, "Viganò's 'Giovanna d'Arco' and Manzoni's 'March 1821' in the Storm of 1821 Italy," *Music and Letters* 86/2 (2005): 186–201.

10. On Viganò's *Prometeo* and its critical reception in Milan, see Mary Ann Smart, "Beethoven Dances: Prometheus and His Creatures in Vienna and Milan," in Nicholas Mathew and Benjamin Walton, eds., *The Invention of Beethoven and Rossini: Historiography, Analysis, Criticism* (Cambridge: Cambridge University Press, 2013), 210–35.

11. The ephemerality of sources is a major obstacle to understanding Viganò's creative achievement or the reasons for his success. Libretti for a handful of the Milanese ballets survive, as do scores for three of them, but information about the actual choreography and staging is almost nonexistent. Some sense of the style of movement and scenic effects can be gleaned from reviews, and a little more is recorded by the theater administrator and opera lover Carlo Ritorni in his *Commentarii della vita e delle opere coreodrammatiche di Salvatore Viganò* (Milan: Guglielmini e Redaelli, 1838). However, much of Ritorni's book consists of retellings of the plots (sometimes several different synopses for a single ballet) and enthusiastic but uninformative rhapsodies about Viganò's genius. He rarely says anything about specific gestures or styles of movement, and in fact confesses early in the book that he himself has not seen many of the ballets, and has instead relied on secondhand accounts.

12. Carpani, *Le Rossiniane* (Lettera 1), 36.

13. Reviews of *Il noce di Benevento* and *L'Alunno della giumenta*, in *Giornale italiano*, 12 and 13 May 1812; and 14 June 1812.

14. A[rthur] Michel Saint-Léon, *La sténochorégraphie, ou l'art d'écrire promptement la Danse, avec portraits et biographies des plus célèbres maîtres de ballets anciens et modernes* (Paris: Chez l'auteur, rue Laval 21 et chez Brandus, 1852), 20. Saint-Léon goes on to say that Viganò had little patience for the French style of giving precedence to complex steps for their own sake. Apparently he hated the pas de deux and other "concerted" pieces because the dancers didn't take part in the action, and such numbers thus cooled and slowed down the entire drama. Even so, Viganò made occasional concessions to dancers along these lines. Saint-Léon was a principal dancer at the Paris Opéra, *maître de ballet,* and professor of dance.

15. Volumes of selected numbers (arranged for solo piano) were published for *Prometeo* (1813), *Otello* (1818), *La vestale* (1819), *La spada di Kenneth* (1818), *Bianca, e sia il perdono per sorpresa* (1819), *Mirra, ossia, la vendetta di Venere* (1820), and *Alessandro nell'Indie* (1820), all published by Ricordi.

16. *La creduta vedova, o sia la sposa costante* was designated as a *farsetta* for five characters, first performed at Rome's Teatro Valle in 1785 when Viganò was eighteen years old.

17. *Allegemeine musikalische Zeitung* 19 (16 July 1817): col. 486; cited in Martin Deasy, "Looking North: Carlos Soliva and the Two Styles South of the Alps," in

Mathew and Walton, *Invention of Beethoven and Rossini,* 139–40. Deasy does not identify the author of this review, which was published anonymously, but it was almost certainly Lichtenthal.

18. For more on Lichtenthal's pro-German agenda and the reactions he provoked, see Smart, "Beethoven Dances," 228.

19. This is implicit in many reviews but was stated explicitly by Ritorni when he summed up the differences between the genres of opera and ballet. The first thing he notes is that the choreographer is in charge of all aspects of the performance, while the composer (*"musicografo"*) is slave to the poet, to singers, and to the public. See Carlo Ritorni, *Ammaestramenti alla composizione d'ogni poema ed ogni opera appartenente alla musica* (Milan: Luigi Giacomo Pirola, 1841), 120.

20. It is impossible to ascertain who was responsible for the details of this transcription: it could have been Viganò himself, but it might also have been one of his habitual collaborators Lichtenthal or Brambilla. No matter who actually executed the transcription, we know enough about the close control Viganò kept over all aspects of his production to attribute the musical conception of the number to the choreographer himself.

21. See Rossana Dalmonte, "'Une écriture corporelle': La musica e la danza," in Ezio Raimondi, ed., *Il sogno del coreodramma: Salvatore Viganò, poeta muto* (Bologna: Mulino, 1984), 145–240, here 196.

22. *Corriere delle dame,* 4 March 1819.

23. "Musica e parola," *Lo spettatore* 9 (1818): 152–54. The author continues: "If music is to be anything other than empty sound, which expresses no determinate thought, no poetic idea, then we must ask with Fontenelle, 'Sonate, que me veux-tu?'"

24. See, for example, Melina Esse's discussion of Signora Lattanzi's commentary on Rossini in the *Corriere delle dame,* 1816, in "Rossini's Noisy Bodies," *Cambridge Opera Journal* 21 (2009): 27–64, here 32–34.

25. Carpani, "Appendice alla Lettera VII, Sulle differenze e carattere morali degli stili e sul linguaggio musicale" [1824], in *Le Rossiniane;* reprinted in Carlida Steffan, ed., *Rossiniane: Antologia della critica nella prima metà dell'Ottocento* (Pordenone: Edizione Studio Tesi, 1992), 106. "Roscii" refers to the Roman actor Quintus Roscius Gallus (c. 126–62 B.C.E.), who was considered such an adept of communication through gesture that his many imitators became known as Roscii.

26. Steffan, *Rossiniane,* xvii–xxvii; cited in Esse, "Rossini's Noisy Bodies," 34. Esse (38) shows that Carpani flirts with a sensualist aesthetics but ultimately pulls back to integrate neoclassical values of beauty and imitation.

27. James Johnson, *Listening in Paris: A Cultural History* (Berkeley: University of California Press, 1995), 226; Richard Taruskin, *Oxford History of Western Music* (New York: Oxford University Press, 2005), vol. 3: 25–26; Esse, "Rossini's Noisy Bodies," 27–31; Emily Dolan, *The Orchestral Revolution: Haydn and the Technologies of Timbre* (Cambridge: Cambridge University Press, 2013), 234–35.

28. "The music is openly anti-realistic because openly anti-mimetic: its repetitive mechanisms highlight the gap between the stage and the real world, forcefully

negating any realistic dimension to the musical action unfolding on the stage"; Emanuele Senici, "Introduction: Rossini's Operatic Operas," in Senici, ed., *Cambridge Companion to Rossini* (Cambridge: Cambridge University Press, 2004), 1–9, here 4. See also his "'An Atrocious Indifference': Rossini's Operas and the Politics of Musical Representation in Early Nineteenth-Century Italy," *Journal of Modern Italian Studies* 17/4 (2012): 414–26.

29. In the chapter on *L'italiana in Algeri,* for example, Stendhal praises a Venetian woman who refused to let anyone bring a copy of the libretto into her box, and of his own listening practices, writes: "I always rewrite the words of an opera to my own taste. I take the situation the poet has invented, and I require from him beyond that just one word, one only, to identify the emotion." Elsewhere he claims to be reading the libretto of *La gazza ladra* for the first time as he drafts his chapter, and only because it would be ridiculous to print a line of printed music at the bottom of the page to indicate a specific aria. Stendhal, *Vie de Rossini*, in *Oeuvres complètes de Stendhal* (Paris: Michel Lévy, frères, 1854), 56 and 221.

30. Stendhal, *Vie de Rossini,* 54. This is one of Stendhal's many disgruntled remarks about the inadequate performance of Rossini's operas in Paris and their resulting reception by audiences at the Théâtre-Italien.

31. For a brilliant discussion of Stendhal's recourse to enthusiasm and superlatives in his writing about Rossini, see Benjamin Walton, "1824. Deciphering Hyperbole: Stendhal's *Vie de Rossini*," in his *Rossini in Restoration Paris: The Sound of Modern Life* (Cambridge: Cambridge University Press, 2007), 24–67.

32. Stendhal, *Vie de Rossini,* 131–32. Stendhal here uses the word *"arrière-boutique,"* which was popularized in the 1830s by Balzac and Musset as a site of vulgar, uncultivated speech and behavior.

33. The preface to Caigniez's play explains the plot's connection to real-life events; discussed in Emilio Sala, "De *La pie voleuse* a *La gazza ladra,*" in Sala, ed., *I libretti di Rossini,* vol. 2: *La gazza ladra* (Pesaro: Fondazione Rossini, 1995), 9–51, here 15.

34. On the competition, see Chapter 1 and the introduction to Alberto Zedda's critical edition of *La gazza ladra* (Pesaro: Fondazione Roissini, 1979).

35. Stendhal, *Vie de Rossini,* 224.

36. Stendhal, *Vie de Rossini,* 136. See Esse, "Rossini's Noisy Bodies," 35–38, for a nuanced analysis of Stendhal's somewhat inconsistent views on musical expression and the dynamics of listening.

37. On the history and values of *opera semiseria,* see Stefano Castelvecchi, *Sentimental Opera: Questions of Genre in an Age of Bourgeois Opera* (Cambridge: Cambridge University Press, 2013); and Emanuele Senici, *Landscape and Gender in Italian Opera: The Alpine Virgin from Bellini to Puccini* (Cambridge: Cambridge University Press, 2005).

38. The passage continues:

> For example, the strettas [of the trio, duet, and quintet in the second act] ... strike me as anything but dramatic, even though the scenic climaxes [*punti di scena*] and the

emotions that animate the souls of the characters are extremely dramatic. If someone were to object that moving and vivacious gestures were necessary in order to depict agitation, I would answer that there is a great difference between passionate vivacity and comic vivacity.

Gazzetta di Milano 153 (2 June 1817): 672; cited in Chiara Marin, "La presenza delle arti figurative e sceniche nella stampa periodica lombardo-veneta (1800–1848)," doctoral thesis, Università di Padova, 2006, 429.

39. Ritorni, *Commentarii della vita e delle opere coreodrammatiche di Salvatore Viganò*, 120n.

40. Ritorni, *Commentari*, 120n.

41. Stendhal, *Vie de Rossini*, 222.

42. Stendhal, *Vie de Rossini*, 223.

43. On the tempi at the Théâtre-Italien, see Stendhal, *Vie de Rossini*, 225.

44. Stendhal, *Vie de Rossini*, 206. See also the related passages on *L'italiana in Algeri* ("Rossini, terrified of boring his audience, made it exceedingly short," 59) and *Barbiere* ("We see here that with an idea, no matter how agreeable it may be, Rossini fears boring the listener," 146).

45. The original title of the libretto that won the competition at La Scala was *L'Avviso ai giudici* (Advice for the Judges), which suggests that this particular moment may have been a key element of the libretto's structure from the beginning.

46. Writing about the appearance of this waltz theme in the opera's overture, Stendhal explicitly connected the snare drum with realism: "The introduction of the snare drum as a principal sonority lends the overture a reality, if I dare to express it thus, whose sensation is unlike what I have experienced in any other music"; *Vie de Rossini*, 204.

47. He dispenses with the Act 2 aria in a single sentence of praise but treats the character in general as a symptom of all that is wrong with Italian society. ("The Podestà's aria and especially the chorus that concludes it would have made the reputation of a composer far less distinguished than Rossini"; Stendhal, *Vie de Rossini*, 218.)

48. *"Rossini a été peintre fidèle dans tout le role du Podestà"*; Stendhal, *Vie de Rossini*, 214.

49. Stendhal, *Vie de Rossini*, 213.

50. "Dialogo sulle unità drammatiche del luogo e del tempo," *Il conciliatore* (1819), www.classicitaliani.it/ottocent/visconti_unità_drammatiche.htm; accessed 22 February 2015.

51. Between 1811 and 1822 Leoni (1776–1858) published translations of seven Shakespeare plays. The collected edition published by the Società tipografica of Verona in 1822 bears a dedication to King Ferdinand I of the Two Sicilies.

52. Michele Leoni, "Opinioni intorno alla musica di Gioacchino Rossini di Pesaro," *Antologia* 10 (October 1821): 40–58; cited in Claudio Toscani, "Di tragedia in bacchanale: *La gazza ladra* e l'astrazione del realismo patetico," program book for *La gazza ladra*, Teatro la Fenice (1998), 71–79, here 78.

53. Barbieri's translations were made from the French rather than the original English and were published by the Milan firm Vincenzo Ferrario. The first volumes to appear were *Kenilworth* (1821, trans. Barbieri), *Waverly* (1822, trans. Virginio Soncini), *The Abbott* (1823, trans. Barbieri), and *The Antiquary* (1823–24, trans. Pietro Borsieri) followed by several more volumes translated by Barbieri, including *The Bride of Lammermoor*. Historian Raffaele Barbiera was convinced that Barbieri was sent to France to spy on Italian exiles and expatriates there (including Cristina Belgioioso), submitting his reports under the names "Pietro Dolce" and "Pietro Svegliati." Barbieri gave his true identity away, Barbiera claims, by throwing into his reports quotations from classical tragedies that he himself had translated and by using occasional Modenese dialect spellings such as *"vomo"* for *"uomo."* Barbiera, writing at the pinnacle of pro-Risorgimento feeling around 1905, tends to paint matters in black and white, and his assessment of Barbieri is no exception: an account by the director of police, Carlogiusto Torresani, he says, offers a profile of "one of the many damned souls of that time, emerging from one political intrigue only to immediately throw himself into another, and butting up against systems that had changed, and living without a moral compass and without dignity." Barbiera, *Passione del Risorgimento: Nuove pagine sulla Principessa Belgiojoso e il suo tempo con documenti inediti e illustrazioni* (Milan: Treves, 1903), 75ff. The accusation is supported by John Rosselli, *The Opera Industry in Italy from Cimarosa to Verdi* (Cambridge: Cambridge University Press, 1984), 145, who draws on Barbiera and on Alessandro Luzio, "Della Massoneria sotto il Regno italico," *Archivio storico Lombardo* 44 (1917): 241–52.

54. [Barbieri], *Rossini e la musica, ossia Amena biografia musicale: Almanacco per l'anno 1827* (Milan: Stella, 1827), 43. In 1827 *I teatri* attributed the anonymous pamphlet to Giovanni Gherardini (librettist for *La gazza ladra),* including it in a list of his works (*I teatri,* Tome 1 Parte 1 [1827], 80, Fascicolo 3). However, Luigi de Benedetto has convincingly shown that the author must be Barbieri, who plants certain clues to his identity (including his own initials) in the preface to the essay. De Benedetto hypothesizes that as editor of *I teatri,* Barbieri wanted to point attention away from himself and perhaps damage Gherardini with the attribution; de Benedetto, *Arrigo Beyle Milanese* (Florence: Sansoni, 1942), 62–64. Similar analogies between novelistic description and Rossini's orchestral preludes were drawn by Carlo Varese and Stendhal; on attitudes to musical description in Rossini, see Edward Jacobson, "Rossini: Narrate or Describe?," paper delivered at the Second Transnational Opera Studies Conference, Bern, July 2017.

55. [Barbieri], *Rossini e la musica,* 54n.

56. "As the arts have flowered and been enriched, song and pantomime, which were equal accessories of drama in the ancient theater, have become separate dramas unto themselves" (228); Ritorni, *Ammaestramenti alla composizione d'ogni poema e d'ogni opera appartenente alla musica* (Milan: Pirola, 1841), 228.

57. Giuditta Pasta is said to have studied gesture with Viganò's prima ballerina Antonia Pallerini; see Paolo Russo, "Giuditta Pasta, cantante pantomimica," *Musica e storia* 10 (2002): 497–534; and Susan Rutherford, "La cantante delle passioni:

Giuditta Pasta and the Idea of Operatic Performance," *Cambridge Opera Journal* 19/2 (2007): 107–38.

58. *"Come una Pallerini, ma senza coreografo che l'ammaestrasse, esprimeva la pantomima della cecità, da cui delirando credeva essere stata presa, secondando tutto l'andamento dell'istrumentale espressione"*; Ritorni, *Ammaestramenti*, 123.

59. The letter probably first appeared in an anonymous pamphlet published in Florence in 1843, entitled *Sull'estetica di Vincenzo Bellini-Notizie communicate da lui stesso al Gallo*. It was reprinted the same year in the Palermo newspaper *L'Occhio* and several other Italian newspapers before being picked up in Filippo Cicconetti's 1859 Bellini biography. The letter has been reprinted in most Bellini biographies since. It appears in Luisa Cambi's collection of the composer's letters (*Epistolario* [Milan: Mondadori, 1943], 181–82), with a footnote questioning its authenticity, but is not included in the most recent edition of the correspondence, Carmelo Neri's *Caro Bellini . . . Lettere edite ed inedite a Vincenzo Bellini* (Catania: Prova d'autore, 2001).

60. For an imaginative and affirmative view of how romanticism may have contributed to political activism in Italy, see Ginsborg, "Romanticismo e Risorgimento," 5–67, especially 38–48. Specifically, Ginsborg perceives romanticism as contributing to a culture in which young men were willing to devote their lives to a cause that at times seemed hopeless, and even to die for their beliefs.

CHAPTER 3. ELIZABETH I, MARY STUART, AND THE LIMITS OF ALLEGORY

1. The original source for such portrayals of Elizabeth I was probably a French publication of 1678/1680 called *The Secret History* in which women (in spurious first-person confessions) tell their love-secrets to confidants. This was widely reprinted over the next century and formed the basis for John Banks's 1681 she-tragedy *The Unhappy Favourite, or the Earl of Essex*, which in turn influenced James Ralph's *The Earl of Essex* (1731), Henry Jones's *The Earl of Essex, A Tragedy* (1753), and Henry Brooks's *Earl of Essex* (1761). See Michael Dobson and Nicola J. Watson, *England's Elizabeth: An Afterlife in Fame and Fantasy* (Oxford: Oxford University Press, 2002).

2. Rossini and Tottola's *La donna del lago* (1819) predated the 1821 publication of Scott's poem in Italian translation; Tottola adapted his libretto instead from a French translation. The first Italian adaptation of a novel by Scott was Giovanni Galzerani's 1823 ballet *Il castello di Kenilworth* in Turin in 1823; the first opera was Donizetti's *Elisabetta al castello di Kenilworth* (1829). On dramatic and operatic adaptations of Scott, see Henry Adalbert White, *Sir Walter Scott's Operas on the Stage* (New Haven: Yale University Press, 1927); Jerome Mitchell, *The Walter Scott Operas* (Tuscaloosa: University of Alabama Press, 1977); and Ann Rigney, *The Afterlives of Walter Scott: Memory on the Move* (Oxford: Oxford University Press, 2012).

3. Franco Moretti, "Conjectures on World Literature," *New Left Review* 1 (2000): 54–68; reprinted in *Distant Reading* (London: Verso, 2013).

4. On Donizetti's experience in Naples, see Paologiovanni Maione and Francesca Seller, *I reali teatri di Napoli nella prima metà dell'Ottocento: Studi su Domenico Barbaja* (Bellona: Santabarbara, 1994); and William Ashbrook, *Donizetti and His Operas* (Cambridge: Cambridge University Press, 1983).

5. Rosselli, "Materiali per la storia socio-economica del San Carlo nell'Ottocento," in Lorenzo Bianconi and R. Bossa, eds., *Musica e cultura a Napoli dal XV al XIX secolo* (Florence: Olschki, 1983), 369–79, here 370.

6. Martha Feldman, borrowing a term from Clifford Geertz, has called eighteenth-century Naples a "theater state," in which the opera house and the royal palace were part of the same physical structure and functioned as mirrors of each other, and the power of the Bourbon monarchy was cemented by pageantry both on and off the stage; see her *Opera and Sovereignty: Transforming Myths in Eighteenth-Century Italy* (Chicago: University of Chicago Press, 2007), 188–89.

7. John A. Davis, "Opera and Absolutism in Restoration Italy," *Journal of Interdisciplinary History* 36/4 (2006): 569–94, here 573–76.

8. Harold Acton, *The Bourbons of Naples, 1734–1825* (London: Methuen, 1956), 642.

9. *Giornale del Regno delle Due Sicilie,* 7 December 1815.

10. *Giornale del Regno delle Due Sicilie,* 12 September 1816.

11. Giovanni Simone Mayr and Urbano Lampredi, *Il sogno di Partenope* (Naples: Flautina, 1817).

12. *Cantata pel faustissimo parto del S.M. la regina delle Due Sicilie* (libretto by Leopoldo Tarantini) (Naples: Flautina, 1838). Other occasional cantatas by Donizetti include *Preghiera per un popolo* (July 1837) and *Cristoforo Colombo, o la scoperta d'America* (April 1837). The same period saw gala performances of *L'Assedio di Calais* (for the queen mother in July 1837) and *Gemma di Vergy* without its tragic finale (for the birthday of Queen Maria Teresa of Austria, 31 July 1839). Many of these performances are discussed in Maione and Seller, *I reali teatri di Napoli.*

13. Lampredi was a well-known classicist and conservative, editor (with Ludovico Valeriani) of *Poeti del primo secolo della lingua italiana* (Florence, 1816), editor of the *Giornale constituzionale del Regno delle Due Sicilie* from 1813 to 1815, and the butt of Foscolo's epigrammatic poem "Contro Urbano Lampredi." On his conservatism, see Cesare Malpiga, "[Necrologia] Urbano Lampredi," *Giornale agrario lombardo-veneto* 2/9, fasc. 3–4 (April 1838): 254–55.

14. As the stage direction for the cantata's first scene specifies, *"in lontananza il Tempio delle Muse, o sia il Teatro di San Carlo"* (7). In Scene 2 of the first act, in the midst of an angry monologue by the evil spirit Poliflegonte, a personification of the Campi Flegrei who will burn the temple cum theater, a stage direction instructs, "We see the theater, and hear a few chords taken from the ballet *'La virtù premiata'"* (10).

15. In Naples Colbran had already appeared in *Elisabetta, regina d'Inghilterra* (Teatro San Carlo, 4 October 1815), *La gazzetta* (Teatro Fiorentini, 26 September

1816), and *Otello* (Teatro Fondo, 4 December 1816). Rossini's own version of the Cinderella story was to be unveiled at the San Carlo just a week after the gala, on 25 January 1817, with Colbran in the title role.

16. Stendhal, *Rome, Naples et Florence* [1826], ed. Pierre Brunel (Paris: Gallimard, 1987), 314 (13 February 1817) and 319 (23 February 1817). Stendhal arrived in Naples about a month after this performance and altered the date of the gala in the pseudodiary of his 1817 Italian journey to make it seem as if he had been in attendance. A few weeks later he wrote about a performance of *La virtù premiata* at a benefit for the choreographer Louis Duport in which the applause, led, as was the convention, by the king, went on for forty-five minutes.

17. Stendhal, *Rome, Naples et Florence*, 319.

18. Portraits by the eighteenth-century court painters Francesco Liani (c.1770) and Francesco Saverio Candido (c.1785) echo this style, all including the scepter and the crown set upon a cushion. On the evolution of Bourbon iconography, see Giulio Brevetti, "Tra-Volti dalla Ristaurazione: La ritrattistica dei Borbone delle Due Sicilie da Ferdinando I a Francesco II," *Temi di critica letteratura artistica* 8 (2010), www.unipa.it/tecla/rivista/8_rivista_brevetti.php; accessed 22 July 2014. My argument about the modernization of the monarchy in this section is indebted to John Davis, "Opera and Absolutism in Restoration Italy" (see n7).

19. In royal portraits painted in 1818–19, Vincenzo Camuccini reproduces almost exactly the same constellation of signifiers, and Jacques Berger copies the same costume and pose but replaces the window with a theatrical curtain and a table that looks like a stage prop.

20. This reading of the props comes from Daniela Tarabra, *European Art of the Eighteenth Century* (Los Angeles: Getty Publications, 2008), 203.

21. The discussion of allegory and romantic painting here is indebted to Paul de Man, "The Rhetoric of Temporality," in *Blindness and Insight: Essays in the Rhetoric of Contemporary Criticism*, 2nd ed. (Minneapolis: University of Minnesota Press, 1983), 208.

22. Barbara Johnson, *The Wake of Deconstruction* (Oxford: Blackwell, 1994), 54.

23. Cited in Daniel Fischlin, "Political Allegory, Absolutist Ideology, and the 'Rainbow Portrait' of Queen Elizabeth I," *Renaissance Quarterly* 50 (1997): 150–206, here 180. Elizabeth's self-characterization, from a speech reportedly made at Tilbury at the time of the Armada in 1588, is also discussed by Louis A. Montrose, *The Subject of Elizabeth: Authority, Gender, and Representation* (Chicago: University of Chicago Press, 2006), 148–52. Montrose has suggested that while Elizabeth's femininity always needed to be controlled and compensated for, her famous virginity became a way to transform the problem of her gender into the source of her power, as well as to identify her as a personification of the inviolable island nation; Montrose, *Subject of Elizabeth*, cited in Fischlin, "Political Allegory," 180.

24. Ernst Kantorowicz, *The King's Two Bodies: A Study in Medieval Political Theology* (Princeton: Princeton University Press, 1957). For a recent reevaluation of Kantorowicz, see *Representations* 106 (Spring 2009), special issue, "Fifty Years after the King's Two Bodies."

25. Marco Spada has cut through a thicket of implausible claims about Rossini's literary source for his opera, to show beyond doubt that *Elisabetta* was based on Carlo Federici's play *Il paggio di Leicester*, which was in the repertory at Naples's Teatro Fondo from 1813 through 1815; Spada, "*Elisabetta regina d'Inghilterra* di Giaocchino Rossini: Fonte letterarie e autoimprestito musicale," *Nuova rivista musicologica italiana* 24/2 (1990): 147–82, here 149 and 152. On Federici, see Alexander Weatherson, "Queen of Dissent: Mary Stuart and the Opera in Her Honour by Carlo Coccia," program note for Teatro Donizetti, Bergamo, www.donizettisociety .com/Articles/articlemarystuart.htm; accessed 4 June 2014.

26. The full stage direction reads:

The sentries on the towers give out the signal with their trumpets, announcing that they have seen the royal cortège approaching. A cannon shot is heard from the fortress. Several of Leicester's guards enter and stand in formation [*vanno a formare doppia ala*] on the path where the queen will enter. All the servants and ladies in waiting in festive attire gather on the bridge, and brimming with pleasure, they take turns exclaiming: *Eccolà*.

Andrea Leone Tottola, *Il castello di Kenilworth* (Naples: Flautina, 1829), 11.

27. In placing Elizabeth in the midst of a love triangle and countering her with a more conventionally feminine rival, Rossini and Donizetti (and their librettists) participated in a strategy of softening and feminizing the queen that had been going strong since early in the eighteenth century. As Michael Dobson and Nicola J. Watson have put it, "Eighteenth-century anxieties about producing Elizabeth as both an eligibly grief-stricken heroine of sensibility and at the same time a more-than-adequate sovereign precipitated a completely new plot-structure." These depictions "rescu[e] Elizabeth's femininity" by prominently exploring her feminine and romantic qualities and also by association with her more conventionally feminine rivals, who perhaps function affectively as extensions of the queen. Dobson and Watson also note that "writers regularly tried to exonerate Elizabeth by representing her indecision over executing her rival as emotionally driven rather than politically motivated." Dobson and Watson, *England's Elizabeth*, 88 and 103.

28. Martin Deasy has suggested that the queens in these two operas are "equally at ease singing in public or private, and never threatened by others' intrusive gaze," unlike the Elisabetta of Donizetti's *Roberto Devereux* (1838). Donizetti's later Elisabetta, he argues, keeps her private feelings secret in a manner more in tune with "traditional conceptions of sovereignty, which understood royal power as sustained by the monarch's mask-like demeanour... [and believed that] the divinely appointed sovereign was accountable to none but God, and the workings of her mind thus concealed from the gaze of men"; Deasy, "Bare Interiors," *Cambridge Opera Journal* 18/2 (2006): 125–50, here 127–28.

29. The two poets were close contemporaries, who for most of their careers worked together as official librettists for the Neapolitan theaters. Very little is known about Giovanni Schmidt except that he was one of the official poets at the Teatro San Carlo and that he supplied the libretti for three other Rossini operas as

well as for works by Zingarelli and Mercadante. The other Rossini works were *Armida* and *Adelaide di Borgogna* (both 1817) and *Edoardo e Cristina* (1819). Schmidt seems to have been active from just before 1800 until about 1825.

Tottola was active as a librettist from 1796 until his death in 1831; he wrote the libretti for *Ermione, Zelmira,* and *La donna del lago,* as well as for several of Donizetti's early Neapolitan operas. Bruno Cagli calls Tottola Schmidt's superior at the theater. Franca Cella, who contributed the entry on Tottola to the 1980 *Grove,* notes that in the nineteenth century "his name became a byword for librettists' bad taste by reason of his naively framed ideas, his frequent lack of stylistic and dramatic coherence, his hasty rhyming and his careless meter."

The updating of Tottola's entry and the addition of one for Schmidt in the 2001 *Grove* (both by John Black) did not occasion any upward revision of their achievements: Black characterizes Schmidt's libretti as "prolix, pedestrian and cliché-ridden" and Tottola's as "clumsy . . ., monotonous and prolix," concluding that the two together dominated libretto production in Naples in the first third of the century and have received "deservedly bad press." See Cagli, " . . . 'Questa povero poeta esordiente': Piave a Roma, un carteggio con Ferretti, la genesi di *Ernani,"* in Pierluigi Petrobelli, ed., *Ernani ieri ed oggi: Atti del convegno internazionale di studi* (Turin: EDT, 1987), 1–18, here 1; and Cella, "Tottola, Andrea Leone," in *New Grove Dictionary of Music and Musicians,* vol. 19 (London: Macmillan, 1980), 91.

30. For a comparison of these two cabalettas from a slightly different angle, see Mary Ann Smart, "The Queen and the Flirt," *Representations* 104 (2008): 126–36.

31. The dress rehearsal took place on 5 or 6 September 1834, and the opera was prohibited by the censors immediately afterward, the announcement made on 7 September. It was recast as *Buondelmonte* and given only six performances at the San Carlo, the first on 18 October, and achieved a single hearing at La Scala, Milan, in December 1835. See Elizabeth Hudson, "Historical Introduction," in *Maria Stuarda,* critical edition by Anders Wiklund (Milan: Ricordi, 1991); and Annalisa Bini and Jeremy Commons, eds., *Le prime rappresentazioni delle opere di Donizetti nella stampa coeva* (Milan: Skira, 1997), 407–27.

32. On the journalistic neglect of Rossini's *Elisabetta,* see Spada, *"Elisabetta regina d'Inghilterra* di Giaocchino Rossini," 147; and Vincenzo Borghetti, "Notizie storiche," in Rossini, *Elisabetta regina d'Inghilterra* (Pesaro: Fondazione Rossini, 2016), xxv–xlvii. Borghetti suggests that the Neapolitan press regarded Rossini as a newcomer whose innovations were seen as disrupting Neapolitan operatic convention. The *Giornale del Regno delle Due Sicilie* finally published a brief review of *Elisabetta* more than a month after the first performance, on 18 November 1815; Borghetti, "Notizie storiche," xxxiii.

33. Stendhal [Henri Beyle], *Vie de Rossini* (Paris: Michel-Lévy frères, 1854), 126–27. Stendhal's view of absolutism here recalls Mme. de Staël's characterization of Elizabeth I, in *De l'Allemagne* (1813), as "a completely new portrait of the female tyrant," uniting feminine charm, absolute power, and dissimulation. She continues:

The petty concerns of women in general, their vanity, their desire to please, all the qualities imposed on them by their enslavement, finally, contribute to the despotism of Elizabeth; and the dissimulation born of weakness is one of the instruments of absolute power. Without a doubt, all tyrants are liars. One must deceive men in order to rule them; in such a case, they are owed, at the very least, the courtesy of a lie. But what characterizes Elizabeth is the desire to please united with a more despotic desire, and all that is finest in a woman's *amour-propre,* manifested in the most violent acts of sovereign authority.

Mme. de Staël, *De l'Allemagne* (Paris: Firmin, Didot, frères, 1845), 215.

34. See Mary Ann Smart, "The Lost Voice of Rosine Stoltz," *Cambridge Opera Journal* 6/1 (1994): 31–50; and her "Verdi Sings Erminia Frezzolini," *Women and Music* 1 (1997): 33–45.

35. *New Monthly Magazine,* 1 July 1827, 288–91.

36. *Giornale del Regno delle Due Sicilie,* 2 July 1830; in Bini and Commons, *Le prime rappresentazioni,* 208. The *Giornale* registered the same opinion, in similar terms, in an earlier review (18 July 1829); in Bini and Commons, *Le prime rappresentazioni,* 200.

37. *I teatri,* 20 January 1830, and *Il censore universale dei teatri,* 8 August 1829; in Bini and Commons, *Le prime rappresentazioni,* 207–8.

38. *Il caffè del Molo,* 3 July 1829; in Bini and Commons, *Le prime rappresentazioni,* 203. The writer for *Il caffè* calls the Milanese critic "Signor Privo-d'Ali" (wingless, or deprived of wings).

39. On the cantatas *Gesù al limbo* (Salieri) and *Arianna consolata* (Paër), both written in 1803, see John Rice, *Empress Marie Therese and Music at the Viennese Court, 1792–1807* (Cambridge: Cambridge University Press, 2003), 206–7 and 310n. The Viganò collaborations stretched across a decade, from *I giuochi istimici* (Venice, 1804) to *Il nuovo Pigmalione* (La Scala, 1813); see Ritorni, *Commentarii della vita e delle opere coreodrammatiche di Salvatore Viganò* (Milan: Guglielmini e Redaelli, 1838), 230. On Prividali's journalistic activities once in Milan, see Marcello Conati, "I periodici teatrali e musicali italiani a metà Ottocento," in *Periodica musica* (papers from the Fourteenth Congress of the International Musicological Society, Bologna, 1987), 13–23.

40. Competing journalist Francesco Regli would later criticize Prividali for treating the journal as a cottage industry and publishing long-delayed reports; see Marino Berengo, *Intelletuali e librai nella Milano della Restaurazione* (Turin: Einaudi, 1980), 216; and Regli, *Dizionario biografico* (Turin: E. Dalmazzo, 1860), 423.

41. *Il censore universale dei teatri,* 5 January 1831; in Bini and Commons, *Le prime rappresentazioni,* 254.

42. Susan Rutherford cites a number of sources that emphasize the intensity that Pasta could bring to moments of dramatic import "'La cantante delle passioni': Giuditta Pasta and the Idea of Operatic Performance," *Cambridge Opera Journal* 19/2 (2007): 107–38. Rutherford (119) discusses a review from the *Censore universale,* which may be by the same reviewer who wrote about *Anna Bolena,* finding fault in

1829 with Pasta's interpretation of Nina's madness as too realistic and disjointed, out of step with Paisiello's more pastoral vision for the part.

43. *Teatri, arte, e letteratura,* 23 October 1834; in Bini and Commons, *Le prime rappresentazioni,* 416–17.

44. Federico Fornoni, "Creating the Inner Life of a Character," *Opera Quarterly* 28/3–4 (2013): 92–212; and his "'Di un cor che more reca il perdono': Processi psichici di una condannata," in Aragona and Fornoni, eds., *Maria Stuarda: Quaderni della Fondazione Donizetti* 31 (2012): 13–27; and Anselm Gerhard, "'Come in lui rugisse l'anima drammatica di Schiller': Donizetti e il piagnisteo di una straniera," in *Gaetano Donizetti: Maria Stuarda* (La Fenice prima dell'opera, 2009), 11–27. See also Luca Zoppelli, "Tragisches Theater und Oper: Manzoni, Donizetti, und Schillers *Maria Stuart*," *Schweizer Jahrbuch des Musikwissenschaft* 22 (2002): 296–311.

45. The correspondent for *Teatri, arte, e letteratura,* 25 September 1834, 37, names the opera in question as *Giovanna Grey* and announces that it will likely be premièred the following evening.

46. Performing the role of Elizabeth a few years later in Naples, in Donizetti's *Roberto Devereux,* Ronzi de Begnis was lauded for "displaying the dignity worthy of the scepter, the voice of the lover, [and], the rage of the scorned woman"; Achille de Lauzières, *Il globo,* 9 November 1837; in Bini and Commons, *Le prime rappresentazioni,* 659.

47. *Censore universale dei teatri,* 2 January 1836; in Bini and Commons, *Le prime rappresentazioni,* 544–47, here 545. He then adds the charge that Donizetti, for his part, has composed too much "by numbers, without worrying about what comes before and after, simply writing the notes under the words they find there." This preoccupation with royal authority informs even his remarks on the Elisabetta, Giacinta Puzzi-Toso, about whom Prividali writes dismissively, "She has the presence of a queen, but not the portamento" (547).

48. Chenxi Tang points out that Schiller makes Mary the center of the first and last acts, gives Acts 2 and 4 over to Elizabeth, and positions their famous confrontation at the play's center, in Act 3; see his "Theatralische Inszenierung der Weltordnung: Völkerrecht, Zeremonialwissenschaft und Schillers Maria Stuart," *Jahrbuch der deutschen Schillergesellschaft* 55 (2011): 142–68, here 151.

49. Robertson, *Storia del regno di Scozia sotto Maria Stuarda e Giacomo VI* (Naples: Marotta e Vanspandoch, 1830), vol. 6, book 6, 148; and vol. 6, book 7, 82.

50. The earliest translation was made by Pompeo Ferrario around 1816, but it was with Andrea Maffei's 1829 translation that *Maria Stuart* really gained visibility among Italians. On the Italian reception of Schiller's play and its adaptation by Bardare, see Gerhard, "Come in lui rugisse l'anima drammatica di Schiller"; and Paolo Cecchi, "'Per rendere il soggetto musicabile': Il percorso fonte—libretto—partitura in *Maria Stuarda* e *Marino Faliero*," in *L'Opera teatrale di Gaetano Donizetti: Atti del convegno internzaionale di studi* (Bergamo: Comune di Bergamo 1993), 229–77.

51. Alessandro Tinterri, "Brigante e regine: Schiller sui palcoscenici italiani," in Hermann Dorowin and Uta Treder, eds., *Auguri Schiller! Atti del convegno Perugino in occasione del 250e anniversario della nascita del Friedrich Schiller* (Perugia:

Morlacchi, 2011), 165–80. Henry Morley noted the glorification of Mary in Lebrun's play in his *Journal of a London Playgoer:* "Schiller's Mary Stuart is not, like M. Lebrun's, an angel of light, who once in a great scene stands apart from the rest of the play, triumphs as a scold over Queen Elizabeth; she is not only a sad captive, but a sad woman, much hated and much loved, with passions that have brought a stain of murder on her soul"; Morley, *Journal of a London Playgoer, from 1851 to 1866* (London: Routledge, 1891), 182.

52. See Barbieri, "Note critiche intorno alla Maria Stuarda, contenute in una lettera del compilatore al Conte Ludovico Piosasco, Torinese," in his *Nuova raccolta teatrale, o sia repertorio scelto ad uso de' teatri italiani,* vol. 3 (Milan: Pirotta, 1821), 95–102. In this preface Barbieri calls Salvatore Viganò "the Raphael of choreography" and offers the play in informal dedication to him.

53. Lebrun's play diverges from Schiller also in its final scenes. The play ends not with Mary's execution (as in Donizetti), nor with Elizabeth's attempt to duck responsibility for the execution (as in Schiller). Instead Lebrun concludes with the brief scene from Schiller in which Leicester listens from an adjoining room as Mary's sentence is read, as she offers up a final prayer, and as her women lament her impending death. In Schiller, Leicester collapses in a faint as the blade falls on the other side of the locked door; Lebrun heightens the effect with Leicester murmuring, *"Je meurs"* (I die) as he crumples, leaving open the possibility that he has died of sorrow. (The final stage direction reads, *"En proie d'une emotion déchirante, il pousse un grand cri et tombe sans movement dans les bras de Seymour."*)

54. As Reinhard Strohm points out, Donizetti's *Roberto Devereux* has three such objects that serve as proxies for affection: a blue scarf, a ring, and a death warrant that is carried around by ministers, eventually signed by Elisabetta, and then immediately disavowed. This is a mark left on Italian opera of the 1830s by the conventions of French melodrama, which invested sentimental objects with great power; Strohm, "The Earl of Essex, servitore di due padrone," in his *Dramma per musica: Italian Opera Seria of the Eighteenth Century* (New Haven: Yale University Press, 1997), 294–305.

55. Endings centered on a contested death warrant and an execution also occur in Coccia's *Maria Stuarda* (1827), Mercadante's *Il conte d'Essex* (1833), and Pacini's *Marie Tudor* (1843), as well Niedermeyer's *Marie Stuart* (1844).

56. Space precludes a full discussion of *Roberto Devereux,* which is unique in having Elizabeth abdicate after she signs the death warrant and after she fails in her attempt to halt the execution of Roberto. On the representation of Elizabeth in that opera, see Deasy, "Bare Interiors"; on its ending in contrast with the clemency scenes of earlier Tudor operas, see Winfried Jung and Bodo Plachta, "The Queen Sings Coloratura: Elizabeth I and bel canto Opera," in Christina Jansohn, ed., *Queen Elizabeth I: Past and Present* (Münster: LIT Verlag, 2004), 195–209.

57. Schiller, *Maria Stuart,* Act 4, Scene 2, in *Schiller: Five Plays,* trans. David Macdonald (London: Oberon, 1998), 588–91.

58. Steven Martinson argues that Elizabeth at this point "ostracizes herself completely from the moral sphere and abandons herself to the political realm,"

although he also sees her actions here as privileging the corporeal (the immediate pleasure of signing the paper) in a way that does not correspond to the operatic realization of this scene; Martinson, *Harmonious Tensions: The Writings of Friedrich Schiller* (Newark: University of Delaware Press, 1996), 220–21.

59. Engels, "Outlines of a Critique of Political Economy," *Deutsche; Französiche Jahrbücher* (1844): 86; discussed in Wolfgang Schluchter, *Rationalism, Religion, and Domination: A Weberian Perspective* [1936] (Berkeley: University of California Press, 1989), 325; and Schmitt, *Constitutional Theory* [1928], trans. Jeffrey Seitzer (Durham: Duke University Press, 2008). See also Friedrich Kittler's *Discourse Networks, 1800/1900*, trans. Michael Metteer with Chris Cullens (Stanford: Stanford University Press, 1992), for a discussion of the central role of the civil servant and of the technology of writing in the development of German romantic poetry.

60. Lucy Riall, "Martyr Cults in Nineteenth-Century Italy," *Journal of Modern History* 82/2 (2010): 255–87.

61. Friedrich Dürrenmatt, *Theaterprobleme;* cited in Riccardo Morello, "Da Schiller a Donizetti: *Maria Stuarda*," in Dorowin and Treder, *Auguri Schiller!*, 185.

62. Fornoni, "Creating the Inner Life of a Character"; and Alessandra Campana, "Tracce di gesti," in Aragona and Fornoni, *Maria Stuarda,* 29–41.

63. Carlotta Sorba, *Il melodramma della nazione: Politica e sentimenti nell'età del Risorgimento* (Rome: Laterza, 2015).

64. I am thinking here of the devastating valuation Friedrich Engels delivers on Carlo Alberto in two articles published in the *Neue Rhenische Zeitung* in August 1848; Marx and Engels, *Collected Works,* vol. 7 (London: Wishart, 2010).

CHAPTER 4. READING MAZZINI'S "FILOSOFIA DELLA MUSICA" WITH BYRON AND DONIZETTI

1. *La Minerva,* 1 January 1830. The theater had been operating since 1803 but rarely drew the audiences from La Scala. The year 1830 marked one of the first seasons when the Carcano featured prominent new works that could not be ignored by the operatic elite. One contemporary travel guide in 1833 noted that the theater was *"non molto frequentato per la sua lontananza dal centro della città";* Francesco Gandini, *Viaggi in Italia,* vol. 3 (Cremona: Luigi de Micheli, 1833), 312.

2. *Censore universale dei teatri,* 5 January 1830.

3. This view of the nineteenth-century city originates, of course, with Walter Benjamin, "Paris: Capital of the Nineteenth Century," in his *Reflections: Essays, Aphorisms, Autobiographical Writings,* trans. Edmund Jephcott (New York: Schocken, 1986), 146–62. See also Anselm Gerhard, *The Urbanization of Opera: Music Theater in Paris in the Nineteenth Century* (Chicago: University of Chicago Press, 1998); and Jürgen Osterhammel, "The City as Norm and Exception," in his *The Transformation of the World: A Global History of the Nineteenth Century,* trans. Patrick Camiller (Princeton: Princeton University Press, 2014), 241–48.

4. For recent work that takes up some of these issues in imaginative and convincing ways, see Laura Protano-Biggs, "'Mille e mille calme fiammelle': Illuminating Milan's Teatro alla Scala at the *fine secolo*," *Studi verdiani* 23 (2013): 145–67; Peter Mondelli, "The Sociability of History in French Grand Opera: A Historical Materialist Perspective," *19th-Century Music* 37/1 (2013): 37–55; Flora Willson, "Of Time and the City: Verdi's *Don Carlos* and Its Parisian Critics," *19th-Century Music* 37/3 (2014): 188–201; and Eleanor Clare Cloutier, "Repetitive Novelty: Italian Opera in Paris and London in the 1830s and 1840s," doctoral thesis, University of California, Berkeley, 2016.

5. Soprano Giulia Grisi also in a sense moved to Paris for the sake of artistic freedom: she left Italy to escape an extortionary contract with impresario Alessandro Lanari, who later transferred her management to Crivelli at La Scala; see John Rosselli, *The Opera Industry in Italy from Cimarosa to Verdi: The Role of the Impresario* (Cambridge: Cambridge University Press, 1984), 148.

6. On France's failure to come to the aid of the Italian rebels, see Alan J. Reinerman, "Metternich, the Powers, and the 1831 Italian Crisis," *Central European History* 10/3 (1977): 206–19; and Angeline H. Lograsso, "Lafayette and Italian Independence," *Italica* 35/4 (1958): 225–34, here 228–29 and 232–33.

7. Delphine Diaz, "Exilés et immigrés italiens à Paris, des Trois Glorieuses au Coup d'état Bonapartiste," *Archivio storico dell'emigrazione italiana* 9/1 (2013): 24–29. On the situation of Italian exiles in London, Greece, and Spain (but not Paris), see Maurizio Isabella, *Risorgimento in Exile: Italian Emigrés and the Liberal International in the Post-Napoleonic Era* (Oxford: Oxford University Press, 2009).

8. *Vert-Vert*, 24 January 1835; cited in Mark Everist, Sarah Hibberd, and Walter Zidaric, "Vincenzo Bellini, *I puritani*: Dossier de presse," in Maria Rosa de Luca, Salvatore Enrico Failla, and Giuseppe Montemagno, eds., *Vincenzo Bellini et la France: Histoire, création et réception de l'oeuvre* (Lucca: Libreria musicale italiana, 2008), 407–81, here 474.

9. Tommaseo, *Diario intimo* (Turin: Einaudi, 1946); quoted in Delphine Diaz, *Un asile pour tous les peuples? Exilés et réfugiés étrangers en France au cours du premier XIXe siècle* (Paris: Armand Colin, 2014), 189 and 193.

10. Diaz, *Un asile pour tous les peuples?*, 36. Louis-Philippe escaped, but eighteen people were killed in the attack.

11. Raffaele Barbiera, *La principessa Belgiojoso, da memorie mondane inedite o rare e da archivii segreti di stato* (Milan: Treves, 1922), 96–98.

12. On the historiography of the Risorgimento in the early twentieth century, see Claudio Fogu, "Il Duce taumaturgo: Modernist Rhetorics in Fascist Representations of History," *Representations* 57 (1997): 24–51.

13. "*L'unità d'Italia fu preparata all'estero dagli esuli, chi ad essa conciliavano le simpatie riluttanti degli stranieri.*" Raffaele Barbiera, *La principessa Belgiojoso, i suoi amici e nemici—il suo tempo* (Milan: Treves, 1902), 97.

14. The disagreement is documented in an exchange of letters initiated by Mazzini (from Geneva) in the autumn of 1834. The exchange also touched on the two men's divergent views on the Marquis de Lafayette, who had been instrumental in

introducing a clause into the constitution adopted after the July Revolution stating that France would not intervene in the political affairs of other nations. Gioberti, who was briefly resident in Paris, had cosigned a letter written by a group of exiles to Lafayette's son, thanking him for his stance on Italy, an endorsement that drew Mazzini's ire because he felt that Lafayette's theoretical support had been ineffectual when it came to material support for the 1831 uprisings. Mazzini's letter is undated but was probably written just before Gioberti's reply, which is dated 25 September [1834]. Both letters are reprinted in Giuseppe Massari, ed., *Ricordi biografici e carteggio di Vincenzo Gioberti*, vol. 1 (Turin: Botta, 1860), 336–48.

15. The trio landed first in Marseilles, and from there Mazzini proceeded to Geneva and the Ruffini brothers to Paris and later London. By the 1840s, both Ruffinis had begun to distance themselves from Mazzini, and by 1848 were working with Gioberti. This shift is documented in Ruffini's *roman à clé Lorenzo Benoni;* see also Angelo Nota, *Giovanni Ruffini e il risorgimento italiano, 1807–1881* (San Remo: E. Vacchieri, 1899); Camillo Guerrieri, "Per la storia e la fortuna del 'Lorenzo Benoni,'" in *Giovanni Ruffini e i suoi tempi*, ed. "Comitato per le onoranze a Giovanni Ruffini" (Genoa: Comitato regionale ligure della società nazionale per la storia del risorgimento, 1931), 585–607, here 606.

16. The literature on the Ruffini brothers and their relationship to Mazzini is vast, with an explosion of publishing activity (as usual for Risorgimento topics) at the turn of the century and again during the fascist era. On the literary achievements of Giovanni Ruffini, the more prolific of the brothers, see Martino Marazzi, *Il romanzo risorgimentale di Giovanni Ruffini* (Florence: Nuova Italia, 1991); and Allan Christensen, *A European Version of Victorian Fiction: The Novels of Giovanni Ruffini* (Amsterdam: Rodopi, 1996). For biographical and political issues, see Arturo Linaker, *Giovanni Ruffini* (Turin: Bocca, 1882); and the fascinating letters collected by Arturo Codignola in *I fratelli Ruffini: Lettere di Giovanni e Agostino Ruffini alla madre dall'esilio francese e svizzero* (Genoa: G. B. Marsano, 1925). Finally, most biographical sources devote space to the withering of the close ties between Mazzini and the Ruffinis, a subject treated in depth by Anna Errera in the pamphlet *La fine d'un amicizia (Mazzini-Ruffini)* (Milan: Libreria de 'la Coltura Populare,' 1928).

17. The references to Accursi in Mazzini's correspondence are numerous and complex: Mazzini and intimates spent several years in the early 1830s trying to determine whether or not he was a papal spy. The suspicion originated in the fact that Accursi was imprisoned in Rome and freed by Pope Gregory XVI in 1833, perhaps in exchange for informing on the revolutionaries. The verdict of history seems to be that he was not an informer and was always loyal to Giovine Italia, but the evidence is murky; see the informative biographical note on Accursi in *Scritti editi ed inediti di Giuseppe Mazzini; Epistolario*, vol. 5; Edizione nazionale degli scritti di Giuseppe Mazzini [henceforth M.E.N.], vol. 1 (Imola: Paolo Galeati, 1909), 109. It now seems beyond doubt that Accursi did report to Rome on the activities of the Mazzini circle. Some of his reports to the Vatican are published in Ilario Rinieri, "Le cospirazioni Mazziniane nel carteggio d'una transfuga," Il risorgimento italiano 16 (1923): 173–212 and 439–98; cited in Martin Kaltenecker, "Mazzini et la musique,"

in Giuseppe Mazzini, *Philosophie de la musique: Vers un opéra social* (1835) (Paris: Van Dieren, 2001), 86.

18. These instructions appear in a letter of 29 August 1844. A similar plan is outlined a few months earlier, when Mazzini instructs a correspondent to "send letters to M. G[aeta]no Doniz[etti]. Maître de Chapelle de sa Majesté Apostolique l'Empereur d'Autriche. That 'no' in the 'Gaetano' will indicate to Mich[ele] [Accursi] when he receives them that they are for us" (letter of 30 January 1844); see *Scritti editi ed inediti di Giuseppe Mazzini; Politica,* vol. 2; M.E.N., vol. 3 (Imola: Paolo Galeati, 1907), 93 and 25. Mazzini was also in touch quite energetically with Donizetti's nephew Andrea in 1846–47; but by 21 August 1847 Mazzini's associate Stefano Luigi Canessa writes from Constantinople, where the young Donizetti is resident: "Do not send Doniz[etti] any more letters; he is a good man, but weak"; see *Scritti editi ed inediti di Giuseppe Mazzini; Politica,* vol. 4; M.E.N., vol. 6 (Imola: Paolo Galeati, 1909), 88.

19. Documentation of his political sympathies begins only once he arrived in London in 1837. At that point he continued to see Mazzini and the Ruffini brothers socially and to endorse political initiatives launched by Mazzini. By the mid-1840s, however, Pepoli had doubts about the extremism of Mazzini and Giovine Italia, as his wife Elizabeth Fergus recorded several times in her diary ("Diary of Elizabeth Fergus Pepoli," University of Bologna library, BU 4409.). On ties with the Mazzini circle in London, see Agostino Ruffini's letter of 8 August 1839 to his mother, and Mazzini's letters of 13 September 1843; *Protocollo della Giovine Italia* (Imola: Paolo Galeati, 1916), vol. 1, 95n, and vol. 2, 125.

20. For the connection with Lablache's cook, see letter of 11 September 1841, *Scritti editi ed inediti di Giuseppe Mazzini* (M.E.N., vol. 1). On the politics of the latter two singers, see Elizabeth Forbes, *Mario and Grisi: A Biography* (London: Victor Gollancz, 1985); and Stefano Ragni, "Giuseppe Mazzini e Giulia Grisi," *Bolletino della Domus Mazziniana* 1 (1989): 29–49.

21. Marliani was also a composer, whose opera *Il bravo* was performed at the Théâtre-Italien in 1834.

22. Wayne Conner has argued plausibly that *L'Esule* implicitly took an activist position, distancing itself, for example, from the stance of Catholic submission and resignation espoused in *I promessi sposi;* Conner, "*L'Esule* (1832–1834): Literature and 'Home Thoughts from Abroad,'" *Italica* 40/4 (December 1963): 297–303. Subscribers included King Louis-Philippe, Mazzini, the Marquis de Lafayette, and baritone Antonio Tamburini.

23. The challenge was issued by editor Federico Pescantini, with composer Marliani standing as his second. The offending line was spoken by the queen, Mary Tudor, to an Italian character who seduces an orphan: *"Italien, cela veut dire fourbe! Napolitain, cela veut dire lâche! Toutes les fois que mon père s'est servi d'un italien, il s'en est repenti!... On ne peut tirer autre chose de la poche d'un italien qu'un stylet, et de l'âme d'un italien que la trahison!"* (Italian, that means scoundrel! Neapolitan means coward! Every time my father relies on an Italian he comes to regret it.... One cannot find anything in the pocket of an Italian but a dagger, and nothing in his soul but betrayal!); *Marie Tudor,* Deuxième journée, Scene 7.

24. "Varietà: Seguito e fine dell'articolo a Victor Hugo e Scribe," *L'Esule* 4 (1834): 114–52; "La sfida degli esuli romangnoli a Victor Hugo (Parigi 1833)," *Nuova antologia* (March–April 1902): 313–23; and "Attraverso le riviste italiane: La sfida delle esuli romagnoli a Victor Hugo," *Minerva* 22/17 (6 April 1902): 397–98.

25. Accursi laid out the goals of the new journal in a letter to Enrico Mayer, 26 March 1836:

> We have realized an Italian desire.—A newspaper, a newspaper that can be read in Italy.... The writers who have already agreed to contribute are: prof Meloni, Libri, Tommaseo, Pippo [Mazzini], Giannone, Mamiani, Ghighlione, Ruffini, and others who would be less well known to you, but bright minds.... We are sure that the paper will enter into the papal states, and if so then it can be read anywhere: on the other hand, censorship is already a reality for us; that will be impossible to disarm.

Published in Arturo Linaker, *Vita e tempi di Enrico Mayer,* vol. 1 (Florence: Barbèra, 1898), 365ff.; cited by Carlotta Sorba in "Between Cosmopolitanism and Nationhood: Italian Opera in the Early Nineteenth Century," *Modern Italy* 19/1 (2014): 53–67, here 60. On the journal as a project of the exile community in Paris, see also Ilaria Gabbani, *"L'Italiano:* Un foglio letterario nella Parigi della Monarchia del Luglio," doctoral thesis, Université Sorbonne Nouvelle / Università di Pisa, 2014–15.

26. Quoted in Linaker, *Vita e tempi di Enrico Mayer,* 370.

27. The essay's vision of a newly expressive and socially engaged "music of the future," as well as its depiction of music in the guise of a woman whose purity must be defended against the ravages of decadent culture, have provoked comparisons with Wagner, and it is commonly seen as setting a blueprint for, or even inspiring, the increased interest in local color, an active and individuated chorus, and complex characterization that surface in Verdi's operas beginning with *Macbeth* and *Rigoletto.* Such proleptic readings lean on the slim portions of the essay that propose concrete recommendations for operatic reform and ignore the near impossibility that Verdi could have known of the "Filosofia" before 1851, given the small circulation of *L'Italiano* and the long delay before Mazzini's "Filosofia" was published in Italy. The essay appeared in a Swiss edition in *Scritti letterari d'un italiano vivente,* vol. 2 (Lugano: Tipografia della italiania svizzera, 1847); and in *Scritti editi e inediti,* vol. 4 (Milan: Daelli, 1862).

The most influential voice in shaping the Anglo-American reception of Mazzini has been Gary Tomlinson, in his "Italian Romanticism and Italian Opera: An Essay in their Affinities," *19th-Century Music* 10/1 (1986): 43–60. Sections of "Filosofia" dealing with individualism and collective action are translated as "From 'The Philosophy of Music' (1836)," in Ruth Solie, ed., *The Nineteenth Century (Source Readings in Music History,* ed. Leo Treitler, rev. ed.) (New York: Norton, 1998), 1085–94. Early discussions of the links between Mazzini and Wagner appear in the anonymous article "Mazzini and Wagner," *The Musical Times and Singing Circular,* 1 November 1886, 642–44; Camille Bellaigue, "Les idées musicales d'un révolutionnaire italien," *Revue des deux mondes,* 15 February 1899, 918–34; and Adriano

Lualdi's introduction to his edition of the "Filosofia della musica" (Milan: Fratelli Bocca, 1943), 89–90. Marcello de Angelis authoritatively untangles Mazzini's ideas from Wagner's in his editor's introduction to *Giuseppe Mazzini: Filosofia della musica e Estetica musicale del primo Ottocento: Testi scelti da Andrea Majer, Marco Santucci, Lorenzo Neri, Abramo Basevi, Giovanni Battista Rinuccini* (Rimini: Guaraldi, 1977), 21 and 27–30.

28. Mazzini, *Filosofia della musica,* ed. Luigi Salvatorelli, with an introduction by Stefano Ragni (Tolmino: Pagano, 2001), 60–62. Subsequent references to the "Filosofia" will be to this edition, indicated by page numbers in the main text. For a detailed discussion of Mazzini's philosophy of art, see Imperia Grieco, *La concezione estetica mazziniana e la filosofia della musica* (Naples: Loffredo, 1970).

29. This idea of harmony as opposed to individuality is central also to Mazzini's essay "Byron and Goethe," originally published in English in the *Monthly Chronicle* in 1839, republished in William Clarke, ed., *Essays: Selected from the Writings, Literary, Political, and Religious, of Joseph Mazzini* (London: Walter Scott, 1887), 83–108, here 88. Another consistent element in Mazzini's writing about literature and music in the 1830s and 1840s is the low estimation he accords to imitators and to anything he perceives as merely "summing up the past" rather than ushering in the real new socially engaged art of the future. The impatience with those who complacently sustain past formulas is articulated most strongly in "Fede ed avenire"; but it also permeates "Byron and Goethe," the essay that also offers the clearest vision of the "new poetry of the future," a "new social poetry, which will soothe the suffering soul by teaching it to rise towards God through Humanity" (102).

30. These ideas are articulated most extensively in Mazzini's essays "Fede ed avenire" (mostly written in 1835, with the preface following in 1850) and "Duties of Man" (mostly drafted in 1844, but not published until 1860). On the influence of Saint-Simon, see Marcella Pellegrino Sutcliffe, *Victorian Radicals and Italian Democrats* (London: Boydell and Brewer, 2014), 50; and Simon Levis Sullam, "'Dio e popolo': La rivoluzione religiosa di Giuseppe Mazzini," in *Storia d'Italia,* Annali 22: "Il Risorgimento" (Turin: Einaudi, 2007), 401–22.

31. On Mazzini's ignorance of Hegel, see de Angelis, *Giuseppe Mazzini: Filosofia della musica,* 24–25; and Harry Hearder, *Italy in the Age of the Risorgimento* (London: Longman, 1983), 184–85.

32. Carlotta Sorba suggests that the preference for Donizetti over Bellini, as well as the perception of greater energy and activism in his music, was shared by many of the Italian expatriates in Paris; see her "Teatro, politica, e compassione: Audience teatrale, sfera pubblica ed emozionalità in Francia e in Italia tra XVIII e XIX secolo," *Contemporanea* 12/3 (2009): 421–45.

33. Agostino Ruffini to Eleonora Curlo Ruffini, 10 April 1835; published in Codignola, *I fratelli Ruffini,* 266. Codignola says in a footnote that Ruffini's ideas here are indebted to Mazzini; but as we shall see, the influence may have run in the opposite direction.

34. On the significance of Venice for the Byron of *Marino Faliero,* see Celeste Langan, "Venice," in James Chandler and Kevin Gilmartin, eds., *Romantic Metropolis:*

The Urban Scene of British Culture, 1780–1840 (Cambridge: Cambridge University Press, 2005), 261–85.

35. Considering why *Marino Faliero* engaged Mazzini and whether the opera itself has political content, Francesco Bellotto concludes that Mazzini's interpretation of the opera, and that of many musicologists since, is nothing more than a projection or a wish fulfillment, when Donizetti's opera in fact weakens or defuses potential political messages at several key points; see his "L'Immaginario scenico di *Marino Faliero,*" in *Gaetano Donizetti: Mario Faliero* (La Fenice prima dell'opera, 2002–3), 89–102.

36. Byron intended his *Marino Faliero* as a closet drama, for private reading rather than staged performance, but it was performed without the author's permission at the Drury Lane Theater immediately after its publication in 1821.

37. Burke's *Reflections on the Revolution in France* had appeared in Italian as early as 1795 (with a warning on the title page that it was *"scritta dal protestante inglese Signor Edmondo Burke"*). But histories by François-Auguste Mignet and Adolphe Thiers were translated in 1825 and 1835 respectively: Mignet, *Storia della rivoluzione francese dal 1789 al 1814,* 3 vols. (Italy, 1825); Thiers, *Storia della rivoluzione francese,* trans. Ermengildo Potenti, 15 vols. (Florence: Potenti, 1835–39). Paul Ginsborg has identified the question of what cultural forces could inspire Italians to risk their lives for a political cause as one of the most important unanswered questions about the Risorgimento; see his "Romanticismo e risorgimento," 5–67, especially 38–48.

38. In a detailed comparison of the two plays published in 1829 in the *Foreign Quarterly Review,* "K.K." noted that although the adultery plot and all scenes for Fernando and Elena together were the inventions of Delavigne, the French play's debt to Byron was still considerable: "The germ of every thing Faliero utters, whilst he is Faliero at all, may be detected in the English play" (477). Even while copying Byron, the author complained, Delavigne had subtracted all the greatness, passion, and rage from Byron's title character, working on the original like "a waxen bust exposed to the fire"; *Foreign Quarterly Review,* vol. 4 (London: Treutel and Würtz, April/August 1829), 470–75.

39. Carlo Ginzburg notes the parallelism between Faliero and Bertucci as both trying to avenge offenses from nobles; see his "Following the Tracks of Israël Bertuccio," in *Threads and Traces: True, False, Fictive* (Berkeley: University of California Press, 2012), 126–36. For insightful discussions of the differences between the two plays and the libretto for Donizetti's opera, see also Guido Paduano, "L'individuo e lo stato: Byron, Delavigne, Donizetti," in *Gaetano Donizetti: Mario Faliero,* 103–26; and Paolo Cecchi, "'Per rendere il soggetto musicabile': Il percorso fonte—libretto—partitura in *Maria Stuarda* e *Marino Faliero,*" in *L'opera teatrale di Gaetano Donizetti: Atti del convegno internzaionale di studi* (Bergamo: Comune di Bergamo, 1993).

40. The historical facts are sketchy, recorded mainly in Marino Sanuto's *Le vite dei dogi,* published posthumously by Muratori in his *Rerum Italicarum Scriptores* in 1733. Faliero's story was brought to contemporary attention by Pierre Daru's 1819

Histoire de la république de Vénise, which cast events in a Napoleonic, egalitarian light, according to which Venetian oligarchy was evil and elitist, and Venetian pleasure (especially carnival) was representative of the decadence of the aristocracy. Daru mobilized Faliero in his broad-brush critique of the Venetian nobility as corrupt and his apologia for the Napoleonic occupation. He argued that Faliero joined the conspiracy for reasons that were entirely egocentric and cynical—unmoved by common interests or ideals, he banded together with the conspirators simply to gain revenge for the affront to his reputation. Byron includes a brief excerpt from Daru in the appendix to *Marino Faliero,* along with the Sanuto chronicle, passages from Petrarch's letters that mention the doge, and an excerpt from Ginguené's *Histoire littéraire d'Italie* (1819). Delavigne appends to his *Marino Faliero* the same excerpt from Sanuto and a different passage from Daru.

On the evolving image of Venice in the nineteenth century, including a brief discussion of *Marino Faliero,* see James Johnson, "The Myth of Venice in Nineteenth-Century Opera," *Journal of Interdisciplinary History* 36/3 (Winter 2005): 533–54; and his *Venice Incognito: Masks of the Serene Republic* (Berkeley: University of California Press, 2011). On historical accounts of Faliero's life and death, see Marijke Jonker, "'Crowned, and Discrowned and Decapitated': Delacroix's *Execution of the Doge Faliero* and Its Critics," *Nineteenth-Century Art Worldwide* 9/2 (2010), www.19thc-artworldwide.org/autumn10/delacroixs-execution-of-the-doge-marino-faliero-and-its-critics—_ftn14; accessed 12 May 2017; and Carla Pomarè, "*Marino Faliero* and *The Two Foscari:* Rewriting the Myth of Venice," in her *Byron and the Discourses of History* (Farnham: Ashgate, 2013).

41. *Marino Faliero, Doge of Venice* (published together with *A Prophecy of Dante*) (London: John Murray, 1821), preface, xii. Byron is here criticizing John Moore, *A View of Society and Manners in Italy* (London: Strahan and Cadell, 1781).

42. Casimir Delavigne, *Marino Faliero, tragédie en cinq actes* (Paris: Marchant, 1835). Delavigne was the author of *Les vêpres sicliennes* (1821), the source for Verdi's 1855 opera and also for Donizetti's *Le Duc d'Albe* (1839), and of the words for the popular song of the July Revolution, "La parisienne." Donizetti also drew on Delavigne for his opera *Il paria* (Naples, 1828). Paolo Cecchi points out that Delavigne's play was translated into Italian by Luigi Raspi and published in Rome in 1829; see his "'Per rendere il soggetto musicabile,'" 229–77, 250.

43. *Revue de Paris* 3 (Paris: Levasseur, 1829), 54–64, here 62–63. Nodier is known for the fantastic tales he wrote in the 1820s, especially *Trilby* (1822), which inspired *La sylphide.* From 1826 to 1830 he convened the Cénacle, a gathering of poets and writers that included among its membership Alfred de Vigny, Lamartine, Hugo, and Sainte-Beuve.

44. *Revue de Paris* 3 (Paris: Levasseur, 1829), 54–64, here 56.

45. Mazzini, "Byron and Goethe," 72.

46. Mazzini, *Filosofia della musica,* ed. Salvatorelli; on *Marino Faliero,* see 70–72.

47. Mazzini, *Filosofia della musica,* ed. Salvatorelli, 70–71. Here Mazzini slightly misquotes the libretto, which reads, *Bertucci: "Ov'è il tuo brando che salvò la patria*

allor? Anco adesso un brando implora. . . ." Faliero: "Si! avrà quello di Falier!" (Bertucci: "Where is that sword that saved our homeland once before? Now again we need a sword. . . ." Faliero: "Yes! you shall have the sword of Falier!").

48. Sismondi reports that when Bertucci approached Faliero about the insult he had received from a patrician, Faliero replied: *"Non sono io oltraggiato al pari di voi ed il preteso castigo del colpevole, non fu forse per me per la stessa corona ducale una nuova offesa?"* (Am I not offended as much as you, and is not the trivial punishment of the offender another insult to the ducal crown?); Jean-Charles-Léonard Simonde de Sismondi, *Storia delle republiche italiane del medio evo,* vol. 2 (Milan: Borroni and Scotti, 1851), 439–40.

49. The cello solo begins the slow movement of Fernando's aria, "Io ti veggio, or piangi e tremi"; the "full, low, and solemn" low notes at the phrase *"Questo schiavo coronato"* occur early in Faliero's contemptuous address to the conspirators, "Bello ardir dei congiurati"; and the high E♭ is heard in Fernando's death scene, "Io . . . vendicarti," which is built around embellishments and extensions of that note for the tenor; all three moments are from the opera's second act and all mentioned in *Filosofia della musica,* 71.

50. See Stefano Ragni, "Giuseppe Mazzini e Giulia Grisi,"43.

51. Letter of 26 January 1835; in Codignola, *I fratelli Ruffini,* 200–201.

52. *Filosofia della musica,* 39 and 63. In "De l'art en Italie: À propos de Marco Visconti, roman de Thomas Grossi," *Revue républicaine,* 10 May 1835, Mazzini grouped Meyerbeer with Donizetti as capable of "translating into notes struggle and emancipation." The "Dernière pensée" was published as Weber's last musical utterance but was actually written by the composer's successor as conductor of the Dresden opera, Karl Reissiger (1798–1859). Its appearance in the guise of a deathbed meditation by Reissiger's more famous colleague seems to have been manufactured by a Paris publisher eager to capitalize on a vogue for Weber in the early 1830s, although copies quickly appeared all over Europe; Camille Saint-Säens, "False Masterpieces of Music," trans. Fred Rothwell, *Musical Times* 62/944 (1 October 1921): 688.

53. 26 March 1835; Codignola, *I fratelli Ruffini,* 248.

54. Drawing on some of the letters cited here, Martin Kaltenecker proposes that Mazzini's essay was the fruit of conversations among the two Ruffini brothers and Mazzini in Grenchen in 1835. Kaltenecker takes the similarity between Ruffini's phraseology and that of the "Filosofia" not as an indication that Ruffini had a role in authoring the essay, but that Mazzini was surrounded by and influenced by supporters of Donizetti, who influenced the direction it took; Kaltenecker, "Mazzini et la musique," in Mazzini, *Philosophie de la musique,* 113, 116–17.

55. From a close reading of Mazzini's correspondence, Marcello de Angelis shows that he finished writing the "Filosofia" on 13 December 1835; de Angelis, *Giuseppe Mazzini: Filosofia della musica,* 7.

56. Ruffini's changes to the libretto were extensive, in several instances decisively redefining the approach to drama and representation. Much of the text for the opera's intimate scenes was written from scratch by Ruffini, including one completely

new aria for Fernando, a new cabaletta in Act 3 for Elena ("Fra due tombe, fra due spettri"), and new text for the lovers' first-act duet. Ruffini's revisions and additions to the original Bidéra libretto are discussed in Francesca Seller, "Il *Marino Faliero* da Napoli a Parigi: Raffronti testuali," *Donizetti Society Journal* 7 (2002): 31–46; this issue of the journal also includes the complete text of the original Bidéra libretto. See also the remarks in Philip Gossett, "Music at the Théâtre Italien," in Peter Bloom, ed., *Music in Paris in the 1830s* (Stuyvesant, NY: Pendragon, 1987), 327–64; and in Paolo Fabbri's article, "'Fosca notte, notte orrenda,'" and Giorgio Pagannone's annotations to his edition of the Paris libretto, both in *Gaetano Donizetti: Marino Faliero,* 73–88 and 11–62.

57. The quick pace and bifurcated texture recall choral scenes of similar constraint in which an energetic string section cycles through repetitions of a major-key melody, attempting to paper over the fragmented, speech-like interjections of characters who are afraid to speak openly, shocked by a sudden turn of events, or otherwise locked into inexpression. *Anna Bolena* begins with a *divisi* male chorus ("Ne venne il re?"), who whisper disjointedly about the king's interest in Giovanna Seymour, their voices woven into a slightly more ominous melody played by violins; a similar texture is central to many of Donizetti's finales, including the tense meeting of the two queens in *Maria Stuarda* and the moments just after Edgardo's unexpected arrival in the midst of the wedding scene in *Lucia di Lammermoor.* After Steno strikes Bertucci toward the end of the scene, the cheerful violin figures and vocal patter resume, communicating even more forcefully the sense of a smooth social surface kept in place with difficulty while characters clash and chafe against the surface restraint imposed by self-preservation.

58. Alberto Banti, *La nazione del Risorgimento: Parentela, santità e onore alle origini dell'Italia unità* (Turin: Einaudi, 2000).

59. That these phrases were interpreted by some as dangerous is confirmed by the fact that it was often precisely these words that were excised when *Marino Faliero* was performed in Italy. In the libretto for the opera's first performance in Bologna in 1837, for example, words that denote class or inequality were systematically replaced with terms that carry an intense emotional charge without reference to power—so *"schiavi"* (slaves), *"tiranni"* (tyrants), *"nobili"* and *"patrizi"* (nobles, patricians) disappear, replaced with words such as *"codardi"* and *"sdegni"* (cowards, scum). A few of Ruffini's incendiary terms (including *"a sollevar la patria"*) were changed to more broadly accepted wordings before even being set to music by Donizetti. For a list of changes made between Ruffini's libretto and the score, see the appendix to Pagannone's edition of the libretto, in *Gaetano Donizetti: Marino Faliero,* 51–54.

60. Byron, *Marino Faliero,* Act 5, Scene 3. The final lyric statement for Elena and Faliero (*"Santa voce al cor mi suona"*) casts Faliero almost as confessor for Elena. In Bidéra's text the stage directions indicate that Faliero should gaze at a crucifix and place his hand on Elena's head; once absolved, she embraces the cross. Ruffini did not alter the dialogue in this scene; but all mention of cross and crucifix disappear in the final version of the libretto, probably in response to strong censorial prohibitions against showing religious icons on stage in Paris.

61. Lucy Riall, "Martyr Cults in Nineteenth-Century Italy," *Journal of Modern History* 82/2 (2010): 255–87.

62. *Le temps,* 23 March 1835, and *Le moniteur universel,* 18 March 1835; in Annalisa Bini and Jeremy Commons, eds., *Le prime rappresentazioni delle opere di Donizetti nella stampa coeva* (Milan: Skira, 1997), 500 and 491.

63. *La gazette de France,* 18 March 1835; in Bini and Commons, *Le prime rappresentazioni delle opere di Donizetti,* 487.

64. *Le constitutionnel,* 16 March 1835, and *Le Charivari,* 15 March 1835; in Bini and Commons, *Le prime rappresentazioni delle opere di Donizetti,* 472–78.

65. Quoted in Sorba, "Teatro, politica, e compassione," 442. Sorba argues that most of the exiles reacted positively to Donizetti's opera, in contrast to the larger French audience; but Tommaseo's is the only voice she cites.

CHAPTER 5. PARLOR GAMES

1. *"Avrei necessità di farti aggiungere qualche verso nel duetto che ho quasi finito, ed è venuto magnifico, e lo squillo della tromba farà tremare di gioia i cuori liberi, che si troveranno in teatro. Addio.* Viva la libertà!!!" To Carlo Pepoli, January 1835; in Carmelo Neri, *Lettere di Vincenzo Bellini (1819–1835)* (Palermo: Publiscula, 1991), 349.

2. Letter to Francesco Florimo of 5 January 1835; Luisa Cambi, *Bellini epistolario* (Turin: Mondadori, 1943), 498; also in Neri, *Lettere di Vincenzo Bellini,* 347.

3. Letter of 26 January 1835; Cambi, *Bellini epistolario,* 501.

4. Mark Everist has suggested that the frenzy was provoked more by the buzzing energy of the two bass voices combined, an unprecedented sonority at the time, than by the duet's political message. Everist, "'Tutti i francesi erano diventati matti': Bellini and the Duet for Two Basses," in *Giacomo Meyerbeer and Music Drama in Nineteenth-Century Paris* (Aldershot: Ashgate, 2005), 281–308.

5. For details of Pepoli's early life, see Sandra Saccone, "Carlo Pepoli," in Cristina Bersani and Valeria Roncuzzi Roversi-Monaco, eds., *Giacomo Leopardi e Bologna: Libri, immagini e documenti* (Bologna: Patron, 2001), 330–39; and Giuseppe Vecchi, "Un poeta e melico: Carlo Pepoli tra Bologna, Parigi, e Londra," in Anna Rosa Poli and Emanuele Kanceff, eds., *L'Italie dans l'Europe romantique: Confronti letterari e musicali,* vol. 2 (Moncalieri: Centro interuniversitario di ricerche sul "Viaggio in Italia," 1996), 585–608.

6. Pepoli also wrote the libretti for Vaccai's *Giovanna Grey* (Théâtre-Italien, 1836) and Michael Costa's *Malek-Adel* (King's Theatre, London, 1837).

7. We owe to Pepoli's inexperience one of Bellini's most informative letters on operatic expression, the 1834 communication that includes the passage, "Carve it in your head in adamantine letters: Opera must make people weep, feel horrified, must kill through singing." The best discussion of Pepoli's contribution to the opera is Pierluigi Petrobelli, "Bellini and Paisiello: Further Documents on the Birth of *I puritani,*" in *Music in the Theater: Essays on Verdi and Other Composers* (Princeton:

Princeton University Press, 1994), 176–92, here 179; originally published as "Bellini e Paisiello: Altri documenti sulla nascita dei *Puritani*," in *Il melodramma italiano dell'Ottocento: Studi e ricerche per Massimo Mila* (Turin, 1977), 351–63. For an alternative reading of the *Puritani* libretto and the dramaturgical opportunities it afforded Bellini, see chap. 3 of my *Mimomania: Music and Gesture in Nineteenth-Century Opera* (Berkeley: University of California Press, 2004).

8. The passage reads in full:

> If music and poetry work in concert, they can vanquish any listener. The proof lies in the Marseillaise. Without the music the poetry is not beautiful: without the poetry the music is not complete: when the poetry and music are joined, it becomes a superb composition! For it the people fought: vanquished, triumphed: Europe and the world shouted Liberty! This is the most important event that can be narrated in the modern history of music.

Pepoli, "Del dramma musicale: Discorso accademico," in *Prose e poesie di Carlo Pepoli: Prose* (Bologna: Zanichelli, 1880), 191. The talk was delivered at Bologna's Liceo musicale in 1830 but was first published only in a collection of Pepoli's works in the 1860s.

9. Pepoli also wrote a number of texts for Paër around this time; see Carmela Bongiovanni, "Bellini e Paër a Parigi: Due musicisti e la loro produzione vocale cameristica a confronto," in Maria Rosa de Luca, Salvatore Enrico Failla, and Giuseppe Montemagno, eds., *Vincenzo Bellini et la France: Histoire, création et réception de l'oeuvre* (Lucca: Libreria Musicale Italiana, 2007), 109–56.

10. *SOIRÉES MUSICALES / Huit Ariettes et Quatre Duos Italiens / avec une traduction française / MIS EN MUSIQUE / avec accompagnement de piano / par G. ROSSINI / Ornés d'une superbe lithographie de Jules David.* (Paris: E. Troupenas et Cie. [1835]). These details are drawn from the Troupenas catalogue for 1835, which also reprinted excerpts from reviews of the publication. The announcement also notes that the songs are available for individual purchase, and with guitar accompaniment. My thanks to Peter Mondelli for sharing this document with me.

The *Soirées italiennes* were probably composed while Mercadante was in Paris for the première of his opera *I briganti* at the Théâtre-Italien (22 March 1836). Schoenenberger advertised the collection under the heading "Musique Nouvelle," as available with text in either French or Italian, in the spring of 1837 (*Journal des débats*, 2 March 1837). Editions quickly followed in Milan (published by Giovanni Canti), Florence (Lorenzi), London (d'Almain), and Mainz (Schott, 1838). The most popular songs were also sold separately.

Liszt prepared transcriptions of both song collections for piano solo, beginning with two pairs of songs from Rossini' *Soirées musicales* (pub. Schott, 1835–36), and continuing with the complete Rossini collection (Ricordi, 1838), and the complete Mercadante set (Schott, 1840).

11. The order of songs and the generic labels for each song given in table 2 are taken from the Troupenas catalogue (for Rossini) and the *Journal des débats* advertisement (for Mercadante).

12. Goethe, *Italian Journey* [1816–17] (London: Collins, 1962), 37.

13. Nelson Moe, *The View from Vesuvius: Italian Culture and the Southern Question* (Berkeley: University of California Press, 2002), 94.

14. Quoted in Moe, *View from Vesuvius,* 114.

15. Patric Schmid noted this allusion in his liner notes for the Opera Rara recording of the Mercadante songs (ORR 206, 1998).

16. Michael Talbot, *The Chamber Cantatas of Antonio Vivaldi* (Woodbridge: Boydell, 2006), 102. Talbot notes that the name does not appear in classical or Renaissance poetry but probably has Spanish associations.

17. Mme. Orfila was the wife of Dr. Mathieu Orfila, the chemist and forensic toxicologist who performed the test that proved that the famous murderer Madame Lafarge had in fact poisoned her husband with arsenic. In *The American in Paris during the Summer* (London: Longman, Brown, Green and Longmans, 1844), 213–14, Jules Janin describes a performance in which Mme. Orfila sings to her husband's accompaniment as an example of the commingling of social status and musical talent that typified the Paris of the 1830s.

18. Rossini biographer Charles Osborne places *his* bet on the Belgioioso salon, which was known to be a gathering place for the Italian exiles and where Carlo Pepoli was a regular; Osborne, *Rossini* (Oxford: Oxford University Press, 2007), 128.

19. David Tunley, *Salons, Singers and Songs: A Background to French Romantic Song, 1830–1870* (Aldershot: Ashgate, 2002), 148. Tunley's lists of repertoire are drawn from reports published in *La revue et gazette musicale* and *Le ménestrel.*

20. The trio performance took place at the Austrian embassy, hosted by the ambassador, Count Rodolphe Apponyi. Anne Martin-Fugier cites Belgioioso's appearance at the Apponyi residence as evidence that commonalities of taste and class trumped political opinion, since the Belgioiosos were fierce opponents of Austria's rule over Lombardy; see her *La vie élégante, ou la formation de Tout-Paris, 1815–1848* (Paris: Fayard, 1990), 316. Dana Gooley gives a clear and well-documented assessment of the politics of Belgioioso and her salon in *The Virtuoso Liszt* (Cambridge: Cambridge University Press, 2004), 18–77.

21. During the 1830s and 1840s she contributed articles to *Le constitutionnel,* founded a newspaper for the exile community, and prepared the first French translation of Vico's *Scienza nuova* (1844). In 1847, when Pope Pius IX declared an amnesty for all exiles connected with the earlier insurgencies, Belgioioso used her wealth to assemble a personal army and, reportedly costumed as Joan of Arc, led her forces into Rome on horseback. By the time she died in 1871, she had published, among other things, a history of the 1848 revolution, a highly regarded set of "Observations" on the current state of Italy (1868), and a study of the contemporary living conditions of Italian women and their prospects for the future (1866).

22. Cristina Trivulzio di Belgioioso, *Ricordi nell'esilio,* ed. Maria Francesca Davì (Pisa: Edizioni ETS, 2001), 94; originally published in *Le national,* 5 September to 12 October 1850.

23. For the classic statements of this view, see Joan Landes, *Women and the Public Sphere in the Age of the French Revolution* (Ithaca: Cornell University Press,

1988); and Dena Goodman, *The Republic of Letters: A Cultural History of the French Enlightenment* (Ithaca: Cornell University Press, 1994).

24. Prince de Feu [Maria de las Mercedes Santa Cruz y Montalvo Merlin], *Les lionnes de Paris* (Paris: Amyot, 1845), 29–30.

25. On this, see Steven D. Kale, *French Salons: High Society and Political Sociability from the Old Regime to the Revolution on 1848* (Baltimore: Johns Hopkins University Press, 2004); and K. Steven Vincent, "Elite Culture in Early Nineteenth-Century France: Salons, Sociability, and the Self," *Modern Intellectual History* 4/2 (2007): 327–51.

26. Bassanville, *Les salons d'autrefois,* vol. 2 (Paris: P. Brunet, n.d. [1862]), 152–53.

27. Janin, *American in Paris during the Summer,* 215–20, here, 217.

28. Bassanville, *Les salons d'autrefois,* vol. 2, 129–30; quoted in Kale, *French Salons,* 188. The riot that Lobau subdued by turning fire hoses on the crowd took place on 5 May 1831; the image of the Maréchal with (or as) a syringe, symbolizing the squirting hose became a favorite with caricaturists; see Charles A. Ramus, ed., *Daumier: 120 Great Lithographs* (New York: Dover, 1978), ix; and David S. Kerr, *Caricature and French Political Culture, 1830–1848: Charles Philippon and the Illustrated Press* (Oxford: Oxford University Press, 2000).

29. Philip Gossett has raised the question of whether these songs were ever heard in salons at all, pointing out that several of the Rossini songs were notated first in various personal albums, as gifts, and only later recopied for publication (personal communication, October–November 2009). However, both the 1835 publication announcement by Troupenas (see n10) and some early reviews of the first edition associate the songs explicitly with amateur performance. Troupenas advertises the songs as "composed expressly to facilitate the study of Italian song for amateurs, who may be intimidated by the length and difficulty of opera arias." Berlioz picks up on this in his review of the *Soirées musicales,* noting that "the vocal part does not present any of the bold features that render so many dramatic compositions inaccessible to salon singers"; *Le rénovateur,* 28 May 1835, reprinted in the Troupenas catalogue, 3.

30. Raoul Meloncelli, "Poesie e poeti della romanza da salotto," in Federico Sanvitale, ed., *La romanza italiana di salotto* (Turin: EDT, 2002), 55–116.

31. The information in table 4 is drawn from the songs discussed in Meloncelli, "Poesie e poeti della romanza da salotto," and from sheet music holdings catalogued in the unified online catalogue of Italian national libraries (OPAC SBN), the library of the Conservatorio Giuseppe Verdi (Milan), the Bibliothèque Nationale (Paris), and the British Library. In my grouping of the songs, I have omitted all the exotic and pastoral styles, partly because it seemed less surprising and noteworthy to find clusters of songs about gondoliers and shepherdesses than it did to discover a similar generic proliferation of tragic situations like the suicidal sailor of "Serenata el marinaro" or the wandering, friendless exile.

32. Renate Suchwiejko has shown that although picturesque scenes of Polish locales were almost nonexistent as a musical topos, the Poles, like the Italians, had a

penchant for titles that alluded to exile and nostalgia—"Loin de sa patrie" (by Stanislaw Katski), "Le mal de pays" and "Reflets de mon pays" (both by Antoine Katski), and "Plainte de l'exilé" (by Edward Wolff) are all by expatriate composers, and all date from the late 1830 and early 1840s. Suchowiejko, "Polish Pianists in Paris: From *couleur locale* to Stylistic Cosmopolitanism," in Rudolf Rasch, ed., *The Circulation of Music in Europe 1600–1900* (Berlin: Berliner Wissenschafts Verlag, 2004), 249–64, here 283.

Historian Maurizio Isabella has shown that nostalgia for the family and for familiar landscapes are key themes in the literary writing of Italian exiles during this period, that "the *patria* thus emerges as a nostalgic construction"; see his "Exile and Nationalism: The Case of the Risorgimento," *European History Quarterly* 36/4 (2006): 493–520, here 501.

33. "Extrait du journal de Salviati," chap. 32 in Stendhal, *De l'amour* (Paris: Michel Lévy frères, 1857), 76–84.

34. Antoine Ronna, ed., *Il parnaso italiano: Poeti italiani contemporanei maggiori e minori* (Paris: Baudry, 1843), 967. The poem's initial publication was in *I versi di G.L. Redaelli, Cremonese* (Bologna: Masi, 1815).

35. The balance between passion and poetic convention recalls the aesthetic situation described by Marshall Brown in a pair of articles on eighteenth-century Anacreontic poetry, in which, he suggests, the very overload of emotional words and images actually works to depersonalize the verse, to distance it from passion and subjectivity. Brown, "Passion and Love: Anacreontic Song and the Roots of Romantic Lyric," *English Literary History* 66/2 (1999): 373–404; and his "The Poetry of Haydn's Songs: Sexuality, Repetition, Whimsy," in Tom Beghin and Sander Goldberg, eds., *Haydn and the Performance of Rhetoric* (Chicago: University of Chicago Press, 2007), 229–50. Redaelli's "Odi d'un uom" is subtitled "Anacreontica"; but it shares with the standard Anacreontic ode only the preoccupation with death, omitting the usual emphasis on wine and easy pleasure.

36. "Scritta a lume di luna nel cimitero della Certosa di Bologna" and "Non prego mai, nè pianto"; all of the Elvira poems are quoted in Francesco Novati, "Una poeta dimenticato: Giovan Luigi Redaelli e il suo canzoniere," in *Studi critici e letterari* (Turin: Loescher, 1889), 137–73.

37. Redaelli's ode was set to music by Donizetti, Rossini, and Francesco Morlacchi but also by now-forgotten composers such as Gennaro Bonamici, Scipione Fenzi, Count Michele Oginski, Fernando Orlandi, Dionisio Pagliano, and Domenico Tescari.

38. A prominent musical example of the genre independent of Redaelli is Meyerbeer's setting of Charles-Hubert Millevoye's "Le poète mourant," probably composed in the early 1830s but published in 1849. Stylistically and generically, Meyerbeer's song belongs to a different tradition: it is more formal and expansive, more of a sculpted funereal utterance, than the simple, direct ode to a particular woman that characterizes the Italian settings of Redaelli.

39. Just a few pages earlier in the *Parnaso italiano* anthology appear four poems by Pepoli, including his "In morte di Vincenzo Bellini" (961–64).

40. In Bellini's sketch for the second and third acts of the opera the heroine is designated as Eloisa; the sketch is transcribed and reproduced in facsimile in Petrobelli, "Bellini and Paisiello," 182–85.

CHAPTER 6. PROGRESS, PIETY, AND PLAGIARISM: VERDI'S *I LOMBARDI* AT LA SCALA

1. Joseph Alexander, Comte de Hübner, *Une année de ma vie, 1848–1849* (Paris: Hachette, 1891), diary entry for 13 May 1848, 185.

2. Hübner, *Une année de ma vie,* 21 March 1848, 96 and 98.

3. Carlotta Sorba has suggested that operatic and melodramatic modes of representation—including the revolutionaries' Ernani-style hats, but also cover designs for cheap novels and theatrical posters—offered accessible frameworks that attracted middle-class and working-class Italians to the cause. Sorba, *Il melodramma della nazione: Politica e sentimenti nell'età del Risorgimento* (Rome: Laterza, 2015). See also her "Il 1848 e la melodramatizzazione della politica," in Alberto M. Banti and Paul Ginsborg, eds., *Storia d'Italia,* Annali 22: "Il Risorgimento" (Turin: Einaudi, 2007), 481–508; and her "Ernani Hats: Opera as a Repertory of Political Symbols during the Risorgimento," in Jane Fulcher, ed., *The Oxford Handbook of the New Cultural History of Music* (Oxford: Oxford University Press, 2011), 428–52. Sorba notes that the hats were common enough—and clearly enough linked to revolutionary cause—that after the 1848 revolutions were suppressed, police in Milan, Cremona, Florence, and Venice all issued injunctions that specifically prohibited the wearing of "hats in the calabrese style, also known as Ernani hats, or hats alla Puritani."

4. Roger Parker, *Studies in Early Verdi (1832–1844): New Information and Perspectives on the Milanese Musical Milieu and the Operas from "Oberto" to "Ernani"* (New York: Garland, 1989).

5. Francesca Vella, "Verdi and Politics (c.1859–1861)," *Studi Verdiani* 14 (2014): 79–120; Michael Sawall, "'Viva V.E.R.D.I.': Origine e ricezione di un simbolo nazionale nell'anno 1859," in Fabrizio Della Seta, Roberta Montemorra Marvin, and Marco Marica, eds., *Verdi 2001: Atti del convegno internazionale, Parma, New York, New Haven, 24 gennaio-1 febbraio 2001* (Florence: Olschki, 2003), 123–31.

6. Philip Gossett, "'Edizioni distrutte' and the Significance of Operatic Choruses during the Risorgimento," in Victoria Johnson, Jane F. Fulcher, and Thomas Ertman, eds., *Opera and Society in Italy and France from Monteverdi to Bourdieu* (Cambridge: Cambridge University Press, 2007), 181–242.

7. See John Rosselli, *The Opera Industry in Italy from Cimarosa to Verdi: The Role of the Impresario* (Cambridge: Cambridge University Press, 1984); John A. Davis, "Italy," in Robert Justin Goldstein, *The War for the Public Mind: Political Censorship in 19thC Europe* (Westport, CT: Praeger, 2000), 81–124; and Davis, "Italy," in Goldstein, *The Frightful Stage: Political Censorship of the Theater in Nineteenth-Century Europe* (New York: Berghahn, 2009), 190–227.

8. Ghislanzoni, "Storia di Milano di 1836 al 1848," in his *In chiave del bairtono* (Milan: Brigola, 1882), 159–60.

9. The best source for information about the Maffei salon is Arturo di Ascoli, ed., *Quartetto milanese ottocentesco: Lettere di Giuseppe Verdi, Giuseppina Strepponi, Clara Maffei, Carlo Tenca e di altri personaggi del mondo politico e artistico dell'epoca* (Rome: Archivi, 1974). See also Raffaello Barbiera, *Il salotto della Contessa Maffei e la società milanese, 1834–1886* (Milan: Treves, 1895). The salon became far more engaged with the question of Italian autonomy after Maffei met Carlo Tenca in 1844.

10. The poem's publication also launched a remarkable pamphlet war. A review of the first five cantos by Felice Romani, under the pseudonym "Don Libero," prompted ten or fifteen responses and imitations within a few months. [Romani], *Sui primi cinque canti de I Lombardi alla prima crociata, di Tommaso Grossi, ragionamento di Don Libero, professor d'umanità, tenuto a mente, e pubblicato di Don Sincero, a lui discepolo* (Milan: Felice Rusconi, 1826).

11. In 1835 Clara Maffei had commissioned Hayez's painting *Valenzia Gradenigo before the Inquisitors* to hang in her public rooms. The three canvases based on Grossi are *Pietro l'eremita predica la crociata* (1826/1829), *La partenza di Saladino* (1835), and *Papa Urbano II in piazza predica la prima crociata* (also 1835). Later Hayez painted *Sete dei crociati vicino a Gerusalemme* (1850). On Hayez and Grossi, see Adrian Lyttelton, "Creating a National Past: History, Myth, and Image in the Risorgimento," in Albert Ascoli and Krystyna von Henneberg, eds., *Making and Remaking Italy: The Cultivation of National Identity around the Risorgimento* (Oxford: Berg, 2001), 27–74.

12. Vincenzo Gioberti, *Del primato morale e civile degli italiani* (Brussels: Méline, Cans, and Co., 1843). Francesco de Sanctis situated Grossi within the Catholic-Liberal constellation in his "Tommaso Grossi e la maniera romantica," in Carlo Muscetta and Giorgio Candeloro, eds., *La scuola cattolico-liberale e il romanticismo a Napoli* (Turin: Einaudi, 1953), 15–45.

13. Basevi, *Studio sulle opere di Giuseppe Verdi* (Florence: Tofani, 1859), 21–22; translated by Stefano Castelvecchi as *The Operas of Giuseppe Verdi* (Chicago: University of Chicago Press, 2014), 28–29. This passage is cited and discussed in Jesse Rosenberg, "Abramo Basevi: A Critic in Search of a Context," *Musical Quarterly* 86/4 (2002): 659ff.; and in Francesco Izzo, "Verdi, the Virgin, and the Censor: The Politics of the Cult of Mary in *I Lombardi alla prima crociata* and *Giovanni d'Arco*," *Journal of the American Musicological Society* 60/3 (2007): 557–98, here 557. Basevi's reference to a "fire" that burned out, burying "all who had stoked it," is probably a reference to the revolutions of 1848, which Pio IX initially supported but was ultimately seen as betraying. The connections between Gioberti and Verdi, or Gioberti and Solera, have been explored by John Rosselli in an essay in the program book for the Royal Opera House performance of *Attila* (1990); Jonathan Cheskin, "Catholic-Liberal Opera: Outline of a Hidden Italian Musical Romanticism: Rossini, Bellini, Donizetti, Verdi," doctoral thesis, University of Chicago, 1999; and Izzo, "Verdi, the Virgin, and the Censor."

14. For a brief discussion of some similarly politicized reviews of historical paintings by Hayez from 1835, see my "Commentary: A Stroll in the Piazza and a Night at the Opera," *Journal of Interdisciplinary History* 36/4 (2006): 621–27.

15. *L'annotatore piemontese, ossia Giornale della lingua e letteratura italiana*, vol. 3 (Turin, 1836), 216.

16. Hayez recalled in his memoirs the work he had devoted to this aspect of the painting, especially the difficulty of endowing the scattered groups in the piazza with the appearance of individuality and distinct emotions:

> The enthusiasm for the holy cause, which reunited so many disparate populations, must have manifested itself in very different ways among people from different regions, ages, and classes.... The figures in the middle ground and background at first seemed not human, but like a herd of sheep, even though I strove to represent even the most distant figures with the various passions that would animate them.

Le mie memorie, ed. G. Carotti (Milan: Reale Accademia di belle arti, 1890), 82–83.

17. The references to Verdi as *"filosofico"* appear in the *Rivista europea* 1/1 (March 1843): 348–51; and in Bermani, *Schizzi sulla vita e sulle opere del maestro Giuseppe Verdi* (Milan: Ricordi, 1846). Vitali takes up the same train of thought, writing that Verdi here abandons the *"leggerezza"* that has for many years marked the Italian style of song, to "cleverly pair grandeur of harmony with fluidity and grace of melody; abandoning the false taste for ornament and fioriture, using art only to express the truth of drama" (*Gazzetta musicale di Milano*, 19 February 1843, 32–35; and 26 February 1843, 35–36). This closely parallels the rhetoric Mazzini had adopted in his 1836 "Filosofia della musica," although Mazzini's views on music were as yet little known in Italy.

18. [Luigi Torelli], *Pensieri sull'Italia di un aninomo lombardo* (Paris, 1846), 274; cited in Franco della Peruta, *Milano nel Risorgimento: Dall'età napoleonica alle Cinque giornate* (Milan: Edizioni comune di Milano, 1998), 68.

19. Elizabeth Siberry, *The New Crusaders: Images of the Crusades in the Nineteenth and Twentieth Centuries* (Aldershot: Ashgate, 2000). See also John Kim Munholland, "Michaud's History of the Crusades and the French Crusade in Algeria under Louis-Philippe," in Petra ten-Doesschate Chu and Gabriel P. Weissberg, *The Popularization of Images: Visual Culture under the July Monarchy* (Princeton: Princeton University Press, 1994); and James Watt, "Scott, the Scottish Enlightenment, and Romantic Orientalism," in Ian Duncan, Leith Davis, and Janet Sorenson, eds., *Scotland and the Borders of Romanticism* (Cambridge: Cambridge University Press, 2004), 94–112.

20. Michaud's history was reissued in multiple editions through the 1840s, with a substantially revised edition in 1841. The six volumes appeared in Italian in 1831 as *Storia delle crociate*, trans. Francesco Ambrosoli (Milan: Fontana, 1831).

21. In his *History of England* (1754–61), Hume famously called the Crusades a "monument to human folly." Voltaire and later Diderot (in his article on the Crusades for the *Encyclopédie*) had also condemned the Crusades as oblivious to the

scientific and philosophical sophistication of Muslim society. In his *Charles V* (1759), the Scottish historian—and champion of Mary, Queen of Scots—William Robertson argued that the only positive outcome of the Crusades was to enrich the coffers of the maritime Italian cities from which the crusaders set sail, a view that was echoed by Adam Smith in *The Wealth of Nations* (1766). For an overview of eighteenth- and nineteenth-century views, see Christopher Tyerman, *The Debate on the Crusades, 1099–2010* (Oxford: Oxford University Press, 2011).

22. Mazzini, *The Duties of Man and Other Essays* (London: Chapman and Hall, 1862), 47; cited in Cheskin, "Catholic-Liberal Opera," 254.

23. The libretti are Giuseppe Nicolini and Gaetano Rossi, *Malek-Adel* (Milan, Teatro Carcano, 1830); Giovanni Pacini and Calisto Bassi, *I crociati a Tolemaide, ossia Malek-Adel* (Turin, 1830); Michael Costa and Carlo Pepoli, *Malek-Adel* (Paris, Théâtre-Italian, 1837); and Andrea de Simone and Leopoldo Tarantini, *Matilda d'Inghilterra* (Naples, Teatro Nuovo, 1841). Nicolini and Rossi's *Malek-Adel* resembles the Pacini/Bassi work quite closely in assigning the title role to a female singer (Giuditta Pasta, at the première of Nicolini's opera) and in the broad outlines of the plot. In 1824 La Scala staged a ballet version of *Mathilde et Malek-Adel,* choreographed by Francesco Clerico. Meyerbeer also worked on a *Malek-Adel* from 1826 to 1829, but the work was never completed.

24. Vitali, *Gazzetta musicale di Milano,* 26 February 1843.

25. Basevi, *Operas of Verdi,* 31.

26. Baruffi, "Istitutzioni ed Opere: Milano, Brescia, e Padova," *Rivista europea* 6 (March 1843): "L'Eco di Milano," 366.

27. Baruffi, "Istitutzioni ed Opere," 367.

28. Camillo di Cavour, review of *Delle strade ferrate italiane e del migliore ordinamento di esse,* by Count Petitti, Counselor of State to the Kingdom of Sardinia; *Revue nouvelle,* May 1846. In the article, Cavour credits the locomotive with the ability to abolish the "inferiority" to which certain regions have been consigned.

29. On this gradual loosening of censorship and the central role of progress, transport, and industry in it, see K. R. Greenfield, *Economics and Liberalism in the Risorgimento: A Study of Nationalism in Lombardy, 1814–1848* [1934] (Baltimore: Johns Hopkins University Press, 1964); Silvana Patriarca, *Numbers and Nationhood: Writing Statistics in Nineteenth-Century Italy* (Cambridge: Cambridge University Press, 2003); and Davis, "Italy."

30. T. [Carlo Tenca], *La moda* 8 (15 February 1843): 9; quoted in Chiara Marin, "La presenza delle arti figurative e sceniche nella stampa periodica lombardo-veneta (1800–1848)," doctoral thesis, Università di Padova, 2006, 187. Marin cites the source as the journal *La fama,* but the review actually appeared in *La moda.* Many thanks to Francesca Vella for tracking down the correct citation, and for her thoughts on Tenca's views and their context.

31. As discussed in chapter 4, the Mazzini article was published in Paris in 1836 but in a journal with a very narrow circulation; it did not become widely known in Italy until well after 1850.

32. Bermani, *Schizzi sulla vita e sulle opere del maestro Giuseppe Verdi*, 36. Bermani's remarks were originally published in Ricordi's *Gazetta musicale di Milano*, as noted on the book's title page.

33. Bermani, *Schizzi sulla vita e sulle opere del maestro Giuseppe Verdi*, 36.

34. M. [Marco Marcelliano] Marcello, "Rassegna musicale: Di Verdi e delle sue opere, e specialmente della *Traviata*," *Rivista contemporanea* 4/3 (Turin: Tipografia subaplina, 1855): 659–77, here 667. Marcello (1820–56) studied composition with Saverio Mercadante, founded the Turinese music journal *Il trovatore*, and wrote several libretti, including those for Mercadante's *Il bravo* and Carlo Pedrotti's *Tutti in maschera*.

35. Marcello, "Rassegna musicale," 667.

36. Marcello, "Rassegna musicale," 667.

37. Pierluigi Petrobelli has noted that Basevi drew a similar connection between the style of *Nabucco* and *Mosè*; see his "From Rossini's *Mosè* to Verdi's *Nabucco*," in *Music in the Theater: Essays on Verdi and Other Composers* (Princeton: Princeton University Press, 1994), 34–47.

38. Solera, "Polemica," *Il pirata*, 28 April 1843. The scandal was set off by a remark in Vitali's review of *I Lombardi* in the *Gazzetta musicale di Milano*, 26 February 1843. Solera responded in *Il pirata* (10 March), and the exchange continued with articles in *Il gondoliere* (15 March, by Giovanni Pullè), the *Gazzetta musicale* (19 March, by Vitali), and *Il pirata* (24 March, 28 April, by Solera). The affair is discussed in Leopoldo Pullè, *Penna e spada: Memorie patrie di armi, di lettere, e di teatri* (Milan: Hoepli, 1899), 264–74; Domenico Giurati, *Il plagio: Furti letterari, artistici, e musicali* (Milan: Hoepli, 1903), 77–81; and Piero Faustini "Il libretto romantico come testo d'uso: Indagine dui melodrammi di Temistocle Solera (1816ca.–1878), poeta e compositore," Tesi di Laurea, Università di Bologna, 2003.

39. Pullè's libretto was written for composer Costantino Quaranta in Brescia in 1840 but was never staged. Solera had collaborated with Quaranta briefly around this time, as he admitted in his 28 April polemic in *Il pirata*.

40. Vitali, "Polemica," *Gazzetta musicale di Milano*, 19 March 1843.

CONCLUSION

1. "Becoming a Citizen: The Chorus in Risorgimento Opera," *Cambridge Opera Journal* 2/1 (1990): 41–64; Peter Stamatov, "Interpretive Activism and the Political Uses of Verdi's Operas in the 1840s," *American Sociological Review*, 67/3 (2002): 345–66. See also Mary Ann Smart, "Magical Thinking: Reason and Emotion in Some Recent Literature on Verdi and Politics," *Journal of Modern Italian Studies* 17/4 (2012): 437–47. Pio IX assumed the papacy on 16 June 1846 and extended the amnesty on 16 July 1846. The pope's popularity was short-lived, eclipsed completely by late April 1848 when, pressured by Austria, he issued a statement proclaiming that the church could not take sides in a conflict between Christian (Catholic)

nations. See Paul Ginsborg, *Daniele Manin and the Venetian Revolution of 1848–9* (Cambridge: Cambridge University Press, 1979), 103–4.

2. On a few occasions, the chorus "O signore dal tetto natìo" from *I Lombardi* was used in similar ways, its allusion to a *"pio"* (pious one, or hermit) reinterpreted to refer to the new pope. Douglas Ipson has shown that in 1847–48 Verdi's music also sometimes featured in a different kind of political demonstration, when audiences simply applauded lines that resonated with events or feelings of the moment, especially references to freedom or to the idea of a unified Italy. He cites an 1847 article by Margaret Fuller in the *New York Herald Tribune* reporting that in Rome the line *"Non vedrò l'amata terra svener lenta e farri a brano"* (I shall not see my beloved country fall to pieces and slowly perish) from *Attila* was wildly applauded and "the music . . . was not the reason"; as well an 1848 report from Naples in the Augsburg *Allgemeine Zeitung* noting that "every passage in the pruned [censored] libretto that smacked of freedom was applauded"; Ipson, *"Attila* Takes Rome: The Reception of Verdi's Opera on the Eve of Revolution," *Cambridge Opera Journal* 21/3 (2010): 249–56, here 254 and 256.

3. *Il pirata*, 18 September 1846; and Achille Gennarelli, *Feste celebrate nella città di Fermo in onore dell'immortale Pio Nono nel settembre MDCCCXLVI* (Loreto: Fratelli Rossi, 1846), 7–8. Gennarrelli reports that in Fermo the words *"Perdono a tutti"* (Pardon to all) prompted "excitement and waving of flags in the boxes, the platea, and on stage, the agitation of the music mingled with that of the audience."

4. The article is signed by "Sior Antonio Rioba." *Sior Antonio Rioba* was the name of a satirical journal that operated in Venice in 1848–49. It took its name from the statue in Venice's Campo dei Mori that had since the thirteenth century served as a surrogate for those who would voice complaints or satirical views anonymously. On the journal, see Robert Justin Goldstein, *Political Censorship of the Arts and the Press in the Nineteenth Century* (Springer, 1989), 97. Goldstein includes the journal in a list of satirical publications that sprang up in 1848 and were suppressed with the return of Austrian (and, in Rome, papal/French) domination in 1849. See also A. Pilot, "Nicolò Tommaseo e il 'Sior Antonio Rioba,'" *Rivista d'Italia* (September 1917): 355–59.

5. On this lament, see my "'Anti-historical, but Nonetheless There': Verdi, 'Tutte le feste' (Gilda), *Rigoletto,* Act II," *Cambridge Opera Journal* 28/2 (2016): 175–78. One version of the lyrics for the Ugo Bassi lament was published on an 1873 broadsheet. A performance of the song by women from the Po Valley town of Medicina was recorded by folksinger and songwriter Rudi Assuntino in 1966 as part of a many-pronged attempt to collect and archive Italian political song, organized by the Institute for Ethnography and Social History at the University of Bologna and by the Milanese music magazine, *Il nuovo canzoniere italiano.* The song's text appears on the website Il Deposito, an archive of Italian political and protest songs, which is where I first came upon it; www.ildeposito.org/archivio/canti/la-morte-del-padre-ugo-bassi. Assuntino's recording is included on the LP *Camicia rossa: Antologia della canzone giacobina e garibaldina* (Dischi del Sole, DS 1117/19, 1979) and can be

heard on YouTube, where one can also find a more burnished, high-art performance from 2008 by the Turin-based Coro Michele Novaro.

6. Eric Drott, *Music and the Elusive Revolution* (Berkeley: University of California Press, 2011); see also Richard Taruskin, "Afterword: What Else?," in Joshua S. Walden, ed., *Representation in Western Music* (Cambridge: Cambridge University Press, 2013), 287–309.

INDEX

Abbiati, Franco, 6

absolutism: allegories of, 95, 97, 101; and operatic spectacle, 65; in Tudor operas, 83–84, 202–203n33

Accursi, Michele, 107–8, 109, 208–209n17, 210n25

activism/activists, 8–10, 14, 110, 127, 131, 172–73

actor-network theory, 15, 190n32

adaptations: of Northern authors, 23; of novels in crusades operas, 161–62; in post-Napoleonic opera, 23; of Rossini's music for ballet, 31–41; Tudor operas as, 73, 74, 89–90

aesthetics: and identity, 11; of Mazzini, 110–11, 121; and morality, 33, 40; in nation-building, 103–4; of political music, 9–10; sensualist, 40–41; in Viganò's ballets, 28–30

affinities of Rossini and Viganò: borrowed music in, 31–35; correspondence of music and dramatic situation in, 35–41; gesture and voice in, 51–59; in Milan, 23–25; and pantomimic ballet, 25–30, 32–33, 40–41

Allanbrook, Wye J., 17

Allegemeine musikalische Zeitung (Leipzig), 32

allegory: as literary mode, 69–71; of monarchy, 60–62, 67–68, 71–101; of patriotism, 7; in portraiture, 68–69

Amati, Giacinto, 44

Anna Bolena (Donizetti and Romani), 86, 102, 111, 215n57

"associationism," cross-Europe, 127

Auber, Daniel: *La muette de Portici,* 9

audiences: and absorption, 27–28, 51; at La Scala, 25; meaning of *I Lombardi* for, 154–55, 157, 174; for salon music, 135–36, 139–43

authors, northern, 2, 29

ballet/ballets: borrowed music in, 25–30, 31–35, 39–40; gestural style in, 26, 30, 33–35; libretti as sources for, 193n11; and romanticism, 18–19, 24, 25–29, 59. *See also* Viganò, Salvatore

banda accompaniment, 163, 165, 168–69

Banti, Alberto, 11–12, 122–23

Barbiera, Raffaele, 106–7, 197n53

Il barbiere di Siviglia (Rossini & Sterbini), 79–81, 190n29

Barbieri, Gaetano, 44, 52–53, 56, 89–90, 197nn53,54

Bardare, Emanuele: *Maria Stuarda,* 19, 82–91, 94–101, 215n57

Baruffi, G. B., 171

Basevi, Abramo, 157, 172

La battaglia di Legnano (Verdi & Cammarano), 14

Beckett, Samuel, 10

Beethoven, Ludwig van: *The Creatures of Prometheus,* 26; Symphony No. 6, "Pastoral," 35, 38

Belgoioso, Christina Trivulzio di, and
salon, 105, 130, 139–40, 218n21
Bellini, Vincenzo: compositional process
of, 58–59; *Il pirata,* 54, 56–58, *57*; *I
puritani,* 13, 20, 104, 128–30
Bellotto, Francesco, 212n35
Berio di Salsa, Francesco Maria: *Otello,*
33–35, *38–39,* 54, 56
Bermani, Benedetto, 173
Best, Stephen, 16, 17
Beyle, Marie-Henri. *See* Stendhal
Biblioteca italiana, 2, 4, 23, 25
Boccabadati, Luigia, 85–86
borrowing: in *I Lombardi,* 174–77; in
portraiture, 79–80, 200n19; of scores
for ballet, 31–35, 39–40; self-borrowing,
79–80, 132, 134, 161–62. *See also*
plagiarism
Borsieri, Pietro, 5
Bourbon monarchy, 65–69, 97, 103
Brambilla, Paolo, 31
Byron, George Gordon (Lord Byron):
Marino Faliero, 105, 112–15, 212–
213n40, 215n60
"Byron and Goethe" (Mazzini), 211n29

Caigniez, Louis-Charles: *La pie voleuse,*
43–44
Cammarano, Giuseppe: *Portrait of Family
of Francesco I of the Two Sicilies,* 68, *70*;
Portrait of Ferdinand I, 69f1
Cammarano, Salvadore: *La battaglia di
Legnano,* 14; *Roberto Devereux,* 90, 97,
201n28, 205n54
cantatas, 51, 66–68, 72
"Canzone del salice" (Rossini), 33–35
Carpani, Giuseppe, 4, 29, 40–41
Catholicism/Catholic Church, 90, 97,
156–57
causality, historical, 20, 112–15
Cavour, Camillo, 12
Cenerentola (Rossini & Ferretti), 43
Censore universale dei teatri (Milan), 86
censorship: of operas, 82–83, 181–82,
202n31; of paintings, 159–60; of the
press, 16, 153–55, 159–60, 177; of public
speech, 7, 12; in the Risorgimento, 12;
standards of, 182

characterization: of Christians and Muslims in Crusades operas, 161–69; of
Elizabeth I, 89–90, 200n23, 202–
203n33; of Mary Stuart, 89–90, 94–95,
97, 204–205n51
characters: archetypal, 63; borrowing of,
161–62; Elvira, *135,* 135–36, 139, 146–47;
individuality of, 110, 115–16; political
and revolutionary uses of, 181–82; in
salon music, 146–47, 151; "the people"
as, 114–15
Chopin, Frédéric: *Hexameron,* 129–30
choruses/choral scenes: discussed in "Filosofia della musica," 110, 122, 210n27; in *I
Lombardi,* 158–59, 163–69, 170; in
Malek-Adel, 162; in *Marino Faliero,*
123–24; pacing of, 122, 215n57; as patriotic and martial music, 154; and politics, 177, 179–80; in the pro-Unification
movement, 154; in Tudor operas, 73, 74,
94; as universalism, 174; "Va pensiero,"
6–7, 21–22, 153, 179
cinque giornate revolution, 152–53
Colbran, Isabella, 83–84, 85
collectivity, harmony as, 110, 173, 211n29
*Commentarii della vita e delle opere coreo-
drammatiche di Salvatore Viganò*
(Ritorni), 193n11
Compagnia Reale Sarda, 89
complacency, 11, 173, 211n29
Il conciliatore, 25, 26–27, 50–51
Confalonieri, Federico, 5
Corriere delle dame (Milan), 1–2, 29, 39–40
Cosmorama pittorico (Italy), 134
Costa, Michael: *Malek-Adel,* 161–62
Cottin, Sophie: *Mathilde et Malek-Adel,*
161–62
couleur locale, 29, 61, 65
Creatures of Prometheus (Beethoven), 26
critics: on borrowed music for choreogra-
phy, 32–33, 35, 39–40; on gesture and
pacing, 182–83; on innovation, 172–73;
on *I Lombardi,* 157–60; on *Maria
Stuarda,* 97; on musical affect, 39–41;
on Rossini's music, 32, 40–51; second-
ary employment of, 15, 86, 197n53
I crociati a Tolemaide (Pacini), 161
Crusades, 155–69

marches/march melodies, 116, 129, 163, 165–66, 168–69

Marcus, Sharon, 16, 17

Maria Stuarda (Donizetti & Bardare), 19, 82–91, 94–101, *96–100*, 215n57

Maria Stuart (Schiller), 89, 91, 93

Marie Tudor (Hugo), 109

Marino Faliero (Byron), 105, 112–15, 212–213n40, 215n60

Marino Faliero (Delavigne), 112–14

Marino Faliero (Donizetti & Bidéra), 19–20, 104, 105–8, 111–27, *117–18, 125*, 182, 212n35, 215n59

Marino Faliero (Donizetti & Ruffini), 111–12, 122–24, 214–215n56

Marseillaise, 131, 151, 216–217n8

martyrdom, 89–90, 94, 97, 105, 124

Mary Stuart, Queen of Scots, 82–83, 86–87, 89–90, 94–95, 97, 204–205n51

Mathew, Nicholas, 187–188nn15,17

Mathilde et Malek-Adel (Cottin), 161–62

Mattinson, Steven, 205–206n58

Mayr, Giovanni Simone: *Il sogno di Partenope,* 66–68

Mazzini, Giuseppe: "Byron and Goethe," 211n29; correspondence with Ruffini, 120–24; on Donizetti, 105, 111–20; *Duties of Man,* 161; "Filosofia della musica," 20, 23, 102–27, 210n27; and Gioberti, 107, 207–208n14; "Giovine Italia" movement, 107–8; idealism of, 12; identification of with the crusaders, 160–61; on *Marino Faliero,* 111–20, 182; on romantic individualism, 109–11

Meloncelli, Raoul, 143–44

Mercadante, Saverio: *Soirées italiennes,* 20, 131, 132, *132,* 134–36, *137, 138*

Méric-Lalande, Henriette, 54

Merlin, Comtesse de, salon of: *Les lionnes de Paris,* 140–42

Merruau, Charles, 126

Metastasio Pietro, 131

Michaud, Joseph: *Histoire des croisades,* 160–61

Milan: 1840s political mood in, 18, 152–55, 188–189n21; *cinque giornate* (1848 revolution) in, 152–55; as Jerusalem in *I Lombardi,* 155–60; libretto contests in,

1–2; localism of opera in, 103–4; musical tastes in, 31–32; rise of national sentiment in, 152–55; romanticism in, 25–28; Tudor operas in, 82–83, 88–89

Mirra (Viganò), 26

Moe, Nelson, 134

monarchs/monarchy: allegories of, 60–62, 67–68, 71–101; bureaucratic, 90–95; depiction of, in Tudor operas, 60–62; dual bodies of, 71–82, 116; impersonation of, 83–84

Le Moniteur (Paris), 126

Monti, Vincenzo, 1, 185n1

Moretti, Franco, 16

Morsut, Zuleika, 21

Mosé in Egitto (Rossini), 171

motivations for rebellion, 112–15, 126, 212–213n40

La muette de Portici (Auber & Delavigne), 9

Music and the Elusive Revolution (Drott), 187n17

music criticism: of aesthetics, 40; and censorship, 153, 159–60; dancers' performances in, 32–33; fear of excess in, 52–53; of Italian opera in Paris, 109, 115, 118–20, 124, 126–27; language of, 159, 177; and plagiarism, 174–77; and romanticism, 59; of Rossini, 32, 40–51; of Tudor operas, 82–89

Muti, Ricardo, 22

mythology, 29–30, 172–74

Nabucco (Verdi & Solera), 6–7, 21–22, 158–59, 171, 174, 176–77

Naples: Bourbon control of, 65, 103; centrality of opera in, 66–68; political atmosphere in, 18, 65–70; and *Il sogno di Partenope,* 62, 65–71; Tudor operas in, 60–61, 85–88

Napoleonic period, 18, 65–66

nationalism, 13, 152–55, 156–57, 172–73, 174

nation-building, 6–7, 9–12, 68, 103–4

neoclassicism, 40, 41

New Monthly Magazine (London), 85

Niccolini, Antonio, 66, 67

Il noce di Benevento (Viganò), 25–26